JAPANESE WAR ART AND UNIFORMS

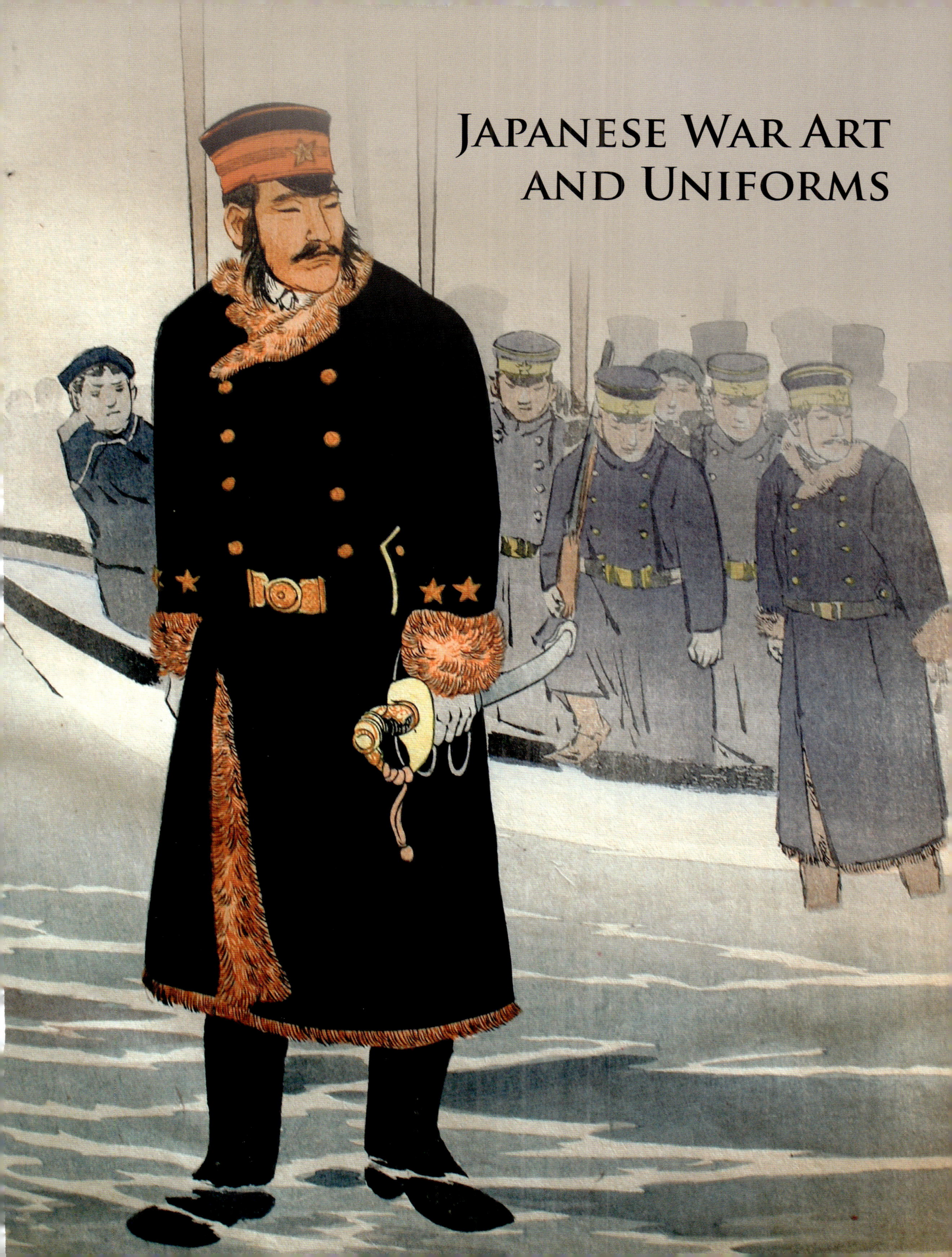

JAPANESE WAR ART AND UNIFORMS

1853-1930

René Chartrand

Schiffer Military History
Atglen, PA

DEDICATION

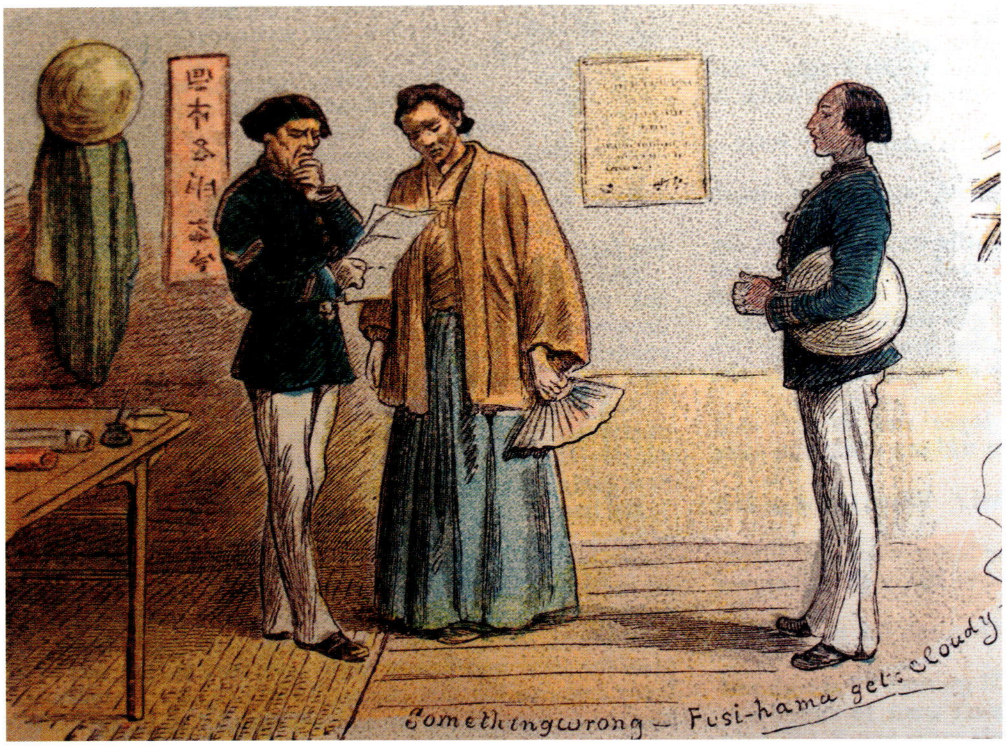

To my sons Louis and Alexandre,

who have appreciated all things Japanese since they were small boys.

Book Design by Stephanie Daugherty.

Library of Congress Control Number: 2011936151

Printed in China.
ISBN: 978-0-7643-3957-8

We are interested in hearing from authors with book ideas on related topics.

Published by Schiffer Publishing Ltd.
4880 Lower Valley Road
Atglen, PA 19310
Phone: (610) 593-1777
FAX: (610) 593-2002
E-mail: Info@schifferbooks.com.
Visit our web site at: www.schifferbooks.com
Please write for a free catalog.
This book may be purchased from the publisher.
Please include $5.00 postage.
Try your bookstore first.

In Europe, Schiffer books are distributed by:
Bushwood Books
6 Marksbury Avenue
Kew Gardens
Surrey TW9 4JF, England
Phone: 44 (0) 20 8392-8585
FAX: 44 (0) 20 8392-9876
E-mail: Info@bushwoodbooks.co.uk.
Visit our website at: www.bushwoodbooks.co.uk
Try your bookstore first.

CONTENTS

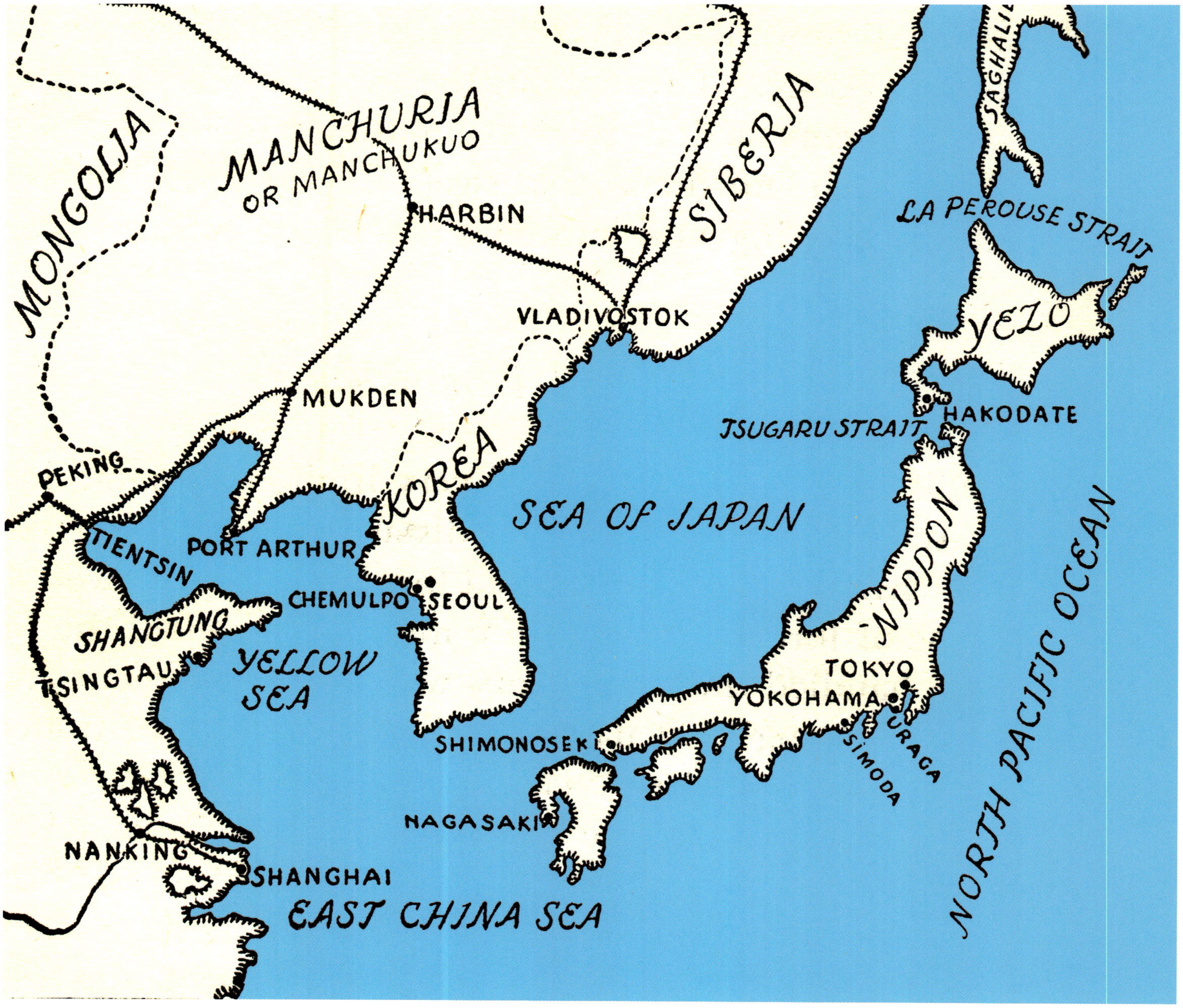

Map of North China and Japan, late 19th century and early 20th century. Many localities are indicated by the name used in sources until the late 20th century and reproduced here as such for the ease of the reader.

INTRODUCTION

AND ACKNOWLEDGEMENTS

"No great art has ever yet rose on earth but among a nation of soldiers."

– John Ruskin (1818-1900)

So stated the great British art critic and historian of the 19th century. His "unwelcome sentence" nevertheless seemed "historically irrefutable – so far" to Sir Kenneth Clark, the distinguished art historian, in the last third of the 20th century. A few decades have since passed and, for most observers, the verdict remains as Ruskin stated it.

This book is about the war art and military uniforms of one of history's most martial nations: Japan. Was Ruskin very familiar with Japanese military art? We doubt it. Like artists such as Van Gogh, Gauguin, Mannet, Monnet, Degas, Whistler, Cassat and many others, the more peaceful renderings with their remarkable aesthetic qualities in design and treatment of color were certainly the overwhelming number of works seen by Ruskin and other westerners. Indeed, even today, it is difficult to find books in other languages than Japanese, and perhaps in Japanese too, that delve into that nation's military art and military costumes.

The notion to write a book on those topics was entirely due to unforeseen circumstances. I am basically a "musket period" military historian of North America and Western Europe specialized in military material culture and tactics. However, an interest in the transformation of Japan during the Meiji period initially led me to write a short and well-illustrated article on the evolution of the Japanese army between 1854 and 1904. It appeared at the end of 2009 in the French military review Tradition. A few months later, I was attending the trustees meeting of the Brown University Library in Providence and took the opportunity to delve into yet more research in the marvelous Anne S.K. Brown Military Collection housed at the university's John Hay Library. In spite of repeatedly researching in that collection since the late 1960s, when it was then housed in Mrs. Brown's residence on Benefit Street, I have always discovered new wonders every time I went there. This time, I wondered what there might be on Japan. Kindly led by Peter Harrington, the curator of the collection whom I value as an old friend after all these years, I was shown shelves full of rather odd-looking volumes. I gasped as I glanced at very rare uniform regulations and a superlative collection of triptych prints, complete or parts thereof, that nearly all dated from the late-19th or early-20th centuries. I was astounded.

My amazement was not destined to be over with those discoveries. There were also a number of the "Todd Albums" on Japan's army and navy on the shelves. These albums were collated by Colonel Frederick P. Todd, former professor at the West Point Military Academy and director of its museum amongst his many distinguished assignments. They cover almost every nation and, being a great friend of Mrs. Brown, who herself was probably the most outstanding collector of military illustrations in the 20th century, he prepared these albums, replete with all that he had collected, for inclusion into her collection at the Brown University Library.

The Japan albums turned out to be extremely interesting and far richer than I would have ever expected. Not only do they contain all manners of notes and useful data therein, but also, exquisite and quite rare prints, some dating back to the samurai era. Some are cut up or else have obviously been acquired incomplete. They often lack data about what they are and who made them. Another part of the albums is a series of large watercolors showing Japanese army uniforms from 1886 to the 1920s in a rather naïve but clear style. Colonel Todd added many notes on the sources and army organization in his albums. They reveal that he had been an "historical officer" with the U.S. Army staff "in Japan and Korea" at the end of the Second World War; in 1946, he had seen these watercolors in Tokyo's imperial war museum. As a result "arrangements were made to have facsimile copies painted." On her side, Mrs. Brown had also acquired remarkably good prints. All this made it possibly the finest collection of war art and uniform renderings outside of Japan.

For my part, having a certain appreciation for Japanese art, I was familiar with the outstanding collection of prints at the Library of Congress as well as in other collections that are often reproduced in art books. What struck me was the paucity of warrior or battle prints reproduced in most art books compared to those showing very elegant women and superb landscapes. When there were military subjects, nearly all were about the fabled samurais and hardly any showing post-1850s fighting men and battles. There were a few art museum catalogues of temporary exhibitions showing military prints of the Sino-Japanese War and the Russo-Japanese War produced, but these were rather isolated if most worthy art studies. However, none made a link between military material culture and art.

Yet, looking at the outstanding collection of post-1850s prints in the Brown Collection, it was obvious that the style was the same with the men's wild looking faces and heroic postures just like those shown in earlier prints. The most basic difference was the men's dress and weapons. Pre-1850s prints showed them wearing armor and wielding traditional samurai swords; post-1850s prints had the men in European style uniform shooting rifles or brandishing European style swords. But everything else about them and around them was largely Japanese in its art form. Amazingly, the artists lauded for their landscape and samurai prints were often the same individuals that, in the early Meiji period, produced the "uniform" war prints. A most surprising feature of art books dealing with Japanese prints, paintings and sculpture was that they hardly ever featured warrior or military themes. Furthermore I had never seen a book that dealt with both Japanese military art and uniforms in the 19th and early-20th centuries.

That week, Schiffer editor Bob Biondi happened to visit the Brown Collection and we got into a discussion about this topic. Bob is not the sort of man that beats around the bush. "Make me a proposal with a book plan," he said. I did and you now hold the results of our labors.

Certainly, it has an unparalleled wealth of illustrations on this topic as well as a few on related subjects such as the influence of Japanese art on western artists and aesthetics or even on what a 1905 cruiser actually looked like. Except for the many items from the Library of Congress and the few from Richard Kriml and Wikimedia, all the photos of the various prints and objects were taken by myself.

There are of course some documentary gaps due mainly to my total ignorance of Japanese in its ancient or modern forms. Thus, the inscriptions often found on the prints will remain a total mystery to me. This was also the case of those western individuals who compiled the collections such as Mrs. Brown and Colonel Todd although they did note whatever they had found identifying artists and topics, but this was relatively uncommon. Fortunately, French is my mother tongue and there are a number of remarkable art studies and historical accounts on Japan published in that language (see the bibliography).

At this conjuncture, the study of uniforms, equipments and flags have proven invaluable when viewing the prints. True, the regulations are also written in Japanese, but there are enough illustrations and related sources to be able to make out the main features of Japan's military dress and thus confirm, and even infirm, what the artists show. I was a curator at Canada's National Historic Sites for some three decades and the expertise that I developed in the study of military material culture often proved decisive in identifying and dating works of art. This is not fail safe, but it is a tremendous if somewhat unsuspected tool for art curators and historians. Hence the addition of "and uniforms" in the title. This work is in fact designed for a dual audience: those who appreciate Japanese art and the enthusiasts of militaria.

After reviewing all the material presented as well as all that was not included, more than ever it can be affirmed that Ruskin's statement was founded on careful observation and it certainly extended to Japan.

In closing, it would have never been possible to put such a work together without assistance. I am pleased to acknowledge, first and foremost, the outstanding help given by Peter Harrington, curator of the Anne S.K. Brown Collection. This study could have never been presented without his encouragement and patience. Through him, I am also grateful to Mrs. Brown and to Colonel Todd, both now departed, and both of whom I knew as a younger man; I am still discovering their far-sighted dedication and wisdom. My sons Louis and Alexandre, because of their long-standing interest in Japan's martial history, philosophy and culture, have been quite helpful. The Library of Congress in Washington is to be lauded for its outstanding policies of dissemination and access to its superlative collections. Other institutions and their staff provided great help. I am most grateful to the Research Centre of the Canadian War Museum in Ottawa, the Gatineau Municipal Library, the University of Ottawa Library, the Washington County Museum of Fine Art in Hagerstown, Maryland, the Art Institute of Chicago, Denis Darmanin of Malta, the Musée d'Orsay and the Musée Guimet in Paris, the Museum of the Royal Military College of Canada at Kingston, Ontario, the Museo de Armas in Buenos Aires, Argentina, the Musée Ingres at Montauban, France and Richard Kruml, the outstanding Japanese art dealer in London. Many thanks to Bob Biondi and the staff at Schiffer who turned a pile of dvds and computer files into this handsome publication. And last but not least, Dr. Luce Vermette, who is versed in history and in fine arts as well as a practitioner of Japanese Ikebana, for her patience and advice to the fortunate and grateful spouse that I am. As always, all efforts were made to have as few errors as possible, but they always do seem to creep in somehow and the author, who is truly horrid at proof reading, sincerely apologizes to the readers.

René Chartrand
Gatineau (Québec), Canada

Calendars used in Japan:

Until 1872, the lunar calendar system was used officially in Japan. The Gregorian calendar was officially adopted at the time. The day after the 2nd of the 12th month of 1872 (of the lunar calendar) became the 1st of January 1873 (of the Gregorian calendar).

Japanese eras:

Edo or **Tokugawa** (1602-1868)
Meiji (1868-1912)
Taisho (1912-1926)
Showa (1926-1989)

Chronology

8000 BC to c. 300 BC	Caucasians originally from Siberia appear to have formed most of Japan's population. They are followed by people from the South Pacific.
3rd Century AD	Mention of warrior clans.
4th Century AD	Sizeable population migration into Japan from China and Korea.
6th Century AD	Buddhism introduced in Japan.
604	Prince Shotoku introduces a Chinese-style constitution based on Confucian principles, which inaugurates the Japanese empire.
792	Emperor Kammu abolishes the obligation for all men to perform military service.
9th Century AD	Mention of "samurai" warriors.
940	Taira revolt crushed; evidence of a warrior class.
1185	Minamoto Yoritomo of the Hojo clan seizes power, becoming the first shogun of Japan in 1192, while the emperor (or "Mikado") becomes a figurehead.
1191	The "Zen" sect introduced in Japan.
1274	Mongols of Kublai Khan try to invade Japan, but are repelled by "kamikaze" hurricane.
1480s	Tea drinking, introduced in Japan from China since 815, becomes a ritual ceremony for the shogun and elite samurai warriors.
1542	Portuguese discover Japan and introduce firearms; Catholic missionaries reach Japan in about 1549.
1588	Peasants forbidden to own weapons; swords now only worn by nobles and samurais.
1603	Emperor appoints Ieyasu as shogun and founds the Tokugawa dynasty of shoguns that divides Japanese society into five hereditary classes (lords, samurai, farmers, artisans, merchants); Christianity banned in 1614.
1633	Shogun Iemitsu forbids traveling abroad and reading foreign books; forbids building ocean sailing ships from 1638.
1853	U.S. warships arrive at Yokohama, provoke opening of Japan to foreigners.
1863-1864	Western powers warships bombard Choshu and Shimonoseki to open more Japanese ports to foreigners.
1866	Yoshinobu Tokugawa, also called Keiki, ascends to the shogunate in Kyoto.
1867	Emperor Komei dies on 30 January and is succeeded by his fourteen-year old son Meiji (whose personal name was Mutsuhito); Japanese prints exhibited at the Paris World's Fair raise much interest in the French artistic community; shogun Yoshinobu Tokugawa resigns on 9 November.
1868	On 3 January, Emperor Meiji officially assumes power, which is actually exercised by a government council of reformers. Outbreak and defeat of dissidents to the imperial government during the Boshin War.
1869	Rebels last holdout at remote Hakodate falls to imperial troops in May; reformer Yukichi Fukuzawa's 1866 and much reprinted "Things Western" launches the wave of Westernization for all national institutions.
1870	Imperial guard created.
1871	The feudal system is abolished and replaced by a division of the country into prefectures; the feudal lords forbidden to retain private armies; Emperor Meiji declares that all Japanese children will attend schools for free.
1872	Western dress is prescribed for official ceremonies; conscription law passed to recruit the armed forces.
1873	Japan grants religious freedom and adopts the Gregorian calendar.
1874	Expedition to Taiwan.
1875	Military academy for training officers founded on the French model of St. Cyr; Japanese Red Cross Society founded; incident with, and expedition to Korea.

1877	Satsuma (or samurai) rebellion against the imperial government is defeated by the regular army.
1878	Army general staff created along the German model.
1879	Japan holds regional elections, the first democratic elections held outside of the West
1880	Murata service rifle made in Japan.
1882	China sends troops to defend the Korean government and Japan sends troops there to protect its delegation after a mob attacks it; in 1885, China and Japan agree to pull out their troops from Korea.
1888	Division organization created in army.
1893	Navy general staff created; Japanese shipyards now capable of building large warships.
1894-1895	Sino-Japanese War; Japanese forces victorious in Korea, Port Arthur, northern Chinese coast and Taiwan. Taiwan and Pescadores islands ceded by China to Japan; China leases Lianing Peninsula to Japan; pro-Japanese government in Korea.
1896	European powers force Japan to surrender the Liaotung peninsula of China.
1898	Port Arthur leased by China to Russia for twenty-five years.
1900	Boxer rebellion in China; Japan is the main participant making up the international force that takes Peking (Beijing); Russian military occupation of Manchuria.
1902	Alliance with Great Britain.
1904-1905	Russo-Japanese War; Russia cedes lease over Port Arthur and interest sphere of southern Manchuria to Japan. Korea declared Japanese protectorate.
1910	Japan annexes Korea.
1912	Emperor Meiji dies on 30 July and new emperor Taisho (whose personal name was Yoshihito).
1914	World War I breaks out in August, pitting Britain, France, Italy, Russia, Serbia, USA and (from 23 August) Japan against Austria, Germany and Turkey; German possessions in China and Pacific taken by Japanese forces during the fall of 1914.
1917	Japanese navy squadron based at Malta operates in the Eastern Mediterranean.
1918	End of World War I in November; Japan obtains mandate over former German territories in Pacific; Japanese troops participate in allied intervention against Russian Bolsheviks in eastern Siberia.
1922	Troops withdrawn from Siberia; Japan accepts to limit the size of its warships at the Washington Conference.
1925	Japan introduces universal male suffrage increasing the number of voters from three to twelve million, but in reality becomes a de facto military dictatorship under nominal imperial rule.
1926	Emperor Taisho dies; succeeded by Emperor Showa (whose personal name was Hirohito) on 25 December. Reigns until his death on 7 January 1989.
1930	Japan accepts again to limit the size of its warships at the London Conference.

Statue of a warrior, 6th century AD. This large earthenware statue, possibly from the Kanto region, is one of the earliest representations of a Japanese fighting man. Musée Guimet, Paris.

1

LAND OF THE NIPPONS

TO 1853

The Japanese archipelago is made up of some 20,000 islands including its four main islands: Hokkaido, Honshu, Shikoku and Kyushu. Its present limits, like its cultural homogeneity, are the result of a long and gradual process going back to prehistoric times. From about 8,000 BC, groups of men and women from Siberia settled in Japan followed by others from the South Pacific in about 300 BC and, from the fourth century AD, many more from China and Korea. The political unity of the various clans came about during the seventh century.

From the earliest times, the island nation of Japan was the scene of conflict and the home of warriors. Powerful clans had carved out domains protected by redoubtable warriors that were often in conflict became increasingly aware that they could be invaded from outside and sought some sort of political unity. The model chosen was that of imperial China, but it evolved very differently in Japan. In China, the "Mandarins" who were the senior bureaucrats of the empire eventually controlled its government during most periods of its history with its emperor sometime taking part in temporal affairs. In Japan, the emperor (or "Mikado") eventually became a living god on earth that was above temporal and political concerns. By the 13th century, he was deeply revered as a symbol of the nation and of its religious faith. The nearly continual conflicts between the various lords were thus beneath the imperial family and it was an unforgivable sacrilege to even suggest that the emperor be coerced or harmed in anyway. He reigned, but did not rule. This largely defined the concept of Japan's national entity, which rested on the notion that the country was divinely chosen and that its emperor's ancestry went back to the age of the ancient gods. Political reality was actually more complex, but on the whole, this doctrine has not changed much to this day.

Rulers of the nation were found in the clans of the powerful lords that, through alliances and battlefield success, would rise to become "shoguns" who would govern in the name of the emperor. By the Middle Ages, the power struggles at court between soldiers and bureaucrats had been resolved in favor of the warrior caste. In 1192, the shogun's central government was set up. The primary warrior qualities such as obedience to the will of the emperor, heroism, honor, abnegation, self-sacrifice and death rather than shame in defeat became national values. These were eventually consigned in

Top: Bronze spearhead, 1st century AD. This ancient Japanese object is approximately three feet long and originates from the Kyushu region. Musée Guimet, Paris. **Bottom:** Warrior's sword guard, end of the 6th century AD. It is intended for the "Hoto" style sword in vogue between c. 550 and 800 AD. The grip is covered with a layer of gilded bronze and the pommel is of the same material. Musée Guimet, Paris.

the "Bushido" code during the 16th century. Thus, the nation had developed a very strong vision of itself as a united country presided by a holy emperor, which did not prevent the less saintly shoguns and lords to bicker amongst themselves in their temporal and, in a Buddhist sense of the world, vain pursuits.

The art of war developed in an outstanding way. Samurais were trained from infancy in archery and swordsmanship. The latter was especially important. The sword had a great symbolic importance in all societies because it defined its wearer as a warrior. In Japan, samurai warriors carried two swords, a long one for combat and a short one that could be used for the ritual "hara-kiri" suicide in order to die with honor in defeat, be it military or political.

The Japanese sword itself, the most exalted symbol or the warrior, was certainly the finest and most lethal weapon of that type ever devised. There were several types of long and short swords, the "o-katana" and the "wakizachi" respectively being possibly the main models in use. What especially distinguished the Japanese sword was its extraordinary blade that featured a curvature, which was developed in the 10th century. Master sword makers would fold and hammer its red-hot steel thousands of times to achieve a solidity and cutting power that was second to none. Well handled, it could sever limbs and heads in one blow and even the best armor was no guarantee against such a weapon. There were naturally various qualities offered. The making of a fine sword could require many months. It was also mandatory that it be an object of great beauty. The finest swords were naturally very expensive. They often were handed down from generation to generation so that swords, such as those illustrated in this book, may have been carried by successive samurais for several centuries.

Personal armor was worn by all who could afford them. Unlike European armor made of fairly large steel plates and consequently quite rigid and very heavy, Japanese armor was flexible being arranged in intertwined small metal plates fixed with cord on leather or fabric. There were various types of armor including ceremonial armor not intended for use on battlefields. Some could even be folded for storage, an unthinkable feat with Western armor! The helmets had devices of identity, some wore liveries of their clan and might also have pennants bearing clan badges attached to their backs. Armor could also be passed on through generations and the examples illustrated may well have been still used up to the Meiji era.

Fortifications in Japan originally consisted of stockades and earthworks with moats. Wooden superstructures and gates were added and their styles were based on those seen in China and Korea. By the 14th century, they could be termed castles. They were used as combined military defense and command center as well as residences for lords with their samurais and their families. Consequently, the castles became more comfortable and were tastefully decorated outside and inside. It was from the mid-16th century that castles in Japan became numerous in the form that we know them today. Firearms brought by the Portuguese in Japan signaled fundamental changes in castle architecture. There was no siege artillery as yet, but high stonewalls protected garrisons from matchlock musket bullets far better than wooden palisades or earthworks. Castles were henceforth built or remodeled with such stone foundations, their size often expanded and the superstructures built on top achieved unsurpassed artistic style and beauty. The basic design was intended to exhaust enemy assaults by a maze of exterior walls before the main part of the castle with its high superstructure could be reached.

These superb castles were thus quite effective for warfare, as it existed in Japan even after the introduction of firearms. Artillery using gunpowder was not widely used in Japan until the 19th century. Before that time, there were few cannons in the country and they were smaller and less effective than those used by Westerners. Importing cannons was far too expensive and Japanese foundries, though they could cast huge temple bells, did not have the equipment nor the technical expertise necessary to cast good heavy artillery. In Japanese siege tactics, the destruction of walls was not envisaged; often the place would be starved into submission or a battle might be fought outside its walls to decide the issue.

Following the advent of the Tokugawa shoguns in the early-1600s, Japan entered a lengthy peaceful period. Castles now were used primarily as luxurious residences for the local lords. Thus, even the seacoast castles were quite useless against hostile ships because they had no heavy artillery. In the 1840s, however, the Satsuma clan built modern batteries at Fort Tenpozan in Kagoshima mounted with locally made brass cannons including 150-pound pieces, a sign of increased proficiency in gun casting. Odeiba battery, a stone Western type low-lying fort, was built in 1853-1854 to defend the entrance of Tokyo harbor from bombardments by foreign ships.

Contacts with Europeans

In his 16th century history of the Indies, Father Maffee mentioned that, "many Portuguese had claimed for themselves the glory of having discovered the Japans. But according to the opinion of Antonio de Galva … it was Antonio Mota, Francisco Zeimet and Antonio Pexot, who [were sailing] for China, were carried by the wind to the Japans, in the 42nd year of the century [1542]." The Portuguese were impressed by what they saw and soon, more ships sailed from their main base of Goa, India, filled with European goods and carrying officials anxious to open trade relations with "the Japans."

The Japanese too were quite startled at the sight of the Portuguese and their artists immediately made renderings of the strange ships and men they beheld in their harbors. One of the items that raised great interest for Japanese military officers was the hand held, portable matchlock musket. They perceived the useful potential of such a weapon deployed on a battlefield as well as the realization that it took about a week to train a musketeer to properly use his weapon, while it took many years to develop a good archer or a swordsman. The Portuguese were initially reluctant, but soon were trading

Bishamon, guardian-king of the north, early 13th century. Bishamon is the chief of the four guardian gods who protect the four cardinal directions in a Buddhist sanctuary. This highly detailed and decorated statue of the Buddhist warrior-king guardian of the north gives a hint of the armor worn by samurais during the 1200s, much of it still inspired from China. The right hand originally would have held a weapon such as a spear or a sword to defend the Buddhist law. His left hand holds a miniature reliquary. Statue of lacquered wood decorated with gilt, the eyes are of crystal. Musée Guimet, Paris.

Kusunoki Masashige and his warriors barricading themselves into Chihaya Castle. They were loyal to the emperor and, being overwhelmed at Minatogawa, Kusunoki Masashige and many of his men committed hara-kiri on 22 May 1333. Masashige was thereafter revered for his virtues as a warrior and for his absolute loyalty to the emperor, qualities that remained paramount amongst the Japanese military. Print after Shuntei Katsukawa. Library of Congress, Washington.

muskets. Before long, the highly skilled Japanese craftsmen were making excellent matchlock muskets and had nothing further to learn from European gunsmiths. It was an omen for the future: the Japanese had all the technical skills, resources and ability to emulate and improve anything that came into their islands.

The question the Japanese faced at that time in their nation's evolution was: apart from a few useful inventions such as the musket, was there any real need to adopt western ways? The answer was no.

First of all, Japan was a very distant country from Europe or America in the age of sailing ships. In the 16th century, sailing to the outer reaches of the Asian mainland was not an easy enterprise due to winds and currents. The early Portuguese and Spanish navigators found the trip north of the Philippines somewhat daunting and only a few ships would reach Japan's southern island. Since it was no "Eldorado" abundant in gold and silver, there was no inclination to occupy it, and besides, early Portuguese reports of the country mentioned a well-organized and well armed military force. The Japanese were also credited with being outstandingly brave with no fear of death.

Furthermore, the Japanese already had their own versions of just about anything the Portuguese brought with them, nor were they terribly impressed by the tales from the distant kingdoms on the other side of the earth. Although often fighting amongst themselves, the Japanese lived in a single imperial nation with a god-emperor and the nearest neighbor was the formidable Empire of China. Japan was therefore a highly sophisticated society when the Portuguese arrived and was unlikely to be overly impressed by Europeans. Because they inhabited an island nation and due to the repeated invasion threats from imperial China over the past centuries, the insular Japanese were somewhat xenophobic to anything foreign. This not only included certain material goods, but also ideas that might corrupt the nation's moral values.

For their part, the Jesuit missionaries that landed in Japan were quite impressed by much that they saw. Again, Father Maffee's history offers many tantalizing descriptions, a few of which are given here:

> The men "follow war [like ways] until they are sixty years old. Few wear beards… They are trained to hunt [from childhood]… they are persuaded that nothing prevents courage more than a soft upbringing…" Their ways "are those of warriors and the whole nation routinely handles weapons, which are about as follows: muskets, bows and arrows, swords and daggers." These last two were meant to be the samurai long and short sword. Weapons were also noted as exquisite, notably the sword blades "that are all pure and without ornaments, which they greatly value and that they estimates at times being worth more than 5,000 gold escudos by the merit or the care of the swordsmith … From the age of twelve, they always carry [swords] … whose blades are so finely tempered that they would easily cut our iron without being damaged."

The Jesuit observers were also very impressed by the power of the art they encountered in Japan. Their explanation was the Japanese's profound commitment to creating beauty, which could only be achieved by mastering the fine arts. This applied to objects, to social behavior and to an education in which art had an outstanding value. "Everything is done in certain ways, which one must know in order to appreciate properly beauty and art." Concerning art, it was observed to apply to any object produced so as to provoke admiration from its craftsmanship and artistic value: a simple cup or vase of beauty would be "as admired as … diamonds … and gold chains by Europeans."

The Jesuits further noted that the Japanese "also have great esteem for paper and they make paper reams that are extremely fine and delicate upon which the finest artists draw birds and trees with such dexterity, and with a black [ink or shade] so unified and equal, that it draws our eye

Woman warrior of the Kamakura period (1185-1333), which was celebrated for its "Amazon" warriors such as Tomoye and Hangaku who were lady samurais in their own right. However, lady warriors were not armed with swords but with the equally lethal "Naginata" spear with a long blade. In this reconstruction made in about 1893, she has put her opponent out of action. After a period photograph. Anne S.K. Brown Military Collection, Brown University Library, Providence, USA.

Samurai warriors escort an altar brought to the sanctuary of Kitano Tenjin, 1538. All the elements of Japanese armor shown hardly changed until the 1850s. The altar bearers wear a red and green livery and are armed with swords. Detail from an unsigned ink and watercolor drawing. Musée Guimet, Paris.

and charms it." These works of art "are bought quickly by all the great lords who show them with great pride to everyone." One should also mention the exquisite art seen on wooden or paper screens, some of whom even depicted the Japanese's vision of the Portuguese and their 'black' ships. Obviously, 16th century Japan had a vibrant and highly sophisticated artistic outlook.

The power of its traditional art was such that European religious images brought as prints or seen in prayer books shown by early missionaries must have seemed unbearably crude and without interest. Rough earthenware and pewter plates seen on board Portuguese ships must have been likened to the worst that could be produced. The emerging European baroque art had nothing to offer to the Japanese sense of aesthetics.

There were many lifestyle and cultural differences that made the 16th century meetings between Europeans and Japanese difficult. The sight and smell of foreigners who hardly ever took a bath was horrific in a society where cleanliness was a national virtue. Nor did the European's use of perfume to mask bad odors were of much help

A mounted samurai in full battle regalia, early-1500s. The horse is also given some protective padding with long tassels. Contemporary print. Library of Congress, Washington.

The central tower of Imeji Castle. Started in 1333, it was remodeled in the 1580s and expanded into a large complex between 1601 and 1618 making it the largest military castle in Japan. In spite of Second World War American bombings, typhoons and earthquakes, Imeji Castle remained relatively intact and was declared a UNESCO World Heritage Site in 1993. Wikimedia.

Warriors of the Toyotomi clan at the Seto-Nai-Kai seaside, c. 1550. They are dressed in full armor and are ready for battle. Woodcut print after Sadahide Gountei. Anne S.K. Brown Military Collection, Brown University Library, Providence, USA.

Feudal troops marching through Kyoto, c. 1600. Feudal lords had to go to Tokyo (then called Edo) every two years to swear allegiance to the ruling Shogun. The warriors depicted wear liveries of their lord. Woodcut print after Yoshimori Ikkousai. Anne S.K. Brown Military Collection, Brown University Library, Providence, USA.

to Japanese nostrils. European-style banquets were as "insufferable" to the Japanese as Japanese-style diners to Europeans. Food itself was "sweet and well cooked" for Europeans compared to "salted … and almost raw" as consumed by the Japanese. Portuguese social conventions dictated that one should stand when guests arrived, but in Japan, one sat down. When it came to heath care, "we often [practice] bleeding, they [the Japanese] never do … Our medicines stink and are bitter, theirs are mellow and agreeably scented."

In conclusion after many more descriptions, the Jesuits felt that "if Europeans seemed ridiculous to the Japanese, by the same token they seemed ridiculous to Europeans because of their cleanliness" and their good lifestyle.

Christian Missionaries

The Japanese initially welcomed the Portuguese traders. From about 1549, Jesuit missionaries arrived, one of which was Father (later Saint) Francis Xavier, and they were welcomed by the shogun. They were allowed to preach their Roman Catholic faith and were granted land in the imperial capital of Kyoto. Soon, missions flourished and hundreds of thousands were converted. However, as time passed and more was learned about the foreigners and their teachings, some Japanese had second thoughts about the value of the ideas that were being imported into their country.

The Christian's critics were famously summed up by the monk and author Suzuki Sochan who tried to

Full armor of a samurai, c. 1650. Note the intricate layering and disposition of the small metal plates with fabric and the fearsome-looking helmet and facemask. This is what the artists were trying to convey in their watercolors and prints. Museo de Armas de la Nacion, Buenos Aires, Argentina.

A samurai armor's iron mask, 17th century. The dramatic expression, exquisitely rendered on this mask by an unknown artist, was intended to induce the opponent's fright. Musée Guimet, Paris.

rationalize the facts that westerners adored, "a single and great Buddha called God … by the name of Jesus-Christ, who was born in a distant land some sixteen hundred years ago to save humanity. By ignorance of this event, [the Christians claim that] other countries revere false gods." Why, Suzuki asked, would God almighty neglect other countries of his manifestation? Why would such a God reserve his wisdom to only one nation? It was "very bad work" for a God that was "master of the universe." Furthermore, Christ was sent into the world, "to be crucified by ordinary men belonging to the inferior world [earth]. The master of the universe! Is it possible to conceive such an absurd event! Christians know nothing of the awakening, the unified state of the original conscience. In their ignorance, they adore a single Buddha. They will not avoid the punishment from Heaven because they have come in this country to spread their false doctrines and diabolical teachings!" Suzuki then mused about the ignorant Japanese being seduced by such logic, asking if this was not, "a national disgrace…that would hurt our reputation in other [Asian, non-Christian] countries?"

Another more militant view held that the Jesuit missionaries were merely the vanguard of a Western invading army. News of the Europeans establishing themselves by force of arms in India, in Indonesia and in the Philippines had warned the Japanese that they might not be immune to such actions. The seemingly well-meaning missionaries might, in fact, be agents of western powers making converts to their values while plotting to overtake the government with the help of their ships and soldiers. Native emperors had fallen in America so why not in Japan? Suspicion spread and, in 1565, Jesuits were banned from the imperial capital, Kyoto. Trading ventures were still welcomed and the southern port of Nagasaki was to harbor the European ships traveling to Japan.

In 1596, a seemingly isolated incident involving the shipwreck of a Spanish galleon on Japan's coast started the movement that would close the country to all foreign influences for over two and a half centuries.

A young samurai is shown "preparing for the first battle." A young woman arranges the long hair of the young man before putting on his helmet. Circa 1713 print by Kiyomasu Torii (d. 1716). Library of Congress, Washington.

Samurai "tsuba" sword hand guards. The "tsuba" hand guards fitted into the sword between the hilt and the scabbard. At left, an extremely rare gilded bronze sword hand guard from the 6th century. At right, a beautifully gold etched example from the 18th century. Musée Guimet, Paris.

Local Japanese authorities seized both the wrecked ship and its cargo, an act that enraged its captain. Hoping to impress and intimidate the officials, he produced a map showing Spain's great world empire. He then proclaimed that Japan would never be as great as Spain because it had no Jesuit missionaries to convert people and thus prepare the way for conquest. Astonished officials immediately reported the captain's boasts to the palace of the regent in Kyoto. On learning of this, the powerful imperial regent Toyotomi Hideyoshi (1536 or 1537-1598) was outraged; it confirmed the view that Christianity was more than a religious matter it was a state security issue. The very existence of the empire might be at stake.

As a result, Japanese converts were arrested and interrogated about their faith and their loyalty to Japan. Some were found guilty and, in 1597, the regent ordered the crucifixion of twenty Japanese Christians as well as six Jesuit missionaries. Another incident with a Portuguese ship occurred in 1610 and Christianity was banned in 1611. The following years and decades witnessed more persecutions, crucifixions, beheading and public renouncements that eliminated Christians in Japan by 1640.

Unity and Isolation

As the most powerful lord in Japan, Toyotomi Hideyoshi was involved in far more matters than dealing with Christians. He is remembered in Japanese history as a "great unifier" because he managed to unify, by diplomacy and force of arms, the nation's political factions. It was a time in Japanese history when the title of shogun was not used but Hideyoshi had the equivalent power as imperial regent, an all-powerful position resulting from decades of civil war between feudal lords. In the 1580s, his troops overcame opposition in many provinces including that of Kyushu in 1587, which had a Christian ruler and this led to banning missionaries there. However, Hideyoshi was also trading with Europeans and he actually tolerated the Christians at that time as long as they did not seem involved in politics.

Many armed peasants had been active in the latest conflict and Hideyoshi decided that this had to stop. Up until 1588, peasants had been allowed to own weapons, especially swords, but this was now forbidden on the basis that it was unnecessary for them to have such a weapon. In effect, peasants could no longer become warriors. The primary result of the ban was a reduction of peasant revolts. Perhaps the most enduring transformation was the rigid stratification of Japanese society that ensued. Henceforth, only nobles and members of the samurai class could carry weapons. However, the samurai were now to reside in castle towns. This resulted in a sizeable and relatively concentrated military force that could be assembled for campaigns such as the two ill-fated invasions of Korea in 1592 and 1598. The Japanese always wanted to control that country as a buffer against a Chinese invasion. They would have more success three centuries later.

Hideyoshi further had a great influence on Japan's government, culture and art. He had the country surveyed and a census taken from which a comprehensive tax system evolved, but individuals were now to stay in their respective places of residence and could only travel with official permission. In 1590, he abolished "forced" labor, in effect, slavery in Japan. A more centralized government system was put into effect and, in 1603, a shogun was once again appointed. A supreme council of the leading clan nobles, the "daimyos", advised the shogun that ruled on temporal issues while the emperor remained aloft as a spiritual leader. It was still a feudal system with ruling clans and clan lords, but the shogun's government strived to keep the various provinces relatively isolated so as to prevent powerful clan alliances that might threaten its power.

Apart from his ability to set up a viable national government, Hideyoshi was a great patron of the arts and sponsored acclaimed artists, had superb residences, shrines and castles built. The noble elite followed suit and the Japanese's already high interest in the arts rose further. Even the highly formal tea ceremony was revamped and Hideyoshi had a gilded portable tearoom accompany him on his travels to entertain his subject lords. These and many more measures were aimed to proclaim the superiority and mastery of Japan's art and culture. It was true in many ways, but it also produced a sense of security that encouraged increasing isolation from the outside world.

Western influence, seen to be either irrelevant or subversive, was thus almost totally banned. Only the Dutch, who had begun trading with the Japanese since 1609, were allowed a very minimal access. They were perceived as being only interested in commerce and did not come with missionaries. The government nevertheless

A superb dress samurai sword hilt and grip, 18th century. This rare luxury weapon was undoubtedly carried by a high-ranking official and is decorated with gold and pearl. Musée Guimet, Paris.

A senior samurai official sent by the prince of Matsay to meet the foreigners at Yokohama in 1853. He is escorted several other samurais. Print by E. Brown after a photograph.

strictly restricted their access to a small island in the harbor of Nagasaki where Dutch traders could maintain lodgings and warehouses on the island, but were not allowed out of it. This tenuous connection with Holland remained the only official link Japan had with the western world until the mid-19th century.

Armed Forces

Because of the policy of isolation, it can be said that Japanese armies made practically no technical progress between the time the Portuguese introduced matchlock muskets to the 1850s when the Western "Black Ships" arrived. Thus, apart from the addition of foot musketeer units in the clan armies, there was no pressure to adopt new tactical doctrines and military thinking remained very conservative and anchored in largely medieval concepts. The right to bear swords being now exclusively the privilege of nobles and samurais combined with the absence of any serious foreign menace created an abyss in military thought for a quarter of a millennium. These men, as evidenced by the martial prints produced in the country, turned to philosophical values mixed with religious beliefs that exacerbated tenacity, heroism and an honorable death in the face of defeat. The example of 1333 samurai Kusunoki Masashige who committed heroic hara-kiri was still hailed as the ultimate military virtue.

Thus battlefield tactics remained "frozen" in Japan while, in the West, the first modern armies were being created in the era of Louis XIV and national conscription widely introduced during the wars of the

Two samurais fully armed and equipped with their armor, c. 1800. Print after Utagawa Toyokini (c. 1777-1835). Library of Congress, Washington.

Archer, early 19th century. Fully armed and wearing armor. He holds a fan and his bow is not stringed. Note the strings holding up a protective armor piece for the lower legs. Contemporary Print. Library of Congress, Washington.

A musketeer as represented by actor Ichikawa Danjuro in the role of Kaya no Sanpei, also known as Yomei Soga Dozaburo, c 1830. Print after Utagawa Toyokuni (c. 1777-1835). Library of Congress, Washington.

French Revolution and Empire. In Europe, hundreds of thousands of men faced each other in battle lines that had little to do with medieval individual combat. They were supported by elaborate and powerful artillery trains. Military engineers had devised, since the 16th century "Italian trace" and especially from the time of the late-17th century French Marshal Vauban, the outstanding fortress attack and defense tactics in accord with the armament used by European armies. The advent of large cannons in the 15th century had rendered European castles and cities with high walls obsolete.

None of this had filtered into Japan. The country was divided into a network of clan castles, all of which were massive structures with large stone foundation walls surmounted by very attractive, multi-leveled and highly decorated wooden buildings. Most were built or rebuilt during the 16th and 17th centuries. Some of these, such as Osaka Castle, were formidable against any Japanese clan army and in this they achieved their objectives for centuries. The art of fortifications in Japan thus remained static.

The armed forces were totally isolated from the outside world until the mid-19th century. The only Western vessels a few soldiers would see were the Dutch trade ships that came into Nagasaki, the only commercial contact permitted by the Shogun. The Japanese military men thus only saw relatively small Western merchant ships until faced with the unthinkable in 1853: large black warships navigating without the help of the wind that carried artillery capable of pulverizing any castle's superstructure, even damage its stone walls and there was no defense against this.

On board Commodore Perry's ships were soldiers and sailors that were totally different from anything the Japanese warriors knew. These ugly looking "white" foreigners soon landed marching in impressive-looking ranks, wearing uniform clothes that were unlike any clan livery and armed with rifled muskets fixed with socket bayonets that totally outclassed any soldier armed with a matchlock musket. At a command shouted by a "leader" the soldiers would all instantly drill with their weapons, move about in step with incredible precision and, at times, might all fire a single blank volley that sounded and looked like an explosion. It may have been a "feu de joie" (firing for joy) to the Western soldiers, but to the Japanese it was a rude awakening to their own incapacity.

Nor was the news that now reached Japan very encouraging to those who felt that seclusion was the best policy. The powerful Chinese Empire had already

Two samurais sitting and relaxing, 18th century. This contemporary print shows the front and the back of their costumes and armor, and their hairstyle is also seen. Library of Congress, Washington.

The castle of Osaka with a view on the river, 1833. The small boats in the river paid a tax on the goods they transported to and from the countryside. While they had massive foundation walls made with huge stones, Japanese castles were totally inadequate against mid-19th century Western warships armed with large naval guns. Richard Kruml, Fine Japanese Prints, Paintings and Books, London.

Pair of samurai swords marked with the badge of the powerful Tokugawa family, whose successive members were shoguns of Japan from the early 17th century until 1868. These remarkable weapons are now preserved in the Douglas Arms Collection at the Royal Military College of Canada Museum, Kingston, Ontario.

An archer in one of the clan armies, c. 1750. Contemporary print. Library of Congress, Washington.

played that card in its dealing with Western powers and lost. In 1840, the British had seized Hong Kong and forced China to lease it for 150 years! The French were showing increased interest in Indochina. The Americans and everyone else wanted to trade. Might they not seize Nagasaki like Hong Kong, which would give them all a foothold in the nation? Much had happened since the 16th century and the Japanese now had to catch up.

Maritime Traditions

Being an island nation, Japan should have been a naval power. Yet at the time of contact with the American and European warships in the mid-19th century, there was no such thing as a Japanese fleet or even a large Japanese ship. The reason for this surprising state of affairs was the nation's policy of seclusion, which was strictly followed since the early 17th century. Indeed, in 1638, Shogun Iemitsu forbade the construction and sailing of large ships in Japan. However, because of the government's willful neglect to built and keep up a national infrastructure of roads and bridges, the

Japanese soldiers at Yokohama, 1853. The uniformity in clothing seen in Japanese prints is not evident in this view taken by a member of Commodore Perry's expedition. Print after W. Heine.

The arrival of Commodore Perry and his officers at a meeting with the commissioners of the Japanese government at Yokohama, 1853. Print after W.T. Peters.

Commodore Perry and his men land at Gore-Hama, Japan, on 14 July 1853. This event was the turning point for Japan in modern history. Print after W. Heine. Library of Congress, Washington.

transportation of bulk goods such as rice had to be carried by small coastal and river vessels. Road networks by land were kept to a minimum because the Shogun's government wished to keep the various parts of the country relatively isolated one from another. It feared, probably rightly, that easy communications would encourage several clans to unite and become strong enough to topple the government. On the other hand, coastal and river navigation by small ships was militarily much less dangerous and the multitude of these small crafts could carry all the needed good all around the island that was Japan. Thus, Japanese landscape prints are replete with depictions of small vessels or even of many small white squares representing sails.

This serves as a reminder that, in spite of its seclusion, Japan had a very strong naval tradition with thousands of coastal villages that were the homes of hundreds of thousands of sailors. For now, they were employed in coastal trade and fishing. But the day was nearing when the national policy makers would harness this maritime heritage to realize Japan's potential as a major world commercial and military power on all oceans of the globe.

The Arts

From the earliest times, the inhabitants of Japan showed an interest in art that became more refined and distinct as centuries passed. Exquisite statues and paintings were produced that were distinct, original and, as time passed, unique in a style that could only be found in Japan. As seen above on Father Maffee's account, the first Europeans that came to the country were impressed by the Japanese's dedication to art.

Many of the renderings showed warriors or military themes that echoed the nearly constant wars that went on between various clans until the end of the 16th century. The period going from the early-17th century was a generally peaceful era and the arts continued to flourish. Kabuki "song-dance-art" theater, which initially had prostitutes as actresses, became more "respectable" once women were forbidden to perform in them. This social acceptance meant that better plays were written for the theater and also for Joruri puppet plays. Most of all, the advent of book printing paved the way for the production of prints that showed images. Hishikawa Moronobu (1618 or 1625-1694) is generally recognized as the first craftsman to produce image print by using wooden blocks that he carved. These prints, called "Ukiyo-e", first published in Edo (later called Tokyo) became the popular art of Japan and their success with the public spawned many excellent artists. The early prints had to be colored by hand. Later on, colored inks besides black were also used. From the mid-18th century, technical progress achieved by Japanese printers allowed them to make color prints relatively cheaply.

The subjects of the prints were extremely varied and aimed at attracting large numbers of clients. They showed

Japanese ships with mount Fudji in the background, mid 19th century. Japan had many harbors and ships at that time. However, because of its policy of seclusion, it had no ocean worthy vessels and absolutely no ships that could oppose modern steam warships. Print after Hiroshige Ando (1797-1858). Library of Congress, Washington.

This "Japanese young man" from a print published in Venice during 1598 is one of the earliest European representation of a Japanese. The European-looking man holds a pole that could be construed as a weapon, but possibly the only somewhat accurate aspect may be the robe he wears, possibly an interpretation of an actual garment brought to Europe. Print from Cesare Vecellio's 1598 Habiti antichi et moderni di tutto il mondo republished as: Vecellio's Renaissance Costume Book (Dover: New York, 1977).

scenes of everyday life, views of famous places, landscapes, animal, flowers and trees, much as on the paper and screen paintings. However, there now was also a substantial production of erotic prints to satisfy a heavy demand for such themes. Historical events and portraits were also very popular and these quickly evolved into scenes of battles showing famous samurais in heroic and bloody combat with foes. Portraits of warriors were also produced in great numbers. A peculiar and very popular Japanese fashion was the production prints showing actors that portrayed warrior heroes. The Japanese public was thus obviously keenly interested in military art and especially: war art.

Military art in Japan had been practiced for many centuries onto various mediums. The paintings done on panels and scrolls depicted battle scenes, military leaders and various types of soldiers mounted and on foot. The composition of these works was always stylistically well measured, the colors used soft or vibrant and the stances designed to draw the onlooker's eye. At the same time, and although details of arms, costume and armor were intricately shown, the expression and posture of the warriors shown were the most important features. All these factors gave these rendering the power and balance associated with great art.

This art tradition continued in the prints produced from the 17th century. Fierce looking and, at times, outstandingly muscular warriors would be set in heroic battle scenes. Individual figures had valiant stances; their arms and dress shown in great detail. It seems that the artists went through much research to produce an accurate record of the material culture, not only of the warriors of their time but also of those of centuries past. Thus, apart from its power to attract the eye, Japan's military art also had great documentary value. There can be no doubt

Early 18th century French print showing Japanese troops entitled "portrait of a horseman and of a soldier of the emperor of Japan" that probably once probably illustrated a travel book. Western traveler's accounts of "exotic" and sometimes forbidden places, Japan for instance, were popular and a mainstay of European publishers. Although they each have the emblematic long and the short sword, the figures shown are more reminiscent of Chinese rather than Japanese soldiers. Some of the horse furniture and headdress as well as the robes seem more Chinese, especially as most Japanese warriors had trousers and distinctive headgear. Of course, accurate images of Japan were all but unknown in Europe so that illustrators tried to adapt the rather vague descriptions to what oriental images they could get, and those would tend to come from China. Anne S.K. Brown Military Collection, Brown University Library, Providence, USA.

that it mirrored one of Japan's most profound values: its warrior ethos.

Before the 1850s, the European view of the Japanese was extremely vague and confused. Only a few sailors and Portuguese missionaries had ventured as far as the "Land of the Rising Sun" and their few written accounts describing what they saw could not be especially clear to even a learned reader in Europe. There was also some confusion between China, Japan and other Far Eastern nation, which all seemed so remote. Sketches must have been made in Japan and costume items brought from there. It is perhaps on such sources that Cesare Vecellio based his figure of a young man, the only Japanese subject in the 500 figures of his costume book published in Venice in 1598. The resulting print mixes is the typical representation of oriental costume of the time worn by a young man that certainly looks like a Venetian. During the next centuries, the few prints made in Europe that showed the Japanese usually tried to reconstruct descriptions given in travel books resulting in somewhat imaginary "oriental" renderings by desperate printmakers. In truth, Japanese art, including its marvelous and powerful war art, was totally unknown in Europe and America.

Japanese view of foreign troops changing guards at Yokohama during the 1850s. The sight of these soldiers was a shock to all Japanese and the source of great curiosity. Japanese artists tried to depict the strange looking men with their clothing and weapons, all of which were totally new to their eyes. This plate appears to represent a change of sentries between squads of marines. They are said to be Americans, but U.S. Marines had dark blue coats. British marines, however, had red coats. Print after Utagawa Yoshikazu. Washington County Museum of Fine Arts, Hagerstown, Maryland, USA.

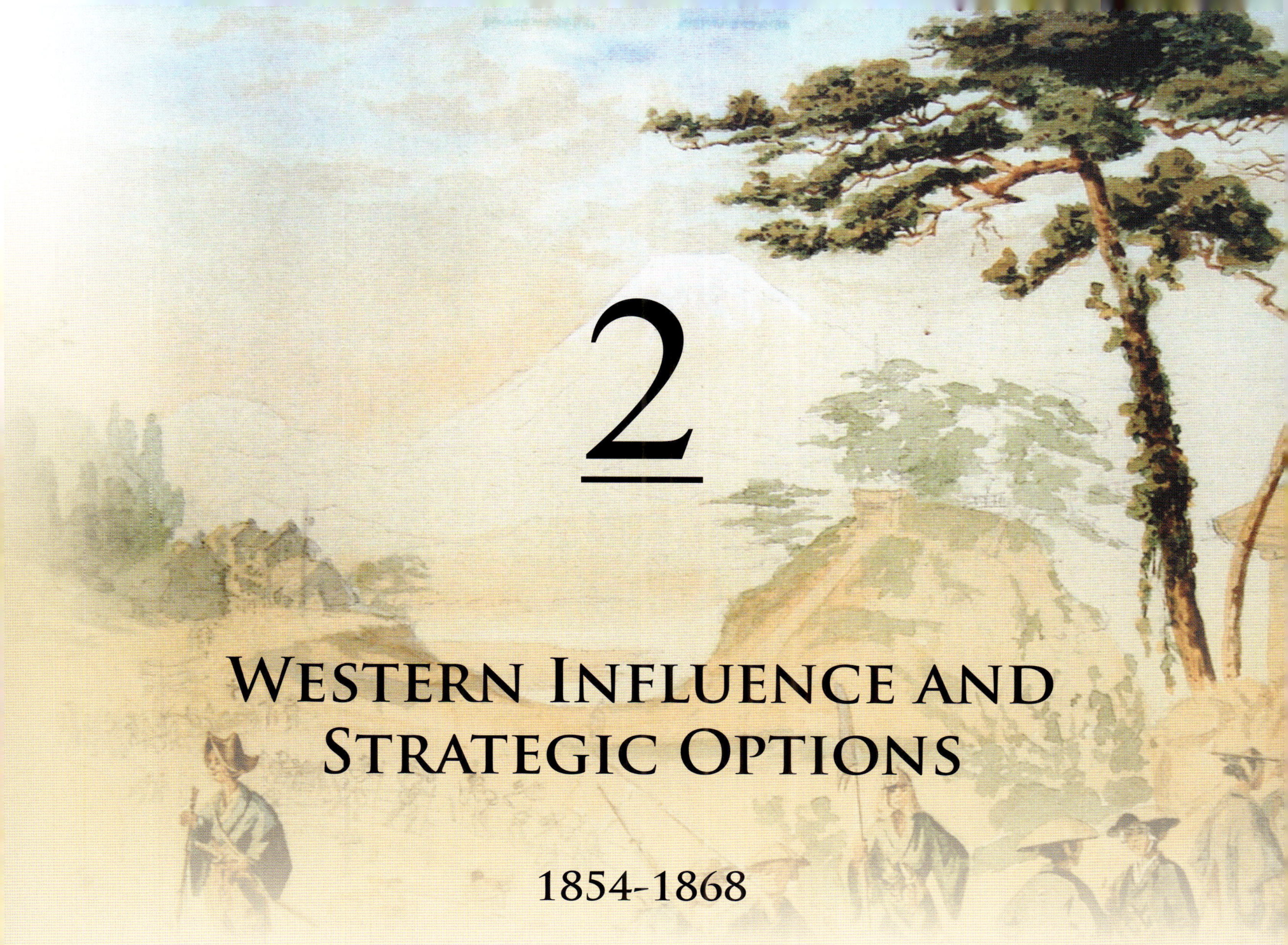

2

Western Influence and Strategic Options

1854-1868

From the time of the 1853 arrival of Perry's "Black Ships" to the outbreak of the Sino-Japanese War in 1894, Japan went through unprecedented changes. Indeed, such a rapid transformation remains a unique event in modern history. Just about anything Western was adopted and transformed. Even Japanese clothes were laid aside and Western fashions were increasingly seen. Even Western food started to appear on Japanese tables. An eminent scholar on Japan, Sir Hugh Cortazzi, pointed out that, "Western influence went much deeper than physical objects. Western ideas and concepts were imported wholesale" and new Japanese words were coined such as "competition" and "freedom" to transmit ideas that were previously undefined in the "inflexible feudal structure of Tokugawa Japan." Many young, educated and brilliant Japanese men traveled to Europe and the United States to learn all they could. Western books translated into Japanese soon had an impact on national literature. New building materials such as bricks brought changes in architecture. Industries increasingly integrated Western engineering and technology.

Such changes were bound to have a huge effect on the nation's military. In 1853, Japan's armies consisted of feudal-style clan armies made up of samurais. Since the early-1600s, they loosely supported the Tokugawa family's succession of shoguns that ruled in the name of the emperor. In the interest of maintaining themselves in power, the successive Tokugawa governments followed the strict policy of having no contacts with the outside world and also keeping internal movements in the country to a minimum by the inadequate road infrastructure and regulations forbidding travel. This so as to discourage the merging of several clan armies that could then attack the shogun as well as to keep the spread of ideas that might be more liberal.

By the mid-1850s, these government options were challenged as never before because of the arrival of the Western power's warships in Japanese ports. The guns they carried were obviously superior to anything found in Japanese castles. The uniformed men on board were, most of all, armed with rifled muskets that totally outclassed anything used by Japanese soldiers. Trade was demanded and now could not be refused. If something was not

Western goods and influences arrive in Japan, 1850s. This remarkable print shows contrasts: the steam powered ship with the square sails of the Japanese sailboats in the distance, the horse drawn carriage going by rickshaws. Note the two western men dark blue and black uniform coats with brass buttons. Some of the bemused Japanese rejected the foreign influences, but most were intrigued and a number of them saw these influences as the key to transforming Japan from a backward feudal country to a rich and powerful world power. Print after Utagawa Kineteru (fl. 1830-1874). Library of Congress, Washington.

done, and done soon, the nation would lie prostrate and defenseless.

In a nation with a strong martial tradition, the answer lay in the two linked concepts of wealth and of strength. The nation had to produce wealth, but what good would that do if its gains were unprotected by redoubtable armed forces? Would Japan sign treaties that could be usurped by Western powers that might chose to bombard a port or seize territory as was being done in China?

The answer, of course, lay in the creation of professional armies and navies on the Western models. Such a program would, however, need the transformation of Japan from top to bottom.

The government needed to be totally changed into a unitary state system. Education needed to be made available to all Japanese. The country's deplorable communications and roads infrastructure had to be modernized as well as a banking system created. The clan armies of suddenly inefficient samurais had to be replaced by a Western-like state-of-the-art national army recruited amongst all Japanese men. A national military navy and an ocean-going merchant marine had to be created out of nothing. Only with such tools could a newly industrialized

Samurai armor, mid-19th century. The advent of westerners did not result in instant changes amongst the equipments of Japan's military men. Armors such as this one continued to be made and used. Musée Ingres, Montauban, France.

economy prosper and be protected from foreign insult. Once this was achieved, Japanese goods and services could be exported with the confidence that comes from being well equipped militarily to face challenges.

The other advantage to having strong and westernized armed forces lay in Japan's geographic position with regards to China, Russia and Korea. In geo-strategic terms, all three countries could be used as springboards for an invasion of Japan. Korea had been used by Medieval Chinese armies in failed attempts to invade Japan. To prevent this, Japan had even made an abortive attempt to occupy Korea in the late-16th century, during the age of sailing vessels. Now, in the age of ever larger steamships, a modern army could quickly cross the Korea Straits or the Sea of Japan from or to the Asian mainland. Sooner or later, Japanese military planners reasoned, the Chinese would have modern armed forces and the Russian's increased interest in Manchuria would also increase their military presence. If Japan was to be secure, it had to have the finest modern army in Asia.

The first years of the opening of trade relations with the western powers were extremely confused for all Japanese, from the emperor to the meanest peasant. Changes started to be seen all over the country in the form of steamships, strange clothes, foreigners in city streets and all sorts of new objects that were being imported into the country ranging from horse drawn carriages to railroad locomotives. Japan was being westernized. If the nation was to survive in the modern world, it had to be modern. And what was modern was defined by the Western powers.

Yukichi Fukuzawa, Japan's former ambassador to the United States and the leading intellectual in favor of total modernization hammered the message that modernization was vital in a series of successive and best-selling publications, notably his "Things Western" that had much success and influence. He also advocated widespread education to gain further knowledge and therefore "civilization" as he saw it. Western dominance, he argued, had been created by the exchange of ideas, education, individualism and a competitive outlook. His ideas were very controversial and he was very courageous in making them known. Conservative samurais were not above murdering opponents by the sword for "sacrilegious" ideas, but he lived on to become almost sainted as one of Japans greatest intellectuals. Fukuzawa's fundamental principle was that national independence was to be achieved by personal independence. In effect, this

Infantrymen of the Shogun, c. 1855. These three privates are dressed in the Japanese fashion. The two at left and center wear the war hat with a clan badge in front. Watercolor by an unknown German artist after a Japanese original. Anne S.K. Brown Military Collection, Brown University Library, Providence, USA.

Troops of a clan army drilling, c. 1860. The infantrymen are all armed with European muskets, equipped with cartridge boxes and are performing a musket drill. The European field gun is fired by gunners equipped with ramrods. However, all are wearing traditional Japanese costume, the infantrymen having a blue and white livery. Detail from a triptych after Gountei Teishu (Sadahide). Anne S.K. Brown Military Collection, Brown University Library, Providence, USA.

called for the abolition of the class system. To reformers, and especially those wishing radical military reforms, it was the philosophical stance they needed to push through their arguments for totally Western style armed forces in a radically transformed nation.

Political Revolution and Dissent

Such rapid change naturally created a counter-reaction that resided mainly in the feudal governments and, to a certain extent, in the shogun's rule. An early conservative attempt by some clan leaders to keep foreigners out of their ports backfired in 1863 when the British, French, Dutch and American governments sent warships to bombard Choshu. In 1864, they bombarded Shimonoseki. These made the government open more ports and, more fundamentally, convinced most Japanese including the politically liberal groups that the 250-year-old Tokugawa shogun's feudal rule had to go. The liberals, which included many samurais who realized there was no future in isolation, pressed for the end of the shogun's rule and the advent of imperial government. In Japan, the emperor did not rule. He was above politics, had a god-like status and was the living symbol of the nation. The imperial party promoted the instauration of a new government that would have sweeping powers to reorganize the nation into a modern state. It was desirable that the emperor be agreeable to this change. Otherwise a large and bloody civil war might engulf the nation and that would wipe out all chances of creating a modern nation.

In 1866, the old Shogun Lemochi Tokugawa passed away and was replaced by Yoshinobu Tokugawa. He was committed to reform and sought help especially

Infantry of a clan unit, c. 1860. The soldiers wear Japanese costume, but are armed with European muskets. English print after a Japanese artist. Anne S.K. Brown Military Collection, Brown University Library, Providence, USA.

Two soldiers relaxing, c. 1860. English print after a Japanese artist. Anne S.K. Brown Military Collection, Brown University Library, Providence, USA.

from France in that regard. It was especially important to modernize the shogun's "Bakafu" troops and, in 1867, a French military mission sent by Emperor Napoleon III arrived in Japan. French and American military equipment was bought and a start was made at reorganizing the army. French engineers also started to build a modern shipyard at Yokosuka. The shogun's actions were certainly progressive, but he was also committed to preserving the old form of government, denounced as Medieval by critics at home and abroad.

Emperor Komei was likely as confused as any Japanese as to which way to go. But on 30 January 1867, he passed away and was succeeded by his son Mutsuhito, who would become better known as Meiji. The new emperor was only fourteen. As the year progressed, the position of the shogun was becoming untenable in the face of changes to government demanded by just about everyone. A compromise was found: the shogun would resign his title and become president of a national council made up of the clan leaders, the daimyos. On 9 November 1868, Yoshinobu Tokugawa resigned his post as shogun and formally returned power to the emperor. The imperial reformers did not agree with the new daimyo's council and opposed its president; real power was to be at the imperial court, not in the former shogun's palace.

The Boshin War

Things now came to a head and troops on both sides started to assemble. Yoshinobu with dissident daimyos was openly mobilizing the former shogun's Bafuku army to regain power. The new imperial government favored a peaceful settlement, but its Satsuma, Chosu and Tosa supporters also prepared for the worst. Some daimyos rallied to the emperor, others remained neutral. Early on, there were more troops for the dissident daimyos, but a first clash on 27 January 1868 at Tori-Fushimi, near the imperial capital of Kyoto, ended in an outstanding imperial victory. Its effects were enormous. Yoshinobu fled, the morale of the former shogun's Bafuku army collapsed and neutral clans now sided with the imperial government. Osaka Castle was abandoned by the Bafuku troops and occupied by imperial troops who later defeated attempts to retake it. Meanwhile, Imperial troops led by Saigo Takamori marched towards Tokyo (then called Edo until renamed on 26 October), defeated Bafuku troops at Koshu-Katsunuma and entered the city in May without opposition. The imperial troops took over the former shogun's castle. Emperor Meiji moved in with the imperial family and, from then on, Tokyo was the national capital.

Imperial troops went on to secure most of the country except for the northern domains supporting the Aizu clan. They formed a dissident "Northern Coalition" that boasted an army of about 50,000 men led by prince Kitashirakawa Yoshihisa and raised their own flag (a black five point figured star on white). They were relatively well armed, but not as well as the imperial troops. It is interesting to note that most officers of the French military mission joined the dissident troops and they now found that Japanese imperial officers were quite astute in the art of war. The coalition's troops were consistently defeated over the summer of 1868. The coalition collapsed in October and November.

The remaining dissident forces, including five French advisers, retreated to the Hakodate peninsula on Hokkaido Island, declared the "Republic of Ezo" on 25 December and built fortifications during the winter. The new republican army was under the command of Otori Keisuke seconded by French Captain Jules Brunet. It was organized into four brigades, each commanded by a French army officer, the eight half-brigades having Japanese leaders leading about 3,000 men. Two former French navy officers were in charge of fortifications and organizing a republican navy. In early April 1869, an imperial fleet with 7,000 troops on board appeared off the Hakodate peninsula, landed troops that attacked and gradually secured the positions held by republican troops. Imperial warships won the naval battle of Hakodate Bay that lasted for several days in early May. Having lost most of its ships and about half of its troops, the remaining forces of the Ezo Republic surrendered on 17 May.

Although it mobilized up to 120,000 men on both sides and caused the death of about 3,000 of them, the Boshin War was really a political struggle by two relatively small factions vying for power rather than an all-out Civil War such had been seen in the United States. There were relatively few battles and damages were minimal and restricted to a few places. The nation was otherwise unscathed and now firmly in the grip of the reformers at the imperial court.

The Military Organizations

At the time of Commodore Perry 1853 visit to Japan, the country did not have a national army. Some fifteen years later, the military structure was still largely medieval because the nation itself was still organized in fiefdoms

Infantry of clans supporting the Shogun, 1860s. From left to right: private, officer and two NCOs. The officer has a western style single-breasted jacket with buttons and one of the NCOs has a pair of trousers with a stripe. Watercolor by an unknown German artist after a Japanese original. Anne S.K. Brown Military Collection, Brown University Library, Providence, USA.

Troops of a clan supporting the Shogun, 1860s. These appear to show the Aizu clan. All have a dark blue or black uniform. English print after a Japanese artist. Anne S.K. Brown Military Collection, Brown University Library, Providence, USA.

Band of a clan unit, 1860s. Note the presence of a drum major's cane and the European style drums. The blouses are also of a lighter hue, indicating distinctive uniforms for musicians like European troops. English print after a Japanese artist. Anne S.K. Brown Military Collection, Brown University Library, Providence, USA.

dominated by clans who retained groups of samurai warriors to form their respective clan armies and, in some cases, navies. The lords, or "daimyos" that ruled each clan thus enjoyed substantial military powers in their own areas. Their troops were often dressed in their own family livery and they carried their lords' insignias on their flags. Since time immemorial, this had been the way in Japan and it had produced a nation of warriors and it was warriors that ruled the nation. As seen above, the strongest clan since the early-17th century was that of the Tokugawa family and its successive leaders were the shoguns, the military dictators that actually ran the country.

The clan armies maintained by the daimyos varied in strength and may have amounted to as many as 370,000 infantry and 40,000 cavalry that could be mustered under the orders of the shogun in case of a national emergency such as an invasion. There were also about 60,000 men in the service of the shogun.

The shoguns were aware as anyone that the armed forces needed to be modernized, but how to do this without infringement on the clans and their vested interests was an almost insoluble problem. Eventually, by the early 1860s, the shogun opted to organize his own "modern" army. It was possibly to be used as a deterrent in the case of foreign intervention and as a sort of model army for the clan troops. It was recruited amongst retainers favorable to the Tokugawa regime and also represented a modernization of that clan's already powerful army. Its officers came largely from the Tsukiji Military Academy founded in Tokyo since December 1854.

The shogun's modern army was organized from 1862 and augmented and improved over the next years. In 1864, its strength was 13,625 and men divided as follows:

1,406 officers
8,306 infantrymen
1,068 cavalrymen
800 field artillerymen
2,045 garrison artillerymen

Soldiers of the Shogun's army, 1862. The clothing and equipment is traditional if uniform in color. However, the men also carry modern European rifled muskets as well as Japanese swords. Watercolor by Herbert Knötel. Anne S.K. Brown Military Collection, Brown University Library, Providence, USA.

Recruits being drilled, c. 1864. All wear typical Japanese costume and carry wooden drill muskets. Note the drillmaster wielding a small whip! English print after a Japanese artist. Anne S.K. Brown Military Collection, Brown University Library, Providence, USA.

Troops of the Shogun, 1864 and 1865. At left, two officers or NCOs wearing their traditional war hats, shirts and sandals, but also clothed with somewhat western style coats and trousers. Both have their swords slung at the waist. The black war hats were painted with unit designation in gold (or yellow). At right, soldiers in drill order wearing jackets, trousers and shoes or boots. One has a western pattern saber. Watercolor by an unknown German artist after a Japanese original. Anne S.K. Brown Military Collection, Brown University Library, Providence, USA.

Officers at Yokohama, February 1866. A British correspondent sent a sketch that resulted in this print, showing a party of Japanese officers "met in the street the other day, and you will see the difference by comparing their costume with that of an officer of the old school, who looks on with astonishment at the degenerate habits of his fast young countrymen." Print after Wingman. Illustrated London News, 7 April 1866.

These troops were organized into regiments, battalions and companies. However, this new army did not have much benefit from Western officers as instructors. A few did serve individually in it, always accompanied by five cavalrymen as an escort. It was only with the arrival of the sizeable seventeen member French military mission in 1867 that formal training really started to take place. At about that time, a contingent of imperial court troops was formed, surely to insure the safety of the emperor as the political situation worsened.

The shogun's army was initially probably armed with various types of European muskets with bayonets, most having been imported from the Netherlands since the 1840s and 1850s. These were the only relatively "modern" muskets available in numbers at the time. The daimyo of Nagaoka had, on his side, obtained several thousands modern rifled muskets for his clan army and, in about 1867, a couple of Gatling machineguns. His troops supported the shogun's government. In 1866, the shogun ordered 30,000 Dreyse "needle" rifled muskets from Prussia, but most of this order does not appear to have been delivered. Some 2,000 excellent Chassepot rifles were received from France in about 1867 and they were used to arm the shogun's guard. Only a minority of soldiers carried such modern weapons. During the 1868 Boshin War, some of the shogun's troops were known to have only ancient matchlock muskets for lack of anything better. All carried the traditional swords.

Uniforms

Information on early uniforms is vague. Artworks of the period, both of Japanese and of foreign origin, do not convey a sense of much uniformity existing during the 1850s. Heine's prints of the Perry expedition show Japanese soldiers in varied costumes. On the other hand, Bayard Taylor who was with the Perry expedition recalled seeing Japanese sailors in liveries of "blue gowns, with white stripes on the sleeves, meeting on the shoulder, so as to form a triangular junction, and a crest, or coat-of-arms, upon the back. Others had gowns of red and white stripes, with a black lozenge upon the back. Some wore upon their heads a cap made of bamboo splints, resembling a broad, shallow basin inverted, but the greater part had their heads bare, the top and crown shaved, and the hair

Troops at Yokohama, early 1866. A British correspondent noted that the troops were, "now dressed in a queer imitation of the uniform of our soldiers … their caps, which are made of black velvet, are the most original thing about them. Altogether, their attire now presents a total contrast to the former fashion." Print after Wingman. Illustrated London News, 19 May 1866.

Maneuvers of Japanese troops near Yokohama, 1866. The Japanese soldiers wear their distinctive hats, but are armed and equipped with modern European weapons. French navy personnel are present at right, training with the Japanese soldiers. Print after Wingman. Illustrated London News, 12 January 1867.

A detachment of the shogun's troops guarding the British minister's residence at Osaka in late 1866. The shogun's troops, who had been primarily trained by a Dutch military mission, were defeated by the Choshu clan in 1866. At that time they had a dark blue uniform trimmed with white with black hats as shown in this print. An officer stands at right. Illustrated London News, 12 January 1867.

Shogun Yoshinobu (or Keiki) Tokugawa (1837-1921), c. 1867. He is photographed wearing a French style general's or diplomatic uniform, most likely entirely dark blue with gold lace, epaulets and buttons. He was instrumental in having the first French military mission sent to Japan in 1867. Banned from court after the Boshin War, he went into secluded and quiet retirement. As decades went by, his contribution to modernizing Japan were increasingly recognized. In 1902, he was reinstated by the emperor with the status of prince of the empire. Anne S.K. Brown Military Collection, Brown University Library, Providence, USA.

Infantrymen of the Shogun's forces, 1866. All dark blue uniforms with white stripes on the sleeves and white sashes. The round badge in front denoted the unit's number. English print after a Japanese artist. Anne S.K. Brown Military Collection, Brown University Library, Providence, USA.

Senior officer with escort, 1867. Even in the later 1860s, some Japanese senior officers could be seen wearing the traditional armor. Mr. Wingman, the British correspondent in Yokohama sent a report to London after seeing a, "Japanese grandee, in full costume, mounted on horseback, and attended by his sword bearer on foot, the latter being clad in armor; there was a groom, leading the horse by a blue sash, which serves instead of a bridle." Print after Wingman. Illustrated London News, 1867.

Soldier of the Bakufu Infantry, April 29, 1867. The Bafuku troops were part of the dissident forces led by French officers during the 1868-1869 Boshin War. The soldier show is named Ootsuka Tsukataroo. He wears a dark blue uniform with a traditional black hat and is armed with a rifle with its bayonet and a samurai sword. Print after a watercolor by Captain Jules Brunet, member of France's first military mission to Japan. Wikimedia.

The Shogun's Bufaku troops with Mount Fuji in the background, 1867. In spite of uniforms having been introduced, this print after an unfinished watercolor by Captain Jules Brunet, member of France's first military mission to Japan, shows considerable variety in the soldier's clothing. Wikimedia.

from the back and sides brought up and fastened in a small knot, through which a short metal pin was thrust. The officers wore light and beautifully lacquered hats to protect them from the sun, with a gilded coat-of-arms upon the front part. In most of the boats I noticed a tall spear, with a lacquered sheath for the head, resembling a number or character" as well as soldier in red liveries adding that their "caps and shields were lacquered, and glittered in the sun like polished armor."

The 1862 shogun's army named "Bukafu" appears to be the first sizeable military force in Japan to wear what could be considered uniform clothing. This usually consisted of a dark blue Japanese style jacket, sometimes decorated with white stripes, that fastened with a white sash, dark blue trousers and black socks with sandals. The headwear was typically Japanese consisting of black "battle hat" with marks in front (and which had the shape reminiscent of the British and American steel helmet during the First World War) or a black pointed cap that also had marks to distinguish units and rank.

Aimé Humbert, a Swiss resident in Tokyo during 1863-1864 described the troops he saw as follows: "The common soldiers are men from the mountains of Akoni, who are discharged after two or three years' service. Their uniform is made of blue cotton, and consists of tight trousers, and a shirt like that of the Garibaldian Volunteers, but crossed by white bands on the shoulders. They wear cotton socks, and leather soles fastened by sandals; also a belt, from which hangs a large saber with a lacquer scabbard. A pointed hat of lacquered cardboard completes their costume, but they only wear it when mounting guard, or on parade. The guns of the Japanese army are all percussion, with varied caliber and construction."

There were also summer caps that were radically different being copies of peaked caps covered with "Havelocks" covers that had neck curtains used in the British and other western armies. The Japanese versions were usually dark blue and their curtains sometimes even covered part of the face, a local innovation. As can be seen by the illustrations, there were many variations to this. In 1867, the shogun also received some uniforms as a gift from France described as being black decorated with silver lace. His personal guard probably wore them. The cavalry, as trained by the French advisers, sported lances and assumed a style not unlike the "Chasseurs d'Afrique" wearing kepis covered with large white covers, broad red waist sashes and dark blue or black jackets and trousers.

The political tensions finally led to conflict in January 1868 and the varied clans rallied either with the

Infantry detachment drilling, c. 1865. The men are in a battle formation presenting their rifled muskets with fixed bayonets. They are armed with British Enfield rifled muskets whose equipment included the distinctive cap pouches fixed to the belt. A simple western-style uniform is worn consisting of a green cap, a blue jacket and white trousers. Print after Yashinobu. Anne S.K. Brown Military Collection, Brown University Library, Providence, USA.

Infantry detachment with stacked arms, c. 1865. Standing at attention with British Enfield rifled muskets stacked as in western armies. The silk screen for this print was badly aligned, which shows that not everything was perfect in Japanese printmaking. Print after Yashinobu. Anne S.K. Brown Military Collection, Brown University Library, Providence, USA.

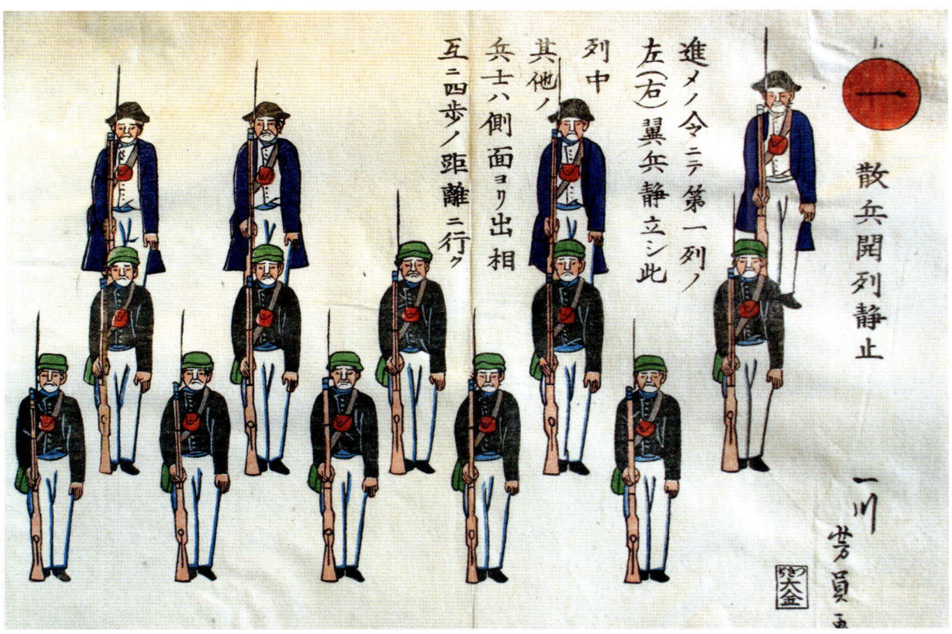

Infantry privates and NCOs on parade, c. 1865. All wear European type uniforms except for NCOs headwear. The figure with blue frock coats at top appear to be NCOs. The men wear green caps, black jackets and white trousers. They are armed with British Enfield rifled muskets whose equipment included the distinctive cap pouches fixed to the belt. The round badge at the upper right appears to show a musket indicating infantry. Print after Yashinobu. Anne S.K. Brown Military Collection, Brown University Library, Providence, USA.

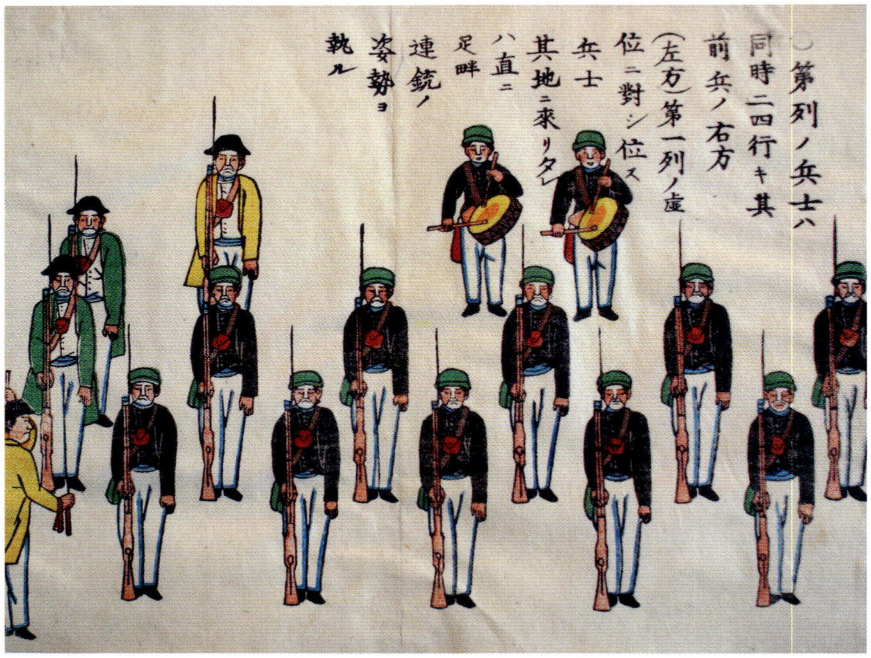

Infantry on parade, c. 1865. All wear European type uniforms except for the officer's and NCOs headwear. The figures with yellow coats appear to be officers. The figures with green frock coats at top might be NCOs. The men wear green caps, black jackets and white trousers. All are armed with British Enfield rifled muskets except the drummers. Print after Yashinobu. Anne S.K. Brown Military Collection, Brown University Library, Providence, USA.

Infantrymen skirmishing and loading rifled muskets, c. 1865. These troops armed, uniformed and equipped like western soldiers are nevertheless give a typically Japanese print mainstay since it has a large tree in its middle background. Nature themes would continue to be prevalent as backdrops in military prints until the early 20th century. Remarkably, some soldiers are shown loading their rifled muskets while lying down, which is rarely seen in illustrations produced in any country of the time. This also proves that these weapons predate the breech-loading rifles issued later. Print after Yashinobu. Anne S.K. Brown Military Collection, Brown University Library, Providence, USA.

Rear view of infantrymen skirmishing, c. 1865. They appear to wear British equipment. The black leather cartridge boxes are shown as green, which might indicate a fabric cover, local manufacture or artistic liberty. Print after Yashinobu. Anne S.K. Brown Military Collection, Brown University Library, Providence, USA.

reformers or the dissidents. The westernized elements in each opposing army had about the same dark blue or blue-black uniforms. Their hats appear to have provided the main difference for identification. For those supporting the imperial government, the Satsuma troops had tall pointed caps and the Choshu contingents had low pointed caps. The troops supporting the dissidents had caps with rounded crowns. These were not hard-and-fast rules and exceptions were seen, a good example being Captain Jules Brunet's 1867 rendering of a shogun's Bukafu soldier wearing a pointed cap. Traditional troops on both sides wore samurai clothes. An added badge for the dissidents appears to have been white armbands although the Aizu clan had them in yellow. Their sashes could be of various colors depending on the status of the soldier. The imperial troops could also have small white banners, some having family clan badges on them, worn on the upper left sleeve for troops wearing uniforms and on the breast for those dressed traditionally. These small banners appear to have been used much more by clans supporting the imperial cause, usually in white with clan badges, but also plain red. Naturally such badges could vary greatly depending on time and circumstance. A final and most peculiar item used by some imperial soldiers were the traditional and fierce-looking headdresses made of long "bear" hair that were red for the Tosa, white for the Choshu and black for the Satsuma clan troops.

Troops supporting reforms and the emperor were much better armed than their opponents, most soldiers carrying British Model 1853 Enfield rifled muskets firing Minié bullets. In 1865, the Choshu clan had acquired 7,500 of these rifles in England. By July 1868, the Tosa troops had received British Snider-Enfield breech-loading rifles and American Spencer repeating rifles were also later used in the northeast. The artillery of the dissident's forces was very poor and wooden cannons might be used. The imperial troops' was far superior because they had many modern British Armstrong breech-loading field guns that were ably served.

As usual with armies formed from various groups, there were all sorts of exceptions. Prince Ninnajinanomiya-Akihito wore his full traditional samurai armor leading the imperial troops in 1868. The imperial court troop detachment had a white and blue traditional livery as well as a standard dark blue uniform with pointed hats. Uniforms there may have been, but uniformity was far from achieved.

The emperor Meiji takes over the government, 1867. This illustration shows one of the most important events in Japan's long history because it propelled the nation into an era of enormous changes. As can be seen, everything was done according to the strict imperial protocol, that included the emperor's face be veiled, with all most senior officers and officials in traditional dress. Print in the Oriental Cultural Society's A Glance... . Anne S.K. Brown Military Collection, Brown University Library, Providence, USA.

The battle of Toba-Fushimi, 3 January 1868. A column of 3,000 imperial troops encountered a much larger Tokugawa force of the Aizu and Kuwana clans on the road between Kyoto and Osaka. The imperial troops led by Prince Ninnajinanomiya-Akihito defeated the Tokugawa army, which then withdrew to Tokyo. The imperial troops armed with modern rifles and bayonets are shown at left wearing black uniforms and pointed war hats. A few sword-wielding Samurais wearing traditional costume with Prince Ninnajinanomiya-Akihito lead them. The dress of the Tokugawa soldiers is generally similar and they have a white armband for recognition. Print in the Oriental Cultural Society's A Glance… . Anne S.K. Brown Military Collection, Brown University Library, Providence, USA.

Prince Arisuga's army leaves Kyoto for Tokyo, 9 February 1868. Following the battle of Toba-Fushimi, more troops rallied to the imperial party and the army took possession of Tokyo without a fight. Note the variety in dress worn by the various contingents shown, some are traditional, some are wearing partly westernized black and blue uniforms and carry modern weapons. Banners with the imperial badge are deployed. Print in the Oriental Cultural Society's A Glance… . Anne S.K. Brown Military Collection, Brown University Library, Providence, USA.

A view of the battle of Toba-Fushimi, 3 January 1868. In this print, the battle scene and its participants is overwhelmed by trees, so typical in Japan's graphic arts, and also the clouds of smoke due to musket fire. This last feature is often "forgotten" by western artists, but it was actually an important feature of battlefields between the end of the 15th and the late 19th century. Print in the Oriental Cultural Society's A Glance... . The imperial troops are at the lower center and right. Anne S.K. Brown Military Collection, Brown University Library, Providence, USA.

Imperial soldiers attacking rebellious troops of the Tokugawa shogunate on Hokkaido Island, May 1869. The Shogun's troops were defeated in what became known as the Boshin War. The imperial troops are depicted in black uniforms and most wear the black and yellow war hat. Print in the Oriental Cultural Society's A Glance... . Anne S.K. Brown Military Collection, Brown University Library, Providence, USA.

The Navy

Much like the clan armies, some clan navies were formed as well as a shogun's navy. As early as 1855, the government bought its first steam-powered warship named the Kanko Maru and, with assistance from Holland, set up a naval training center at Nagasaki. In the following years, students were sent abroad to study Western naval techniques, a practice that went on for many decades thereafter. In 1863, the first steam-powered gunboat built in Japan was launched opening up the nation's shipbuilding capacities. However, the shogun's navy, even if aided by the few small clan gunboats, was in no position to oppose any foreign warship. Following the foreign bombardments in 1863 and 1864, more ships were ordered from Britain, France and the United States. The dissident forces used most of the shogun's fleet during the Boshin War. The naval battle of Hakodate fought in early May 1869 featured eleven steamships of the newly organized Republic of Ezo navy. These included four warships and four transports from the former shogun's fleet manned by about 2,000 sailors under Arai Ikunosuke. They faced ten steamships led by Kuroda Kiyotaka who commanded all the imperial forces; his fleet included the new American-built ironclad Kotetsu, certainly the most outstanding and

The main tower of Osaka Castle. Its construction started in 1583 and it was completed in 1597. This castle was considered a masterpiece of Japanese architecture. After successfully resisting a siege in 1614, the castle was expanded during the 1620s, but was nearly destroyed by lightning in 1660 and 1665. Repairs were made in 1843, but, in 1868, its Tokugawa garrison was overrun on 2 February 1868 by imperial troops and the castle was damaged by fire during the battle and reduced to ruins. Its site was later used as a barrack for imperial troops. The main tower was restored in 1928, but damaged by American bombings in 1945. Its exterior was totally restored from 1995 and 1997. Wikimedia.

Soldiers of the late-1860s. The increasing influence of European uniforms mixed with Japanese costume is remarkable in this print. The head is covered by a European cap and the trousers are mainly western. The tunic has a Japanese cut with badges at the upper back and left sleeve, the waistcoat and sash are traditional as are the sandals. They are armed with swords and muskets. English print after a Japanese artist. Anne S.K. Brown Military Collection, Brown University Library, Providence, USA.

lethal ship on both sides. The Ezo Republican rebels had earlier failed to capture it by a surprise ninja-like raid, the attackers having been repulsed with heavy losses by the ship's Gatling machineguns. Other ships were from the clan navies supporting the emperor. The battle was fought by five Ezo Republican warships against eight imperial warships and lasted from 4 to 10 May. One imperial ship was lost, but two republican vessels had the same fate and the other three were captured. It was an outstanding imperial victory. It was also the signal to formally organize an imperial navy.

The shogun's navy officers adopted mainly dark blue British naval uniforms, much like most of the world's other navies, mixed with various features such as French peaked caps or even Japanese style topknot hairstyle. Rank badges consisted of the usual gold laces at the cuffs, with or without the executive curl. Only the service dress consisting of the double-breasted coat for officers and peaked caps appears to have been actually worn. Petty officers had single-breasted coats. During the Boshin War, officers of the imperial ships had about the same uniform as their opponents. Sailors on both sides were often actually clan soldiers detached for naval duty and wore dark blue jackets and trousers as service dress, not the sailor's style clothing seen in Western navies.

The Arts

The arrival of strange looking foreigners on board large vessels that belched smoke amazed artists just like all other Japanese who saw them. For artists, the challenge to make credible renderings of these human-like creatures covered with mysterious clothes and using all sorts of unfamiliar devices was staggering. As can be seen by the prints published in the 1850s and 1860s, they struggled to render physical details such as long noses and Western clothing. Western military uniforms appear to have been especially bewildering subjects. Utagawa Yoshikazu's print of, supposedly, American Marines in Yokohama would agonize any serious student of uniforms. It is the obvious result of a mixture of notes taken by the artist of various marines and sailors, most likely of several nations, and put together on one plate. The American marines wear red coats like British marines, the shakos have no plates and far from being uniform in appearance, the figures in black coats appear to have been seen worn by naval officers. The improbable wear of sailor's Sou'wester rain hats and cavalry type cartridge boxes and belts eliminates such items as having been taken from life. More precision in military dress and equipment is seen a few years later in three plates showing Japanese soldiers uniformly dressed in black coats with green caps with officers in blue, green and yellow coats, but the artist's unfamiliarity with such clothing, equipment and weapons is still obvious.

Japanese art influence on western art was nascent as yet, but this was about to change. It is said that the first Japanese prints to reach Europe following the opening of trade relations between Japan and western countries were imperfect or torn examples used as packaging material to wrap products such as porcelain. In about 1856, when the packages were unwrapped in France, they caused amazed admiration and some of these damaged prints went to printmakers and artists such as Félix Braquemond. He played a leading role in the revival of etchings in France and produced many with military themes, especially of the works by Ernest Meissonier. By the early-1860s, Japanese "Ukiyo-e" prints were reproduced in French books on Japan. There were now collectors of Japanese objects and an oriental shop on Paris' fashionable Rivoli Street offered prints for sale in 1861. European and American artists that saw them were fascinated by the hitherto unknown and obviously very remarkable artistic culture of Japan.

The Fifer, 1866. This young musician in the French army is one of impressionist painter Édouard Manet's best-known works. The artist was influenced by Japanese art in its composition. In terms of uniforms, the red trousers of the French army were later prescribed for Japanese army bands. Musée d'Orsay, Paris.

Sketch for rose and silver, 1863-1864. This evocative oil on board sketch by the American artist James Whistler while in Paris is one of the early known attempts to discover the power and sensitivity of Japanese aesthetics by a western artist. Worcester Art Museum, Worcester (Massachusetts), USA.

The American James Whistler incorporated certain composition aspects of Japanese art in his work. Indeed, one of the earliest examples may be his 1863 or 1864 sketch of his vision of a Japanese girl almost certainly inspired by a print he would have seen during his residence in Paris. Édouard Manet, an early leader of the transition from realist to impressionist art, saw Japanese artwork during the early-1860s and incorporated some of its aesthetic aspects in two of his masterpieces, "Olympia" of 1863 (not illustrated) and "The fifer" painted in 1866. In both works, the relative flatness of the rendering was inspired by Japanese wood block art prints. Japanese products were now seen in England as well as in France. Japan was not represented in the 1855 Paris World's Fair, but its products were seen at 1862 World's Fair in London. Periodicals such as the Illustrated London News showed the West what its correspondents sketched or photographed in Japan. These included views of Japanese soldiers, many of which are reproduced in this book. Their accuracy may not have always been total, but they gave an idea of the rapid changes occurring in the Japanese armed forces during the 1860s.

The official arrival of Japanese art in Europe was at the 1867 Paris World's Fair. For that important event, the shogun's government ordered a hundred prints to be shown at the fair, half of them showing Japanese women busy at various tasks so as to show the country's lifestyle, the other half being mostly views of Tokyo. The best artists were chosen to work on this government order and their prints created a sensation at the Paris fair. The prints stayed in France because they were sold after the fair closed thus contributing to the first wave of "Japonisme" to reach the French arts community. According to art historian Akiyama Terukazu, the quality of the prints at the 1867 fair was questionable because much of the subtle care in printmaking had been sacrificed to larger production runs since the 1830s. Following the death of such masters as Katsushika Hokusai (1760-1849) and Ando Hiroshige (1797-1858), the quality of Ukiyo-e prints saw a decline. This was combined with increased use of new inks that had very bold colors, especially the reds and the blues, which blotted out the soft tones seen on older prints. Of course, the artists of the French "impressionist" school then had no way of knowing that this art form was past its prime in Japan. They were much impressed by the "Japanese revelation" they saw.

From its first exposure to the West, from prints of the mysterious samurai warriors, the alluring oriental women or the delicate landscape, the young artists of the day such as Whistler and Manet, who would go on to become amongst the world's greatest, were deeply impressed. Such was the power of Japanese art that now arrived in Europe and America.

Prince Arisugawa and his army march into eastern Japan, mid-1868. The troops are dressed in dark blue western style jackets and black traditional war hats. The banner of the emperor is carried in front of the prince. Print in the Oriental Cultural Society's A Glance… . Anne S.K. Brown Military Collection, Brown University Library, Providence, USA.

Generals at a meeting of the imperial council, c. 1871. The senior military men now wore dark blue dress coats with gold lace and epaulets and bicorn hats with white plumes. An amazing print when one considers that only a few years before, these men appeared in traditional dress and carried two samurai sabers. Anne S.K. Brown Military Collection, Brown University Library, Providence, USA.

3

ENLIGHTENED RULE

1869-1893

On 3 January 1869, imperial power was formally restored under young Emperor Meiji Mutshuhito. The nation was about to be thoroughly transformed by gigantic changes decided by a small group of reformers that exercised power in the name of the emperor. No area was left untouched in this vast reorganization of Japan's society, of its institutions, of its economy, of its public services and, naturally, of its armed forces.

The object was to create no less than the most powerful western-style state in the Far East that would become its most influential nation on the world stage. The position of the dominant nation in Asia was then allotted to imperial China by western powers. Although vast and populous, the lumbering "Empire of the Middle" seemed set in its ancient traditions and, in fact, unable to deal with encroachments against western powers as had been seen by the 1860 capture of Beijing (Peking) by a Franco-British force. The French had moved into Indochina in the south and the Russians were eyeing Manchuria in the north. Furthermore, the Chinese and Japanese had been rivals for at least a thousand years and Japan's great invasion scares had always been from China. So there was no "love lost" in Japan for China. Now the opportunity to surpass and, eventually, dominate China was at hand.

The Japanese were determined that their nation would not be further humiliated by western encroachments and, even more important, that a threat from China would be immediately thwarted. China had an immense population. Its armies were huge, but it was generally backwards tactically and technologically by several hundred years when compared to western armies. There were isolated attempts to modernize the Chinese army, but they were piecemeal and they failed. The Chinese navy offered more of a promise to be effective because modern warships were being bought in numbers. In 1871, China created the Beiyang Fleet that became the pride of the Qing imperial dynasty, especially in the 1880s, when it was the most powerful fleet in Asia with seventy-eight ships afloat, some of them German-made battleships. The Japanese felt that this fleet, if successful in war, could lead to a Chinese invasion.

Korea was the most sensitive area because it was the best place for a Chinese force to board ships and cross over to invade Japan. The Korean peninsula was at that time under Chinese influence although an

An early image of imperial guard infantry, c. 1870-1872. In spite of being unclear and somewhat hazy, this photo shows a remarkable sight in Tokyo: infantryman of the guard wearing standard Western style uniforms. They were introduced in 1870 and included red kepis with falling plumes. Note the officers wearing bicorn hats at right. These uniforms were modified in 1873-1874. Anne S.K. Brown Military Collection, Brown University Library, Providence, USA.

officially independent Korean royal government ruled the country. In the early-19th century, Korea had chosen a policy of isolation by closing all its access except for keeping its border with China open. Japanese diplomats and spies thus carefully watched Korea. They always suspected that the Chinese would secretly prepare an invasion from Korea. To the Japanese, only their occupation of Korean peninsula would ultimately solve the problem.

The large Chinese island of Taiwan (or Formosa) at the end of the southern Japanese Riu-Kiu islands was the other area of concern. Japan felt it should be part of its empire, but had never succeeded in taking it over. In 1871, the wreck of a Japanese merchant ship on Taiwan's coast resulted in the beheading of its fifty-four crewmembers by local tribesmen. An outraged Japanese government pressed China for compensation, which the Chinese government rejected because it claimed to have no jurisdiction over remote tribes. A Japanese punitive expedition went briefly to Taiwan in 1874 and, from then on, Japan felt it had to annex the island. It waited for the right opportunity to act.

The Imperial Army

The age of the warrior was ending and the age of the soldier was beginning in 1870s Japan. One of the most important tasks facing the reformers to ensure the nation's future was the creation of a national army. At the end of the Boshin War, the imperial troops were made up of various groups of fighting men, some from clan armies, some from the former shogun's army that had rallied to the imperial cause. Many were samurais, but recent events had shown that proficiency with swords was no longer a vital element for success on battlefields. A commission was appointed to organize a national imperial army that would be mainly set up on the French model. First of all, the French army's published regulations and tactics were translated. The officers and non-commissioned officers were frequently assembled, and instructed in the principles of tactics and military discipline. Camps of instruction were established annually for the purpose of illustrating service in campaign, and teaching the movements of large bodies of troops in the field. Infantrymen and gunner also practiced target shooting. As the second mission of the French officers, which arrived in 1872, did not command, but instructed Japanese officers who retained

Imperial troops, c. 1871-1873. The uniforms showed in this print show the variety seen in the new army from about 1871. The red jackets at left are also seen in other prints and so must have existed for a short time. The mounted general and other officers are shown wearing the French style kepi, a black hussar-type Attila tunic with gold cords, lace and epaulets, and light blue trousers. Behind him are imperial guard infantrymen wearing red kepis (adopted in 1871), blue tunics and red trousers, the flag bearer having a red shako with a red plume. The coloring is not necessarily totally accurate because the leather accouterments, rifle butts and bridles are shown in green. The "War Flag" with its sixteen rays adopted in May 1870 is prominent in this print. Detail from a triptych that shows uniforms superceded by the 1873-1874 regulations although the print itself may have been produced later. Anne S.K. Brown Military Collection, Brown University Library, Providence, USA.

command of their units. Japanese troops initially learned through interpreters (from the French officers) the drill movements they were required to execute. It thus was seen that men trained in a few months with rifles, artillery and machineguns did not have to be born into the warrior profession, train from childhood in swordplay and study the intricacies of the warrior's philosophical codes. In fact, they did not need a privileged position in society to be highly efficient soldiers in a modern army.

Privilege of the clans stood in the way of creating a national imperial army. Clan armies were supposedly restricted to 1,500 men but the Tosa clan had up to 9,000 men. Rather than risk a confrontation, the imperial government opted to create the imperial guard during 1870-1871. This force, which consisted of infantry with small detachments of artillery and cavalry, was recruited mainly from samurais from various clans. It provided a certain amount of security for government members as well as an armed force to enforce its decrees if necessary. Its troops were armed with the latest Western weapons and dressed with a mixture of French and German uniform styles. Besides the imperial guard, other "garrison" line units were created in the wake of the former Tokugawa shogun's forces to guard various castles and military establishments. It was the beginning of a westernized national army.

The government went ahead with far more sweeping national changes. In February 1871, it decreed the end of the old clan fiefdoms and divided the country into French-style prefectures administered by imperial officials. Henceforth, private clan armies were no longer allowed and all who wished to have a military career would have to serve in the new imperial army. For the daimyos that had only recently supported the emperor's reformers, it was the end of an era. For the ordinary people, it was an extraordinary time period with something new appearing almost every month. For instance, the emperor, in one of his very rare "rescripts," had expressed the wish that

Imperial infantry of the early Meiji period, c. 1870-1873. This print titled "Meiji Regime" shows what may be early infantry uniforms, possibly of the imperial guard. The men marching wear dark blue German style forage caps with red bands, nearly all without visors, but the coats are reminiscent of the French army's "basquine" tunic with its short skirt as well as the ample light blue trousers and white ankle gaiters. The mounted officer appears to have a completely dark blue single-breasted tunic with, possibly, a traditional hat. The saddle blanket is also traditional, but with a western style gold lace edging. The officer in the background wears a service dress Attila coat, like French army officers, with a German style peaked cap. Note the very Japanese rendering of the nature around these westernized soldiers. Anne S.K. Brown Military Collection, Brown University Library, Providence, USA.

all Japanese children, and that meant every one of them without regard to class, be freely educated. He wished that there be, "no illiterate family among the people … [because] learning is the basis for all human endavor …" and he asked each of his subjects to "devote yourself to public service in a national emergency."

Education and Conscription

In 1872, the conscription law was passed. All able-bodied men between seventeen and forty years old were liable to military service without regard their social classes. The effect of this law was like a thunderbolt in Japanese society. For longer than anyone could recall, only the nobles and samurais could be armed and assume the title of warrior. This was often a privilege passed on from father to son and had led, in time, to the creation of the largely idle, inefficient, numerous and expensive warrior class whose pensions still created substantial problems to the national treasury. Now, all Japanese men were on an equal standing insofar as military service was concerned. The imperial government was determined to have a highly efficient army. For the most part, the new officers were reform-minded samurais that came from the educated higher classes.

The enlisted men were drawn mainly from the peasantry. It was certainly an extraordinary sight for villagers to see their young men that served in the army come back for a few days of leave with their families decked out in smart-looking uniforms; these young men were transformed by all they had seen, learned and experienced as imperial soldiers and soon must have been the envy of many of their neighbors. They spoke of the great cities they had seen, joked about the terrible sergeants that drilled them, reveled about the rides of troops in railways, confided the respect they had for their truly competent officers and, most of all, stated the blind reverence they had for the emperor. Perhaps for the first time in millenniums, the ordinary people felt they were an essential part of the great leap the nation was taking, going from a feudal and technologically backward fiefdom to a highly centralized and modern industrial state.

To succeed in such an ambitious endeavor, having modern armed forces was a key factor, but only one of the elements. The other basic objective to be achieved was the education of all Japanese citizens of all classes, no matter where they lived. Education was the key to national progress and prosperity. In 1871, the emperor had stated that schooling must be free and compulsory

Imperial guard cavalry and infantry at an official function, c. 1871-1872. The guard cavalry wear the all medium green tunic with red piping and brass buttons, red shoulder straps, red trousers with yellow stripe having a narrow green stripe at the center, red shako with yellow piping and red and white plume, blue schabraque edged with red lace. The guard infantry has blue-black uniforms and red shakos with white plumes. Anne S.K. Brown Military Collection, Brown University Library, Providence, USA.

Japanese boys in a schoolyard playing war games. In 1871, the emperor wished that all Japanese children attend school, which resulted in a vast national educational system being set up in record time. The curriculum included some basic military training to prepare the boys for their future periods of mandatory military service following the enactment of the 1872 conscription law. This 1904 French print shows the boys divided into two groups, one representing Russians wearing fur caps and carrying the Russian white and blue naval standard, the other playing Japanese soldiers with peaked caps and hoisting Japan's white and red flag. The boys are armed with sticks fitted with a ball at the end. Teachers supervise the activity while the girls, who were taught first aid, look on. Le Petit Parisien, 4 September 1904.

for all Japanese children. This objective mobilized the nation. Thousands of schools were built, often with the help of the children's parents and their friends because the access to education, which had been so long barred to ordinary people, was now within reach and was seen as a primary national objective. At the same time, tens of thousands of teachers were selected, rushed through training courses and put into classrooms even in the remotest villages. American educators were also brought in and they made a huge contribution to the organization of Japan's schools. Incredibly, the system was in place and working well within a few years.

For the army and the navy, the benefits were obvious because the conscripts or volunteers that entered the forces would now know how to read, write and be educated in the nation's basic values. Furthermore, the schooling system was expected to provide military training to young boys at an early age. From about the time they were eight years old, their teachers gave them a couple hours per week of very elementary training. Those who went on to higher education were given more advanced training by regular armed forces personnel so that, when they became liable for conscription, the boys were already familiar with the rudiments of military life.

The military and patriotic ethos taught by their schools and acquired during their military training may be summed up in an exchange between a young private soldier and an inspecting general, as witnessed by French traveler and journalist André Bellesort. The General asks:

Who is your leader?

The Emperor

What is the military spirit?

Obedience and sacrifice.

What is great valor?

To never mind the number of opponents and to march forward.

What is little valor?

To loose one's temper for something unworthy and to lower one's self by vile deeds.

(...)

What remains after a man dies?

Glory.

Active service was initially for two years after which the soldiers were released, but were obligated to serve in the reserve army. As reservists, they were called for training periods and an annual inspection. Thus conscription created both a national army for active service and, by 1875, a reserve army of equivalent size. This reserve kept growing as the years went by. By 1893, on the eve of the war with China, a secondary reserve for men over forty years old had also been created. Eventually, there were no exemptions allowed from conscription except for jailed criminals and physically disabled men.

Conscription did not instantly result in a huge imperial army. The system was presented to the people as a democratic social improvement measure. The conscripted recruits were carefully selected and, initially, only a few thousands would be admitted each year. The aim of the reformers was to create a highly disciplined, motivated and well trained force armed that was equipped like the leading European armies. A soldier of the Japanese imperial army enjoyed benefits that were unknown to other oriental armies: pay was regular consisting of five Japanese cents of the time as pocket money, seven cents for various deductions and each man was also given a liter of rice per day, all of which was considered as relatively generous by foreign observers. There were also bonuses for various activities and a decent pension for invalid or retired soldiers. Wives and children of deceased or maimed soldiers were also pensioned, the wives for life and the children until they were twenty years old.

The officer corps was required to be hard working, fit for campaigns and well educated in the latest military theories. To this end, the Military Academy was founded in 1875, its early instructors being mainly French because it was closely patterned after France's Saint-Cyr military academy. This was the work of the second French military mission present in Japan from 1872 to 1880. In spite of many officers from the first mission having fought against the imperial forces in the Boshin War, more missions from France were welcomed; this second mission harmonized relations and was very beneficial to the higher education of Japan's imperial army officers. Furthermore, the French naval mission of 1884-1889 had much influence on the imperial navy.

A policeman (left) and a soldier, 1873. The uniforms of these "Modern Japanese Types" were shown in this print, which appeared in the Illustrated London News. The early dark blue uniform of the police force is shown as featuring double-breasted tunics, baggy trousers, boots and the typical Japanese hat. The soldier appears to be an imperial guardsman because his shako is shown as being a light color, which could be the guard's red headdress. His tunic has longer skirts and piping rather than the shorter skirted and laced garment of the 1873-1874 regulations. Anne S.K. Brown Military Collection, Brown University Library, Providence, USA.

Gone were the freewheeling sword-wielding samurai half-bandits "ronins" that terrorized ordinary citizens in olden days. The soldiers of the new army were disciplined and looked impeccable in their new uniforms. The infantrymen were armed with Snider-Enfield breech-loading rifles like British soldiers and gunners now served a modern artillery park.

Meanwhile, there were still about 400,000 samurai warriors that were receiving pensions under the old system, an unbearable expense for the new Meiji government. In 1873, to provide relief, the government offered voluntary commutation and most of the formerly privileged warrior class accepted this retirement in spite of obvious financial loss. It was a remarkable example of resignation and sacrifice to the will of the emperor. But not all the samurais accepted ...

Shako of the line units, 1874 regulations. They followed the Prussian style and had a small black rear peak. Anne S.K. Brown Military Collection, Brown University Library, Providence, USA.

Shako of the imperial guard units, 1874 regulations. Guard units had red shakos trimmed with black. Anne S.K. Brown Military Collection, Brown University Library, Providence, USA.

Officer's kepis, 1874 regulations. For troops of the line. Dark blue with gold lace. Anne S.K. Brown Military Collection, Brown University Library, Providence, USA.

Officer's tunic, 1874 Regulation. Front and back view. The rank insignia is left off in this plate. Yellow denotes the artillery. Anne S.K. Brown Military Collection, Brown University Library, Providence, USA.

Officer's tunics, 1874 Regulation. At top: engineer corps (white facings); at bottom: cavalry (green facings). The rank insignia is left off in this plate. Anne S.K. Brown Military Collection, Brown University Library, Providence, USA.

Police Force

While not strictly a military force, the Japanese police played a certain military role in the early years of the Meiji Regime. The modernization of the nation led to the creation of a modern, western-style police force to replace the previous town samurai magistrates system that had been in place since the early-17th century. In 1872, the government sent to Europe Kawaji Toshiyoshi, a politician involved in law enforcements systems, to consider its various police organizations. He was especially impressed with the French and the German police forces and used them as models in his recommendations for setting up the new Japanese police, which were acted upon the following year. The nation was then being reorganized into prefectures and the new imperial police force formed part of the new system. It came under the responsibility of the Home Ministry, created in November 1873 to manage the empire's internal affairs. The imperial police force worked within a centralized national government system, but its routine administration concerned mostly the local prefecture. Every prefecture soon had its police component and many new constables were samurai former "policemen" that were trained and integrated in the new imperial police force. It had a quasi-military

Field officer's trousers, 1874 regulations. Dark blue with corps color stripes, in this case red for infantry. Note that field officers had piping and a stripe on each side as shown in this plate. Anne S.K. Brown Military Collection, Brown University Library, Providence, USA.

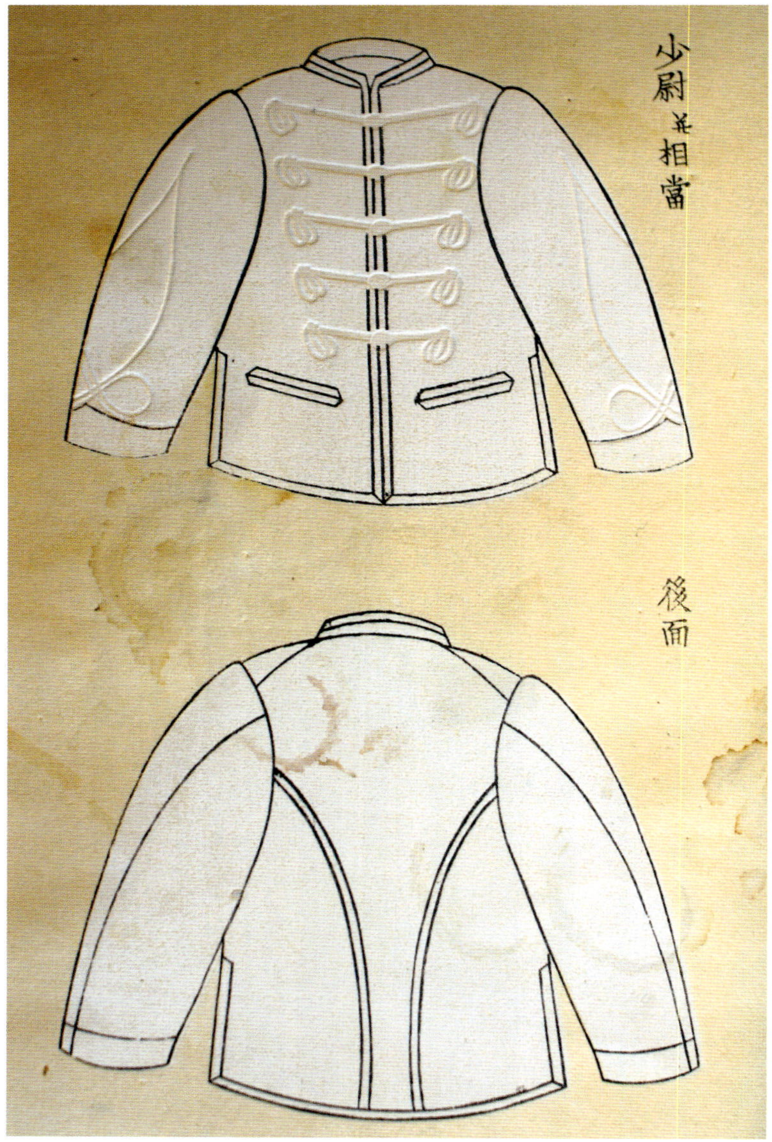

Officer's service dress Attila pattern, 1874 regulations. The flat edging lace is outlined in black and the cords are impressed onto the paper. Anne S.K. Brown Military Collection, Brown University Library, Providence, USA.

Artillery company of junior officer's trousers, 1874 regulations. Dark blue with a single yellow stripe. Infantry had red stripe, artillery yellow, cavalry green, engineers white, train and administrative units sky blue. Anne S.K. Brown Military Collection, Brown University Library, Providence, USA.

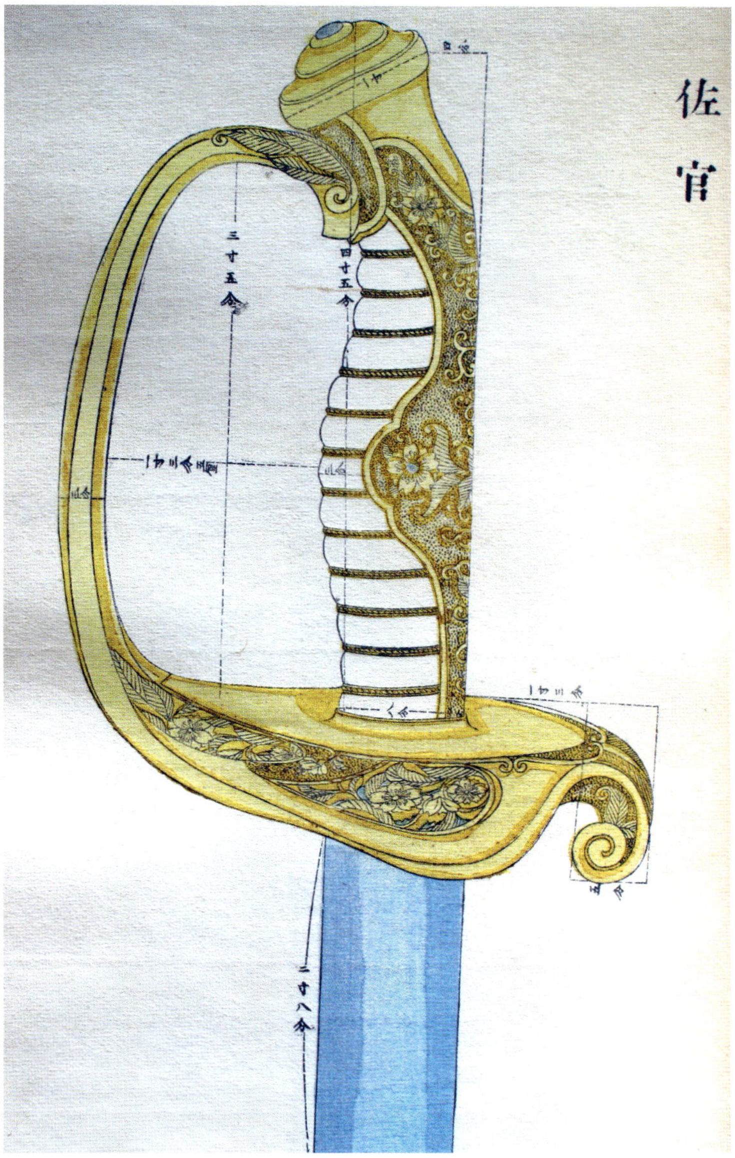

Officer's dress sword belts, 1874 regulations. Anne S.K. Brown Military Collection, Brown University Library, Providence, USA.

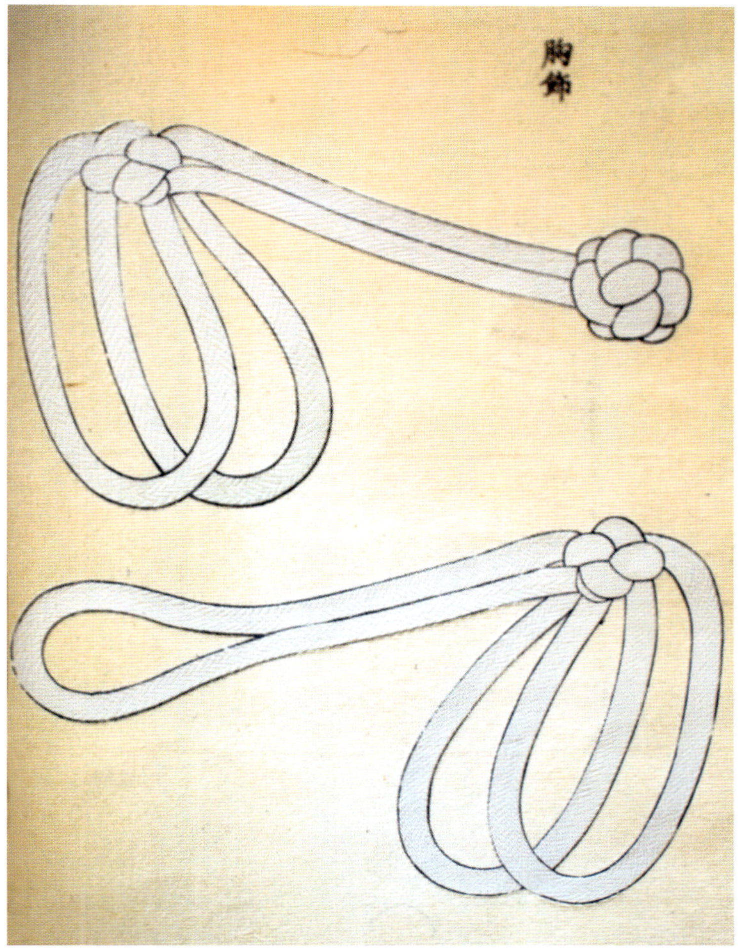

Cord design detail for the Attila, 1874 regulations. Anne S.K. Brown Military Collection, Brown University Library, Providence, USA.

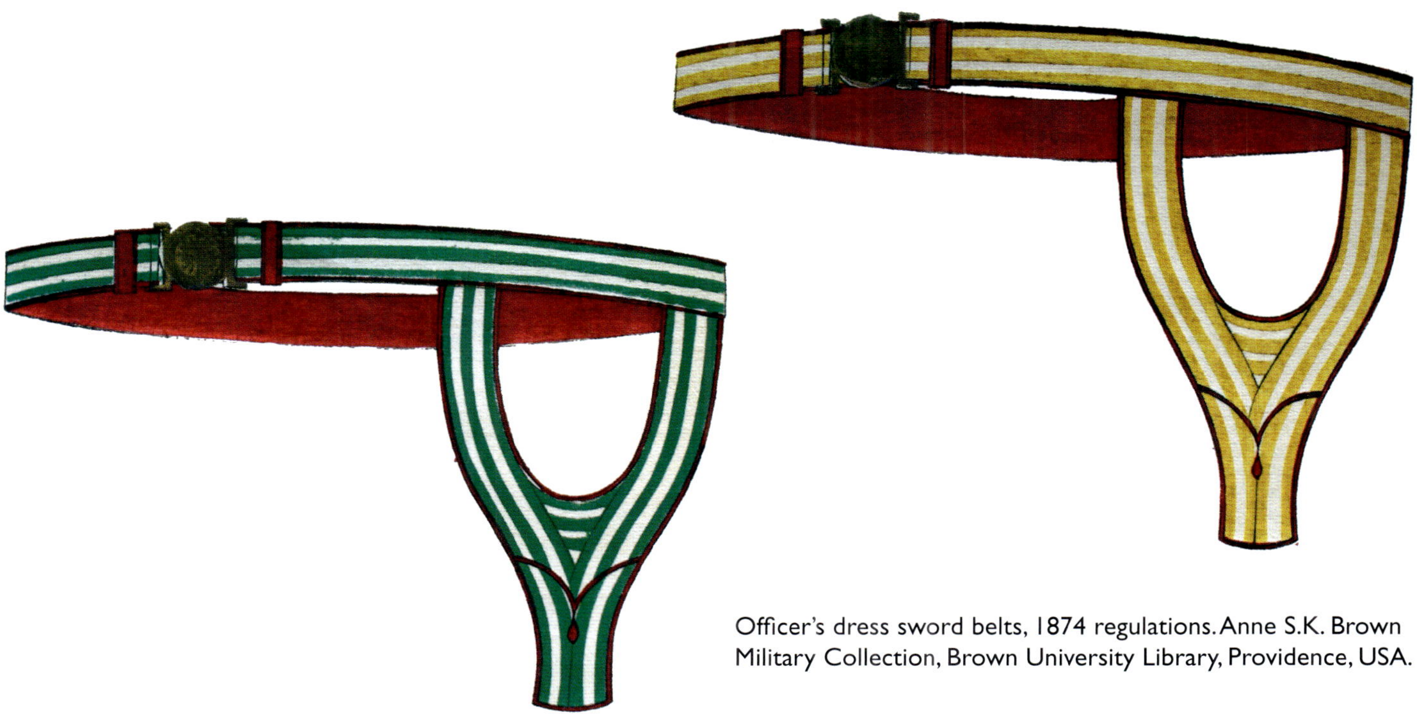

Officer's dress sword belts, 1874 regulations. Anne S.K. Brown Military Collection, Brown University Library, Providence, USA.

Infantry officer's dress sash, 1874 regulations. Anne S.K. Brown Military Collection, Brown University Library, Providence, USA.

Lieutenant general's dress sash, 1874 regulations. The five small silver stars on the tassel's knot denote the rank. Anne S.K. Brown Military Collection, Brown University Library, Providence, USA.

organization with garrison-like posts reminiscent of the French Gendarmerie and it was quite numerous: in about 1880, there were some 23,000 policemen. They wore a dark blue western-style uniform initially consisting of a tunic with two rows of white metal buttons in front, a pair of trousers, a pair of black boots, a low peaked cap and also a traditional Japanese style hat. Japanese policemen were initially only armed with batons.

In 1877, the imperial police force played and important part in the suppression of the Satsuma revolt. Eventually, it was deemed that its professionalism could be improved and, in 1883, a police academy patterned after the one in Germany was opened to increase crime-solving and prevention efficiency. The whole force was also reorganized into a more centralized, yet more local force. The larger garrison-style bases were closed and policemen were reassigned in small groups serving in local city wards or in small villages. It should also be noted that, besides insuring public order, the imperial police also had responsibility for fire prevention and regulated public health concerns, business licenses, workplace safety and mediated labor disputes. It thus had an impact in all aspects of daily life. The imperial police thus enjoyed wide powers to combat criminal activity, which made it both feared and respected by the people.

The 1877 Satsuma Uprising

In 1876, the imperial government abolished the right to wear swords and withdrew the pensions and allowances that were paid to the samurai and nobles, which still represented a sizeable part of the national budget. Both measures were aimed at the die-hard samurais who had not done so voluntarily in 1872-1873. The prohibition to carry swords outraged many and armed outbreaks occurred in several places. Former Marshal Takamori Saigo became the leader of tens of thousands of disgruntled samurais. The new imperial army's first major test came with the Satsuma samurai uprising that broke out on 29 January 1877. Unlike what was seen in Edward Zwick's "The Last Samurai" 2003 movie epic starring Tom Cruise, both sides were using firearms. An important point is that the rebels were armed with fairly modern firearms. They carried muzzle-loading British Enfield and Russian Model 1857 rifles. In the hands of a trained soldier, these rifles could

Officer's aiguillette pattern, 1874 regulations. Anne S.K. Brown Military Collection, Brown University Library, Providence, USA.

fire two to three times per minute. They also had two field guns, twenty-eight mountain guns and some thirty mortars with men that knew how to serve them because Saigo had organized a private artillery school three years earlier. The rebels were nevertheless definitely outgunned by the well trained artillerymen of the imperial army, which had over 100 modern cannons, mostly French and German field guns, as well as American Gatling machineguns. It was not, as seen in the movie, a case of the westernized and well-armed imperial army against the traditionally armored samurais wielding traditional swords; it was nastier than that and there were rifle firefights. It must not be forgotten that the rebellion's leader, Saigo Takamori, had been, a few years earlier, the commander of the new imperial army. He and some of his lieutenants "were dressed in uniforms they had worn in the Imperial army" according to British correspondent A.H. Mounsey. Prints also show Saigo wearing his old pre-1873 general's uniform with a plumed bicorn, a far cry from the "zen" warrior leader portrayed in the motion picture. Some sources put his force at up to 40,000 samurai warriors and supporters, but a figure of about 15,000 to 20,000 would seem more realistic. This was still a sizeable force and many of its men knew how to bear western firearms with the added advantage of wielding with skill that fearsome ancient weapon: the Japanese sword.

The rebellious samurais faced a rapidly growing number of regular imperial soldiers, many of whom had been young peasants forbidden to bear arms only few years before. Now they used the breech-loading British Snider-Enfield rifles that could fire at least six shots per minute and did so with outstanding professionalism and bravery, adding to these qualities the spirit of the warrior traditions that were profoundly Japanese. The imperial army had 34,000 men when the rebellion broke out; reserves were called up to boost army units to war strength and the navy and the marine corps were also deployed. By September, the imperial forces in the field may have numbered as many as 90,000 men. There were some rough engagements, but the extensive training soldiers had received now paid off. The regulars of the imperial army soon seized the tactical initiative and thereafter always kept it. There were a few instances when detachments of insufficiently trained imperial troops were hacked to pieces by sword wielding samurais, but on the whole, superior firepower and discipline prevailed. Aware that it should also have swordsmen, the imperial government called upon loyal samurais, notably those serving in the imperial police force, to battle the rebels and organized some police personnel as temporary military units to help suppress the uprising. As months went by, many rebels realized that it was a hopeless struggle that did not have much popular support. To most people, they were betraying the emperor and thus the nation for their own

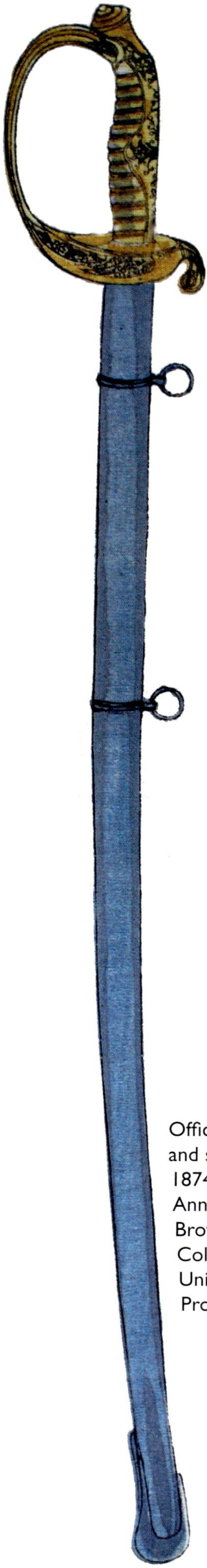

Officer's sword and scabbard, 1874 regulations. Anne S.K. Brown Military Collection, Brown University Library, Providence, USA.

Senior officer's dress sword hilt, 1874 regulations. Anne S.K. Brown Military Collection, Brown University Library, Providence, USA.

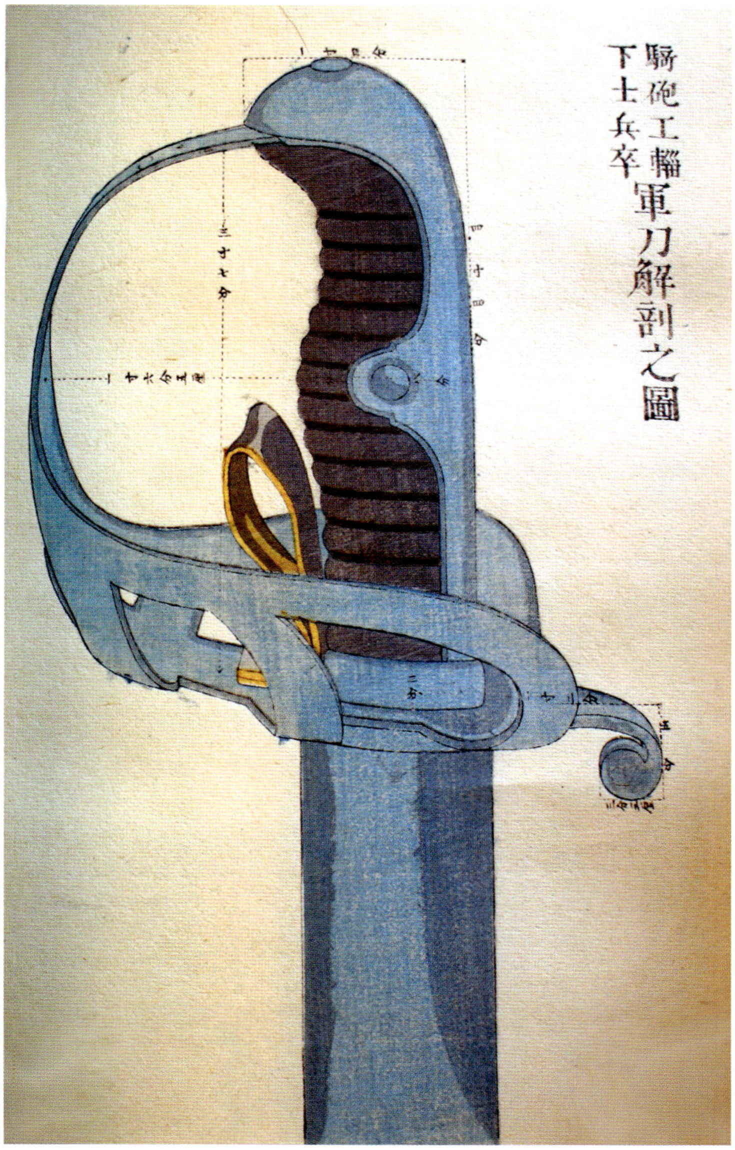

Saber hilt, 1874 regulations. Anne S.K. Brown Military Collection, Brown University Library, Providence, USA.

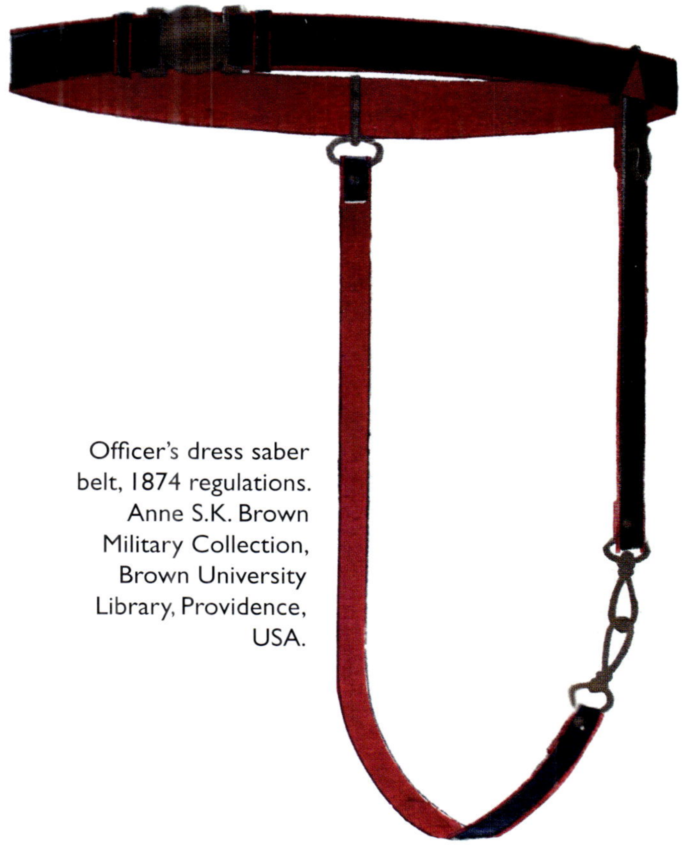

Officer's dress saber belt, 1874 regulations. Anne S.K. Brown Military Collection, Brown University Library, Providence, USA.

selfish goals. Discouraged, many abandoned the rebel camp. The final confrontation occurred at Kagoshima on 24 September where the Satsuma rebellion was crushed after a hard-fought battle. In its last phase, cornered on all sides and wounded in the fighting, Saigo commanded one of his officers to cut off his head, which was accordingly done. About 20,000 rebels and 6,300 imperial soldiers were killed during the uprising while the nation's treasury was practically emptied.

Nevertheless, the regular imperial army mainly composed of peasants had won an overwhelming victory against the ancient warrior caste. All Japanese now knew they had what it took to be excellent combatants. The fighting qualities of the people at large were confirmed. Thus, to one and all, the crushing of the Satsuma rebellion proved that not only samurais, but all Japanese were brave and fearless warriors. The wheel had turned and the archaic past values faded. The nation could now envisage with confidence its ambition of becoming the richest and most powerful country in the Far East.

Army Growth

Even before the Satsuma rebellion, visiting American staff officer Emory Upton was very impressed by the army he saw in 1875 and, in his report published three years later, lauded the imperial government "for its foresight" and prophetically predicted that Japan, "no longer contented with progress at home, is destined to play an important part in the history of the world."

The imperial army remained relatively small during the 1870s. By 1880, there were 3,970 officers and men in the imperial guard and 35,000 in the line army. This was a very small force in a country of some thirty-three million souls according to its first modern census. However, as P. de Lapeyrère, a French officer detached to Japan, shrewdly noted in 1881, the potential to raise a huge army was there: Japan had 6,762,000 men able to bear arms between the ages of seventeen and forty. The imperial government and general staff did not wish a large undisciplined mob of soldiers armed with ancient weapons, such as could still be seen in China. It wanted the Japanese imperial army to be a highly trained, well-armed and efficient force that was second to none. That took time, but as time passed, there were more and more experienced soldiers to train the increasingly educated recruits.

The army grew slowly and steadily during the 1880s. New service corps were added. Amongst the most notable

Kepi with white Havelock cover, 1874 regulations. Anne S.K. Brown Military Collection, Brown University Library, Providence, USA.

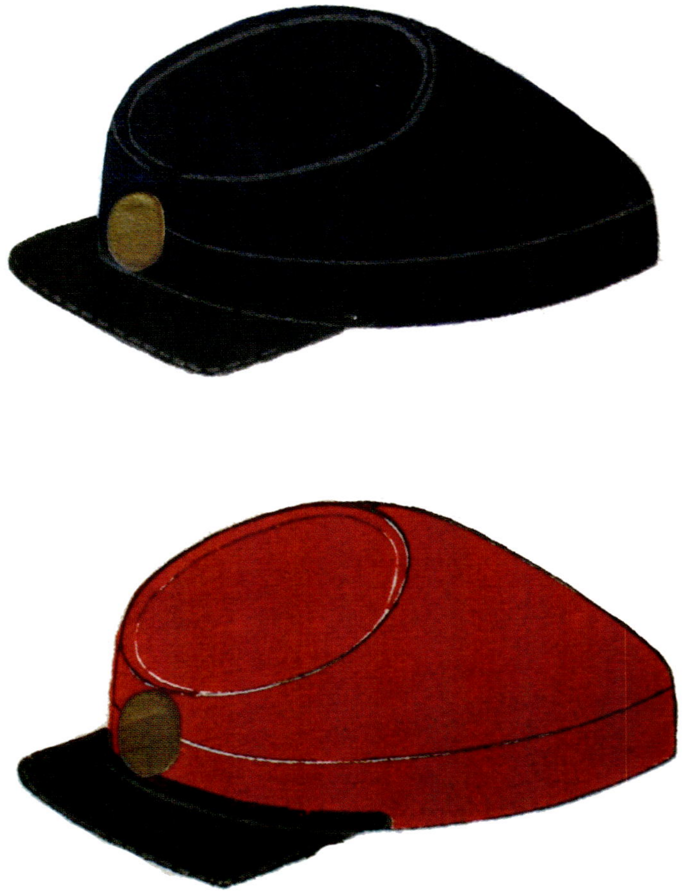

Enlisted men's kepis, 1874 regulations. Top: dark blue for line troops. Bottom: red for the imperial guard. Anne S.K. Brown Military Collection, Brown University Library, Providence, USA.

Field service cap with white Havelock cover, 1874 regulations. Anne S.K. Brown Military Collection, Brown University Library, Providence, USA.

Field service cap with white crown cover, 1874 regulations. Yellow band for the artillery. Anne S.K. Brown Military Collection, Brown University Library, Providence, USA.

Field service caps, 1874 regulations. Enlisted men at top, officers at bottom. Dark blue crown with a band and piping of the corps color, in this case white for the engineer corps. The yellow five-point star was the universal cap badge. Black leather peak. Anne S.K. Brown Military Collection, Brown University Library, Providence, USA.

was the Gendarmerie (or military police) raised from 11 March 1881. Political unrest created by some imperial guardsmen convinced senior authorities that, added to other judiciary factors inherent to a modern army, a provost corps had become necessary and the "Kempeitai" was organized to insure order and maintain discipline in the ranks. One of its functions was to stamp out political activity amongst soldiers, which had been proscribed in 1880. The Gendarmerie had an initial establishment of 1,612 officers and men. In 1882, a judicial department was organized while the medical corps was restructured and expanded.

Command structure too evolved. Following the 1877 Satsuma rebellion, senior officers were not especially satisfied at the way the imperial army had responded in the crisis. It had seemed somewhat haphazard and they wished to know why. The enquiry was entrusted to Colonel (later General and Prime Minister) Katsura Taro, an excellent choice. As a young officer, he had been sent to France, but on the way to Paris learned that it had been taken by the Germans and headed instead for Berlin. Back in Tokyo after several years in Germany, he concluded that the fault lay in the feebleness of the French system of strategic planning, which was also seen as a major reason for the defeat of the France's army in the 1870 Franco-Prussian War. What was needed was a general staff organized like the German imperial army's. Taro's recommendations were accepted and, in 1878, the Japanese imperial army general staff was created. Furthermore, the Japanese government asked Germany if it could send a military mission, which was done in 1885. German Army Staff College major and professor Jacob Meckel led the mission and made outstanding recommendations that were largely

Enlisted men tunics, 1874 regulations. Dark blue with collar and lace of the corps color. Top: cavalry (green); bottom: infantry (red). Anne S.K. Brown Military Collection, Brown University Library, Providence, USA.

Enlisted men tunic, open and back view, 1874 regulations. The skirts of this tunic were very short, like the French army's pattern 1860 "basquine" tunic. The distinctive color shown is for infantry (red). Anne S.K. Brown Military Collection, Brown University Library, Providence, USA.

implemented by the Japanese. These ranged from adopting the divisional structure to increase mobility, making artillery and engineer corps independent commands and even interlinking all army bases with railroads for speedy deployment. These and other reforms paved the way for the army's future battlefield successes.

In 1888, the army was reorganized into seven divisions (including one for the guard) of 12,000 men each with an artillery component of thirty-six field guns. Each division was usually made up of: four infantry regiments, each regiment having four battalions and each battalion had three companies; one regiment of cavalry three squadron strong; a regiment of artillery of six batteries, each battery manning six guns; an engineer battalion and a train squadron. There also was a medical detachment and other support corps. Thanks to this integral organization, the deployment of the army outside of Japan was made much smoother.

The regular imperial army was not the only land force available. Substantial number of reservists could be called back to duty as well the territorial force. In 1893, at the eve of the Sino-Japanese War, there were 104,652 reservists and 83,201 territorial volunteers that could be called on active duty. Thus, the Japanese army could put nearly 300,000 men in the field in a few weeks, all of them well trained, disciplined, equipped and armed like the best and most modern armies of Europe.

Uniforms

With the advent of the Meiji restoration, the newly unified imperial military services were definitively moving towards the adoption of a national army uniform and a

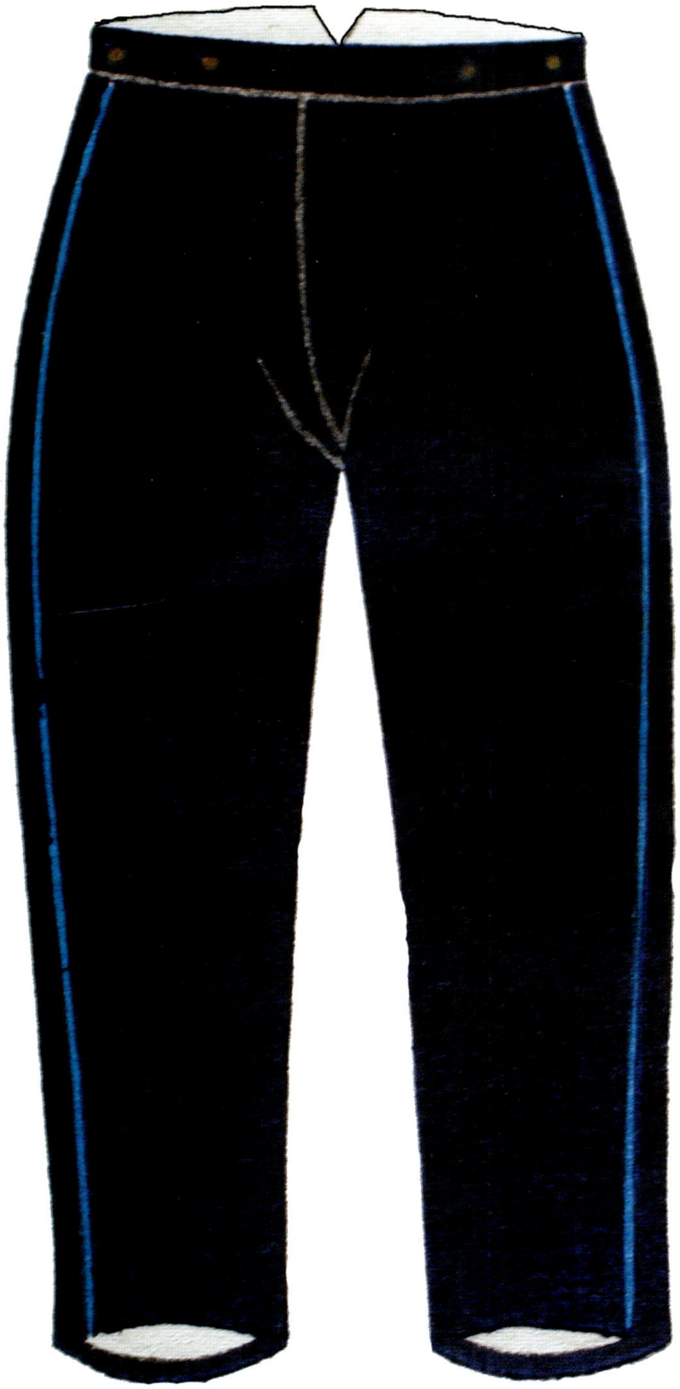

Train, administrative or medical corps private's trousers, 1874 regulations. Dark blue with sky blue piping. Infantry had red piping, artillery yellow, cavalry green, engineers white. Anne S.K. Brown Military Collection, Brown University Library, Providence, USA.

naval uniform. Thus, the first years of the Meiji regime witnessed various experiments. The first uniform was described as "a dingy, shoddy, black tunic, not made, nor apparently intended, to fit him [the soldier]; while the cartouche-box was strapped under the garment, instead of being neatly belted round his waist outside, and thus giving him the appearance of being hump-backed, which was rendered more ludicrous by the protuberant knees and drag of the feet from the wearing of sandals." After various experiments, it was decided to clothe the infantry in a totally Western style. During 1870-1871, the newly formed imperial guard was dressed in a generally French style uniform. The infantry had dark blue tunics with red collar and cuffs and yellow piping and buttons, gray or sky blue trousers with a yellow stripe, dark blue low shakos trimmed with yellow piping to which was attached a red and white plume for dress occasions. There were many variations to the above, for instance gunners had black collars and trouser stripes and cavalrymen had red shakos and trousers with yellow stripes. In 1871, the uniform of the imperial guard cavalry was changed to a green tunic with red cuffs and piping. The infantry's tunic was simplified by the removal of the yellow piping and the trousers were henceforth blue with a red stripe. That same year, the red shako became the distinguishing mark of all the imperial guard units. There was also an infantry service dress consisting of a dark blue jacket, light blue trousers and a dark blue German style service cap with a red band and without a visor.

Meanwhile, troops of the line (at first called "garrison") were also adopting uniforms that were definitely totally European in appearance. In 1870, there were a number of variations, but the dress generally was similar to the imperial guard. The line cavalry continued to wear dark blue tunics with red trousers and shakos after the imperial guard cavalry adopted medium green tunics in 1871. The results of these first steps to provide the army with standard uniforms were generally successful. The basic principle of a single dark blue uniform for nearly all units rather than a distinct regimental dress for each unit was thus adopted. On the other hand, there was not a great deal of distinction between the various branches of the service and one unit, the imperial guard cavalry, had medium green rather than dark blue tunics.

At this time, generals appear to have favored French style full dress uniforms with bicorn hats decorated with white plumes and gold cockade loops. The coats were dark blue trimmed with gold lace, epaulets and buttons and trousers appear to have usually been sky blue with a gold stripe according to period prints. In the field, kepis and hussar-style Attila tunics profusely decorated with gold cords, lace and epaulets were seemingly preferred.

There were as yet no general regulations regarding the dress of the imperial army. Reform-minded officers and military bureaucrats were well aware of the importance of a coherent military dress for the army. The smart appearance of the nation's armed forces was a prime factor in the credibility that the new government sought to convey to western nations. It wished to distance itself from the "antique" look of the Chinese and Koreans troops who were, in many western eyes, inefficient, undisciplined, rag-tag and badly armed. Therefore, the new Japanese army had to have the latest models of western weapons, have faultless maneuvers, drills, training and wear

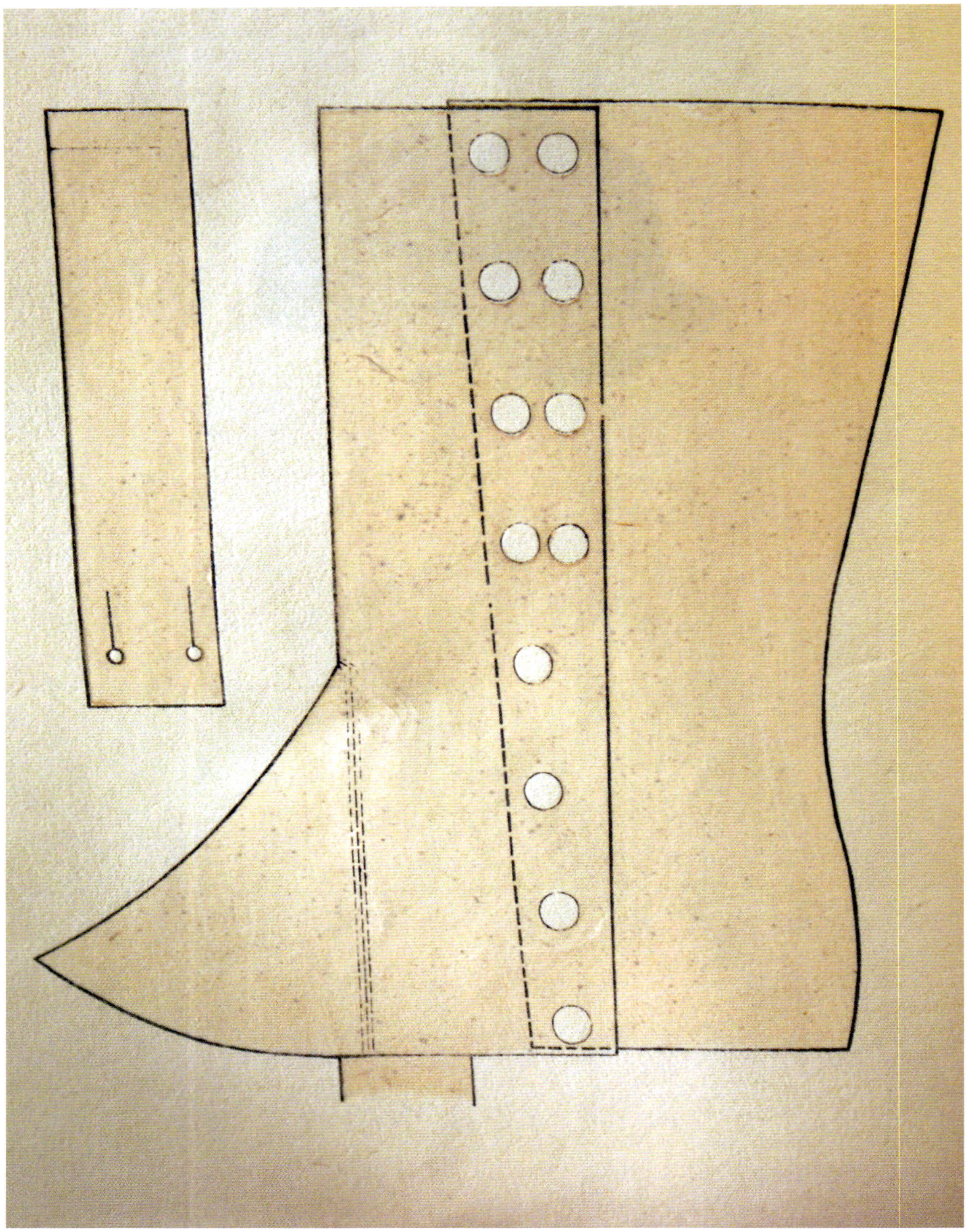

Gaiter pattern for foot troops, 1874 regulations. Anne S.K. Brown Military Collection, Brown University Library, Providence, USA.

western uniforms whose patterns were coherent with the practices in the leading European armies. These were the land forces of Germany and of France.

Although the latter had suffered a terrible defeat at the hand of its German neighbor in 1870, its military reformers were now very busy restructuring the beaten army of Napoleon IIIs vanished empire into the powerful armed forces of the Third French Republic. Across the Rhine, the military forces of the various states were also being reorganized into the new and unified German imperial army. There was thus plenty for the Japanese observers to note and to experiment with between 1869 and 1873, and this included uniforms. For instance, a service cap without a visor like that worn by German enlisted men was seen for a few years. It had a yellow band for infantry and a red band for the imperial guard, but the lack of a visor proved to be impractical. The imperial guard seemingly experimented with red trousers at this time. From October 1870, a five-point star was decreed as the army's service cap badge and the chrysanthemum as its shako plate.

The 1873-1874 Uniform Regulations

By 1873, the patterns were being approved and extensive illustrated regulations were published the following year regarding the uniforms of the army. The new uniforms were somewhat reminiscent of those that had been worn by the French army of Napoleon III during the 1860s, but

Enlisted men's hooded rain cape, 1874 regulations. Anne S.K. Brown Military Collection, Brown University Library, Providence, USA.

Fatigue medium blue linen blouse and plain dark blue cap, 1874 Regulations. Anne S.K. Brown Military Collection, Brown University Library, Providence, USA.

there were also some German features. Like most nations, Japan definitely opted for distinct uniforms per branch of service rather than for each regiment. The national color of the garments was confirmed as dark blue for all units. The facing colors for each branch of the service were:

Infantry: red
Artillery: yellow
Cavalry: medium green
Engineers: white
Train: blue
Medical: violet
Intendance: sky blue
Finance: grey

The cut of the men's tunic featured very short skirts somewhat like the pattern 1860 French infantry tunic nicknamed "basquine" so called because it had short "basques", the French word for a tunic's skirt. The Japanese 1874 version featured the facing color at the collar and by wide laces of the facing color across the chest, around the cuffs, at the tunic's edges and at the back seams. This was a variation of what had been seen on some French army imperial guard units. In the new Japanese army, the enlisted men of all units had the decorative lace. The trousers all had a stripe in the facing color edging each side. This became wider as one rose in rank. The field officer's trousers had a central line of piping and a wide stripe on each side, all of the facing color.

The men's headdress consisted of a low German-style shako with two visors, one in front and one at the back. It had a dark blue crown with black leather trim in the line troops. For the imperial guard, the shako's crown was red and this was its great distinction. All troops had a brass chrysanthemum badge and a white falling plume for full dress on their shakos.

There were also dark blue undress jackets, trousers and peaked caps, medium blue fatigue clothing and white linen jackets, trousers and cap covers for hot weather stations or seasons. The men had single-breasted grey greatcoats and capes with detachable hoods. There were also black rain capes with detachable hoods. Enlisted men were issued with European style black leather shoes and white gaiters. These appear to have been worn for dress and most service occasions. However, during the

Cadet's caps, 1874 regulations. Dark blue with piping of corps color and gilt badge. Black leather visor. Anne S.K. Brown Military Collection, Brown University Library, Providence, USA.

Cadet's coat, 1874 regulations. All dark blue with red (infantry) cuff piping, wide black lace (hardly visible) edging the collar, front and skirts. Black leather visor. Anne S.K. Brown Military Collection, Brown University Library, Providence, USA.

1877 Satsuma rebellion, the Japanese sandal, which was universally worn in the country rather than shoes, was used by imperial troops. This was the first time western uniforms were used in a campaign and the regulation leather boots were found to be unsuitable on long marches. So the men were allowed to, "resume the sandal which is worn by every Japanese of the lower class." As time passed, the sandal became more accepted as the logical footwear on service and for campaigns. The knapsacks were of goatskin, "and similar to those in the French army" and each had a rolled overcoat and a red or green blanket.

The many plates of the 1874 uniform regulations showed each garment in detail. They were rather quaintly drawn up and colored; one can perceive the Japanese artists striving to present a precise picture of the westernized object while retaining their peculiar art style. Although dull by their repetitive nature, the body of these plates nevertheless forms a remarkably interesting statement of Japanese art during the mid-1870s.

The imperial guard had a distinct appearance, but its dress also related to that of the other army units. The imperial guard cavalry traded its medium green tunic for a dark blue one with green collar and lace making it similar to the line cavalry except for the red shakos and kepis worn by all imperial guard units. According to the regulations and the prints produced in Japan between circa 1875 and 1885, the imperial guard infantry had the same uniform as the line infantry except for the red headdress. However, a circa 1880 uniform plate by the noted Italian artist Quinto Cenni, whose specialty was military costume, shows an infantryman wearing a dark blue tunic with white (rather than red) collar and lace, the front and skirts edged with sky blue piping (although this also could be a printer's coloring error) and the dark blue trousers also having a narrow white stripe. The guard infantry's undress uniform is also shown edged with white piping. Some Japanese prints also show guard infantrymen and cavalrymen during the 1877 Satsuma rebellion wearing red trousers with their red kepis and shakos. The uniforms of the bands of music, officially being blue coats with red trousers are sometime shown with green coats. Considering this was the period during which uniforms were introduced in the imperial Japanese army, variations may have crept in from time to time.

Members of the cavalry with some ladies, c. 1875. This plate shows two officers with gold epaulets and sleeve lace, but their tunics have the green lace that decorated the coats of NCOs and privates. The caps are red thus indicating that these are members of, presumably, the imperial guard cavalry. The background also has sentries wearing red caps. This plate is an example of the confusion that artists experienced when faced with, not only the adoption of western style uniforms in their army, but the successive changes in military dress. The ladies dressed in traditional costume play music and dance to the light of a new oil lamp. Anne S.K. Brown Military Collection, Brown University Library, Providence, USA.

A rather Japanese feature was the principle of prescribing a distinct uniform for army's officers. Instead of the short-skirted "basquine" tunic worn by the enlisted men, the officers had, for dress, a fully skirted double-breasted tunic with the branch color at the collar, cuffs and further show by the piping edging the front and the back pocket flaps of this garment. Rank insignia consisted of elaborate "Austrian knot" style laces on the sleeves and lace on the collar. Each side of the dark blue trousers had a wide stripe of the branch color, which, for senior (or field) officers, was wider. The dress headgear was a stiff kepi, dark blue for the line and red for the imperial guard units, that looked somewhat like a small shako when its dress white falling plume was fixed on it; it had lace bands according to rank and small stars outlined in gold on top of the crown: three for field officers and two for company officers. The badge was the gold chrysanthemum with 16 petals. For nearly all units, the buttons, cords and laces were of gold. A bi-colored silk sash with gold tassels at each end was worn around the waist. The color of these sashes was generally white with stripes of the corps colors.

The officer's swords were of western designs. Gone were the samurai swords. The new swords usually had gilt hilts and sword knots. The officer's dress sword belt was white with stripes of the wearer's branch color.

The officer's service dress was also quite distinctive although, in this regard, it followed what was worn by officers of the French army. It consisted of an Attila type

Japanese marines and sailors land on Ganghwa Island, Korea, in 1876. Japan demanded formal excuses for the violent incident against its gunboat at Ganghwa Island in 1875. In January 1876, two warships escorting four transports bearing troops and an embassy arrived at the island. The troops landed, subdued resistance and occupied the place. Bowing to the inevitable, the Koreans made excuses and signed a treaty favorable to Japan. Anne S.K. Brown Military Collection, Brown University Library, Providence, USA.

Troops of the imperial guard fighting Satsuma rebels, 1877. The soldiers are correctly shown wearing the imperial guard's all red kepis. They also wear the service dress dark blue jacket and have red trousers, which were worn before the advent of the 1873-1874 regulations. Assuming this image is fairly accurate, this could portray older trousers still used for service dress. A mounted field officer wearing the full dress tunic is in the background. The war flag his unfurled over the imperial troops. Anne S.K. Brown Military Collection, Brown University Library, Providence, USA.

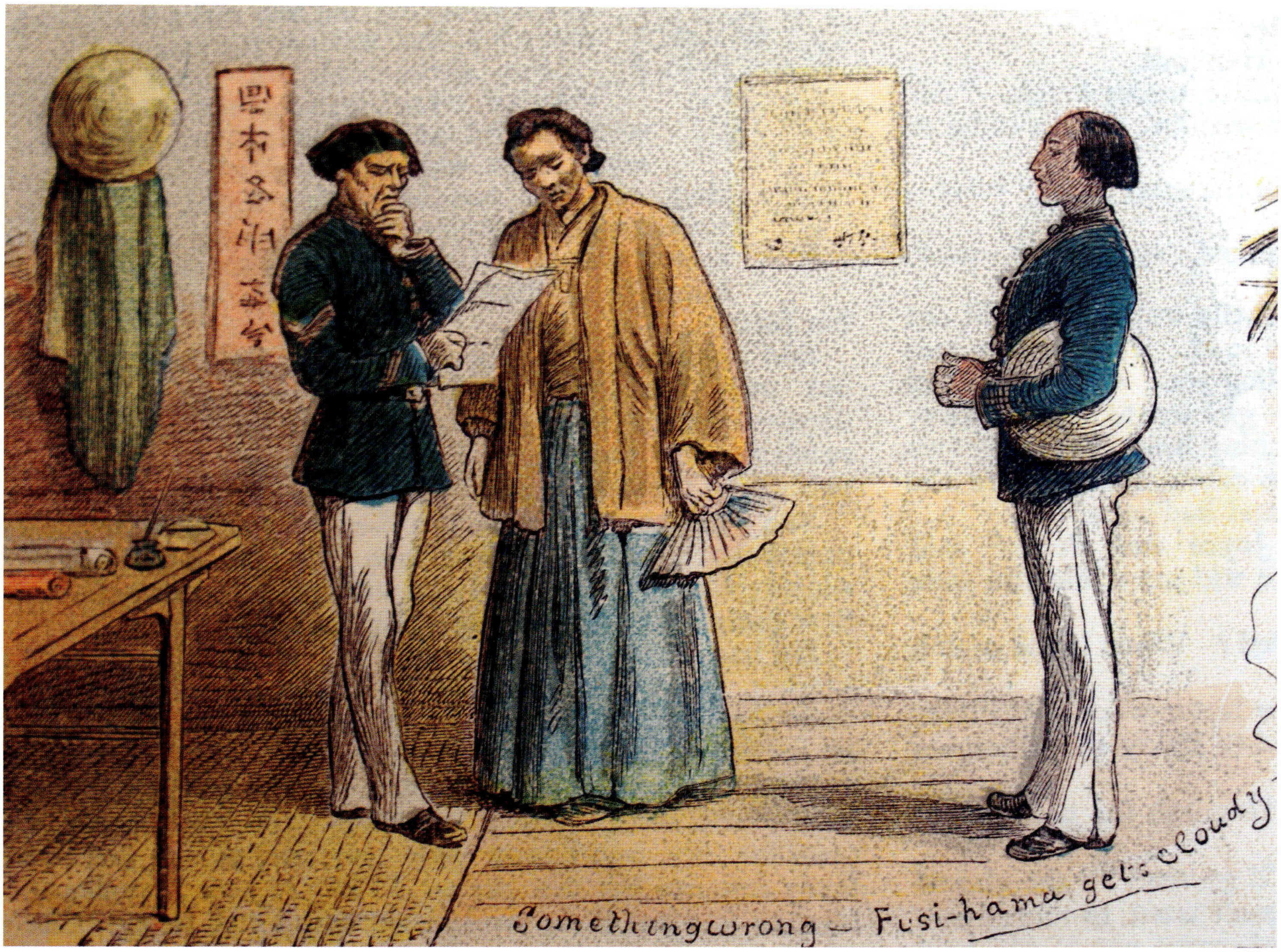

Police officers, c. 1882. Policemen in Japan carried only batons and did not have firearms until 1918. However, many of the early policemen were samurais and those deployed against the Satsuma rebels in 1877 were armed with their traditional swords. English print by W. Ralston after sketches by H.F. Adell. Anne S.K. Brown Military Collection, Brown University Library, Providence, USA.

tunic, generally all dark blue or blue-black, with black cords or flat lace decorating the front and edging the seams. With this was worn a peaked cap with the band of the branch of service color; the center of the band had rank lines indicating the wearer to be an officer. Rank was applied as on the tunic, but with black cord or lace. There was also a white linen uniforms for hot climates; it consisted of a white Attila tunic with white cords the chest, white trousers and the peaked cap had a white cover. The dress greatcoat was dark blue with branch color piping above the cuff and the service greatcoat was grey with a detachable hood, both types of greatcoat being double-breasted for officers. Black knee length boots were worn on service.

All in all, Japanese officers had a remarkably distinct uniform from their men for dress occasions as well as for service. While officers in western armies often had a service dress that had some differences compared to the uniforms worn by the men they commanded, the pattern were generally fairly similar when it came to dress or full dress. Perhaps some of the samurais and nobles that filled the Japanese officer corps wished to retain some distinctions from their largely peasant conscript soldiers.

Generals had a full dress uniform since May 1873 consisting of a completely dark blue double-breasted tunic with the collar and sleeves covered by gold embroidery, lace and buttons. Dark blue dress trousers with scarlet piping and wide band on either side consisted, early on, of a narrow piping edged on each side with a wider band. Full dress white trousers with black high boots could also be worn. Blue and red silk sash with gold tassels, the knots having four or five small gold stars. Bicorn hats were not worn after 1874. Dark blue dress kepi almost covered with gold lace and embroidery and a white falling plume; the crown's top had small stars outlined in gold: five for a lieutenant general, four for a major general.

Army bands were also assigned a distinct uniform in 1873-1874. The tunic was similar to the line infantry's, but the trousers were red with a blue stripe, the shako red and the kepi all red with yellow piping and featuring a

An evocation of the 1877 Satsuma rebellion. This print shows an imperial army infantryman triumphant over the rebellious Samurais. From the dress of the soldier, this print was produced possibly a decade later than when the rebellion occurred. His cap is notably typical of the late-1880s and 1890s; his tunic might be an interpretation of the 1870s undress jacket, in this case edged with narrow red lace. Traditional sandals constitute the footwear, which was used from the time of the rebellion and he carries what appears to be an interpretation of the Snider-Enfield short rifle. A most notable aspect is the portrayal of a samurai woman archer. A group of brave women on Kyusu Island did indeed battle the imperial troops. The bearded leader being taken away could represent Saigo Takamori. Anne S.K. Brown Military Collection, Brown University Library, Providence, USA.

Rebels warriors of the Satsuma rebellion in battle, 1877. This is most likely the final battle at Kogoshima fought on 24 September 1877. Most are shown in traditional dress and wear headbands for recognition. Smaller figures in the background are shown with pattern 1873-1874 army officer's dress coats and the senior officer, possibly Marshall Takamori, wearing a bicorn may be intended to represent the leader of the rebel army. Anne S.K. Brown Military Collection, Brown University Library, Providence, USA.

Ghost of Marshall Saigo Takamori (1827-1877) holding a petition. He was the leader of the Satsuma samurai's rebellion, which was crushed at Kagoshima on 24 September 1877. Saigo was wounded in the leg and his faithful samurai retainer, Beppu Shinsuke, put an end to his life. Saigo was a popular figure and he was later forgiven by the imperial authorities. A statue was erected in his honor in 1899 at the entrance to Ueno Park in Tokyo, and his son was made a Marquis in 1902. This print by Tsukioka Yoshitoshi was issued just under a year after Saigo died. Richard Kruml, Fine Japanese Prints, Paintings and Books, London.

Uniform of the imperial Japanese army, c. 1875-1885. From left to right: soldier, line infantry; soldier, imperial guard infantry; soldier in undress uniform, line infantry; soldier in undress uniform, imperial guard; gunner, imperial guard artillery; soldier, imperial guard cavalry (mounted); soldier, train of the line; general (mounted); staff officers (mounted); rear admiral; officer, line artillery (mounted); officer, imperial guard train; officer, imperial guard infantry; officer, cavalry of the line; officer, line infantry in service dress. Print after Cenni. One wonders where the renowned Italian military artist obtained the information on Japanese uniforms, but, apart from a few obscure details, it is an amazingly good rendering. Anne S.K. Brown Military Collection, Brown University Library, Providence, USA.

white over red plume. Warrant officers and junior officers attached to bands had the infantry officer's tunic with red collar and cuffs.

Later Uniforms

The Gendarmerie raised in 1881 had a dark blue uniform with red collar, cuffs and trouser stripes and, until 1886, a green kepi or service cap. It was a mounted unit and its personnel wore black knee boots and carried sabers. A red kepi with a black band was worn thereafter with red trousers having a dark blue stripe for full dress; dark blue trousers with a red stripe on service. The medical corps appears to have continued wearing the same uniform until 1886 when green was allotted as its branch color. The military justice department, which consisted mostly of officer advocates, appears to have adopted white facings when was organized. In addition to the white Attila tunic, a less ornate white jacket with five buttons in front was introduced for officers in 1883 with the rank indicated on the cuffs by white stars and bars.

The most notable change in the uniforms of the imperial army occurred in the cavalry during 1882. Up until then, the troopers wore, on the whole, uniforms of a similar pattern to those of the rest of the army. In most western countries, cavalry units had distinct uniforms that were more elegant and colorful than the dress of the foot troops. Hussars, for instance, had Attila jackets elaborately decorated with cord. This was the type of dress that was now adopted for the Japanese army's cavalry. Henceforth, the dress uniform of the line cavalry was: dark blue Attila with medium green collar and cuff lace, yellow hussar style cords across the chest and at the back seams, brass buttons; red trousers with green stripe; dark blue peaked cap with medium green band and piping; black shako with chrysanthemum plate and white over red plume. For the imperial guard cavalry: dark blue Attila with medium green collar, red cuff lace, red hussar style cords across the chest and at the back seams, brass buttons; red trousers with green stripe; dark blue peaked cap with red band and piping; red shako with chrysanthemum plate and white

Parade of the Imperial Guard infantry, c. 1880. The enlisted men wear the 1873-1874 tunic with red lace on the breast, the imperial guard's distinctive red shako adorned with a white feather. The officers wear the double-breasted tunic. Print after an unknown artist. Anne S.K. Brown Military Collection, Brown University Library, Providence, USA.

A lunch for officials and dignitaries hosted by the royal family, c. 1880. In a sense, this print shows both the revolutionary changes that swept Japanese society during the 1870s and 1880s as well as the retention of certain traditional values. From the emperor down, all have adopted European uniforms and costumes; they all sit on European chairs and tables, have Western style glasses, bowls and coffee pots and are lighted by oil lamps. However, the tablecloths, curtains, carpets and large urns are of the Orient. Print after an unknown artist. Anne S.K. Brown Military Collection, Brown University Library, Providence, USA.

Imperial Guard, 1886 regulations. Infantry private and officer in the foreground, privates in the right background in field service and drill order dress; all wear the distinctive red cap band. The mounted figures are a trooper, an officer and a trumpeter of the cavalry; all have red shakos. Plate in Toyodo's June 1893 Illustrated Book of Customs of the Imperial Army.

Staff officers and artillery, 1886 regulations. Gunners in campaign dress shown front and back in the foreground; mounted staff officers of infantry and cavalry in the background. Plate in Toyodo's June 1893 Illustrated Book of Customs of the Imperial Army.

General and staff officers, 1886 regulations. In full dress and service dress. Plate in Toyodo's June 1893 Illustrated Book of Customs of the Imperial Army.

Infantry officers, 1886 regulations. Field officers are mounted and shown in full and service dress. An infantry company officer stands at right. Curiously, the soldiers in the background have the yellow artillery collar rather than the infantry's red, possibly a coloring error. Plate in Toyodo's June 1893 Illustrated Book of Customs of the Imperial Army.

Artillery officers, 1886 regulations. Plate in Toyodo's June 1893 Illustrated Book of Customs of the Imperial Army.

Cavalry of the line and guard artillery, 1886 regulations. At top left, a cavalry officer with two troopers. Their collar appears to be colored yellow instead of green. At bottom right, a guard artillery officer with gunners. Plate in Toyodo's June 1893 Illustrated Book of Customs of the Imperial Army.

Administrative support units, 1886 regulations. Administration clerks; mounted judicial corps officer; private and officer, intendance corps. Plate in Toyodo's June 1893 Illustrated Book of Customs of the Imperial Army.

Gendarmerie, 1886 regulations. The mounted officers and the gendarme on foot in the foreground all wear the distinctive shako with a red crown. The infantry private in the background belongs to the imperial guard. Plate in Toyodo's June 1893 Illustrated Book of Customs of the Imperial Army.

Medical Corps, 1886 regulations. Medical officers wearing the attila are shown mounted and standing. A medical corps private is knelt attending an injured soldier. The international Red Cross sign is used for recognition. Plate in Toyodo's June 1893 Illustrated Book of Customs of the Imperial Army.

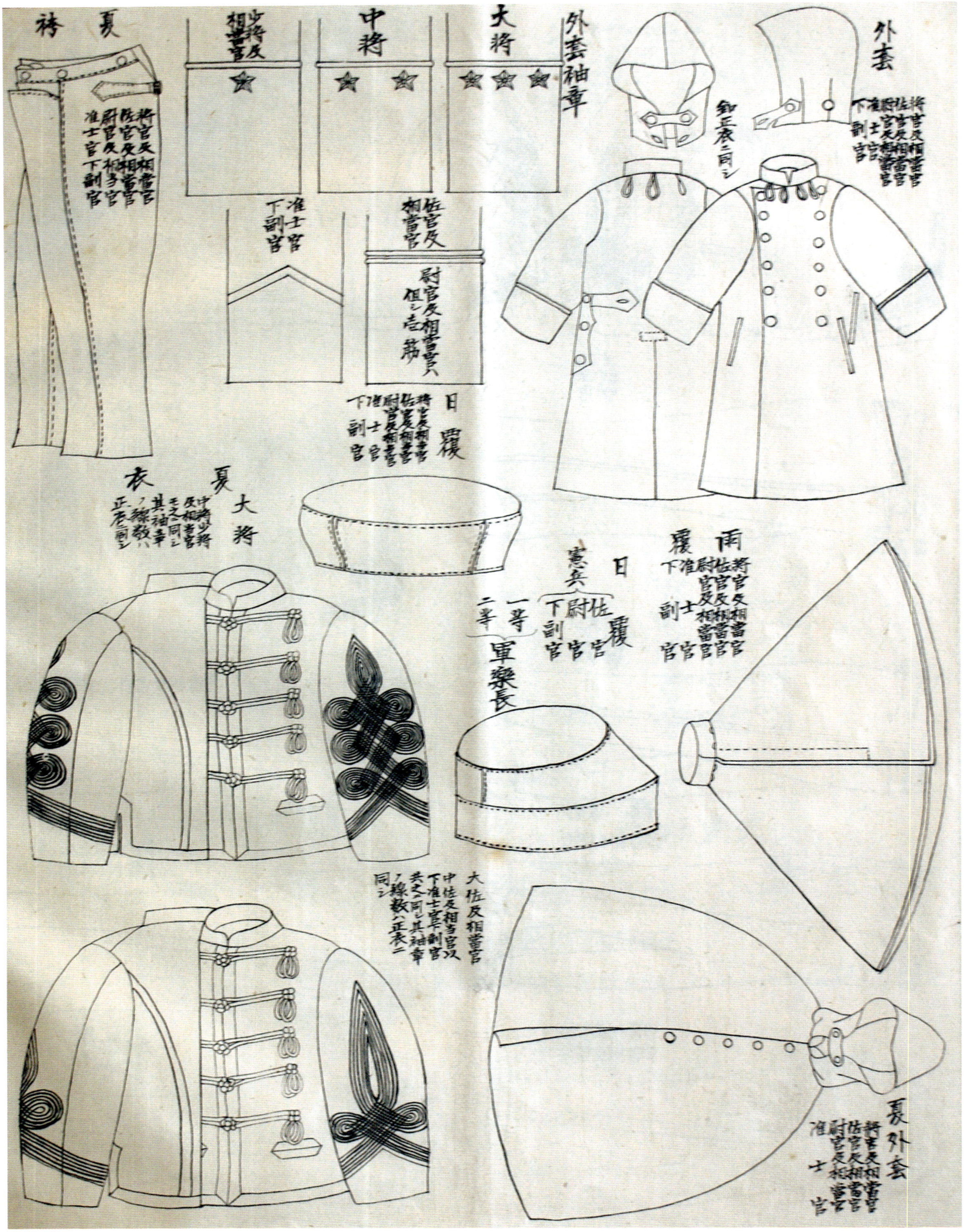

Various patterns of foul weather clothing, cap and kepi covers, and of the officer's service dress attila, 1886 regulations. Plate in Toyodo's June 1893 Illustrated Book of Customs of the Imperial Army.

Uniforms of the 1886 regulations. From left to right: lieutenant general; inspector general; lieutenant colonel of line cavalry; captain, engineer corps. Copies of Imperial Museum uniform drawings. Anne S.K. Brown Military Collection, Brown University Library, Providence, USA.

over red plume. The service dress consisted of a dark blue cap with yellow band and piping for line cavalry and with red band and piping for imperial guard cavalry; single breasted dark blue tunic with medium green collar and, for imperial guard cavalry, red shoulder straps. There was also a white summer jacket with yellow shoulder straps for line units and red for imperial guard cavalry worn with a white cap cover.

From 1882, cavalry officers generally wore the same uniform colors as their men, but their dress Attila was trimmed with black silk cords rather than expensive gold cords. The gold lace was only for the sleeve rank insignia. The officer's field service cap had gold piping and lace.

These changes were an indication that the uniforms of the whole army needed to be reviewed. Time had passed since 1873 and world military fashions had evolved. Furthermore, certain features had been tried and tested in the army with various degrees to success. By the mid-1880s, army bureaucrats were hard at work devising new uniforms.

Uniforms of the 1886 regulations. From left to right: officer, summer uniform; second class lieutenant colonel, intendance corps; infantry adjutant; trooper, imperial guard cavalry. Copies of Imperial Museum uniform drawings. Anne S.K. Brown Military Collection, Brown University Library, Providence, USA.

The 1886 Uniform Regulations

In 1886, new uniform regulations were promulgated for the whole army. Many of the features of the 1873-1874 regulations were profoundly altered or abolished altogether, yet the uniforms retained continuity in design and colors. Indeed, the new uniforms gave the imperial Japanese soldiers an increasingly distinct appearance when compared with the dress of other armies. By shrewdly mixing various features from European uniforms, the imperial army designers created an appearance that was unique to their nation's armed forces.

Starting at the top, the shakos were all but abolished unofficially as the dress headgear for enlisted men. There was a new model shako, black for the line and red for the imperial guard, which had a visor only in front, black leather bands, brass chrysanthemum plate and a white over red tuft in front. It does not seem to have been used, or even issued very much, outside of imperial guard units.

Uniforms of the 1886 regulations. From left to right: infantry officer, campaign dress; lieutenant colonel, medical corps; officer, summer dress uniform; infantry staff colonel. Copies of Imperial Museum uniform drawings. Anne S.K. Brown Military Collection, Brown University Library, Providence, USA.

The enlisted men's service dress kepis also disappeared from view. Henceforth, the field service cap with a visor was the main headdress throughout the army. It assumed a distinctive shape being somewhat higher than most such caps in other armies.

The enlisted men's French-style short-skirted "basquine" coat was replaced by the longer skirted tunic worn by German, British, American and many other armies. In the Japanese version, the tunic's skirts were somewhat shorter. Gone was facing color lace on the chest and edging the tunic. The service branch color was applied basically at the tunic's collar, shoulder straps and trousers stripes. The front closed by five buttons and, except for a few units, there was no piping. The new tunic was a remarkably polyvalent garment meant to be useful on service, yet sufficiently elegant and colorful for parade. With this, the enlisted men wore dark blue trousers with branch color stripes tucked into white gaiters worn below the knees.

Uniforms of the 1886 regulations. From left to right: sergeant, imperial guard cavalry; private, engineer corps; private, imperial guard train; third class clerk, intendance corps; second class gunsmith, artillery. Copies of Imperial Museum uniform drawings. Anne S.K. Brown Military Collection, Brown University Library, Providence, USA.

The distinctive branch colors were:

Infantry:	red
Artillery:	yellow
Cavalry:	medium green
Engineers and pioneers:	maroon
Train:	blue
Medical:	green
Pharmacy:	green
Veterinary:	green
Intendance:	sky blue
Accounting:	light blue (silver-brown from December 1890)
Gendarmerie:	red (from September 1882)
Technical:	yellow (from September 1882)
Justice:	white (from 1882)

These branch colors might also be seen on the cap band and piping and on the stripes above the cuffs, but this was not consistent. For instance, the line infantry cap had a yellow cap band and piping and the tunic's cuffs often had yellow lace rather than its red branch service color. The pioneer battalions did the same. Imperial guard units no longer had kepis, but their field service caps had red bands and piping and their tunic's cuffs had red laces.

The resulting dress must have been confusing to onlookers less familiar with the imperial army, notably artists and colorists who produced artwork and prints at that time. As will be seen in a number of examples reproduced in this book, the coloring was well intentioned but, at times, uncertain in some works. For example, the 1893 "Book of Customs" has some surprising color schemes as do a number of individually published prints. Nor was it only Japanese

Uniforms of the 1886 regulations. From left to right: sergeant, medical corps; infantry private, field service dress; sergeant major, gendarmerie; second class sergeant, fortress artillery. Copies of Imperial Museum uniform drawings. Anne S.K. Brown Military Collection, Brown University Library, Providence, USA.

artists that could be confused. The usually authoritative uniform booklets on many armies published in Liepzig (Germany) at the end of the 19th century by Moritz Rhul present some amazingly curious coloring errors and the failings of the 1896 edition were reproduced in the 1904 reprint. We have noted the outstanding errors or discrepancies in the illustration's captions whenever possible.

Other items such as white summer uniforms, greatcoats and other foul weather items were not changed drastically from the 1873-1874 regulations. Comparing the plates from both the 1874 and the 1886 regulations reveal very little if any differences for the more utilitarian items.

The dress of officers was not changed greatly. For dress occasions, they continued wearing the double-breasted tunic with branch color collar, cuffs and piping as previously. Also for dress, they retained a somewhat stiffened and rather high kepi decorated with lace according to rank to which a white over red plume was added, giving this headgear the look of a small shako. For service dress, the Attila was

Uniforms of the 1886 regulations. From left to right: gunner, field artillery, campaign dress; private nurse, medical corps; private, summer uniform; bandmaster, imperial guard. Copies of Imperial Museum uniform drawings. Anne S.K. Brown Military Collection, Brown University Library, Providence, USA.

obviously popular and they continued wearing it with the field service cap. White summer uniforms, featuring the white Attila and the white 1883 service jacket, continued to be used.

The Gendarmerie, raised since 1881 and considered an elite force, assumed a more distinct uniform in 1888. Its officers and men had the standard dark blue regulation tunic with red branch color, but the trousers were now red with a black stripe and their dress headgear consisted of a stiffened kepi having a red crown, black band, brass chrysanthemum plate and a white over red plume. The dark blue peaked cap with a red band was the usual headwear.

Infantry soldiers at the outset of the war with China, c. 1894. At right, an infantry officer in campaign dress. A general is mounted with, behind him, a regimental color. Anne S.K. Brown Military Collection, Brown University Library, Providence, USA.

Weapons

The standard infantry weapon during the 1870s was the breech-loading British Snider-Enfield rifle. Cavalrymen carried the American seven shot repeating Spencer rifled carbine. Japan wished to make its own arms and, in 1880, introduced the first model of the 11mm caliber bolt action Murata Type 13 infantry rifle named after the engineer colonel who conceived it, being heavily inspired by the Dutch Beaumont Model 1871 and the French Gras Model 1874. It was followed by the infantry Murata Type 18 (Model 1885) that contained eight rounds and, in 1889, the 8mm Murata Type 22 came into service. A cavalry carbine version of the Type 22 (M. 1889) was also approved, but not issued until 1894. Smokeless powder was used from 1891.

The creation of artillery corps in the new imperial army required ordnance for the field batteries. There were nine line battalions and one guard battalion, each battalion having two batteries. During the 1870s, most artillery pieces consisted of French field 4- and

Naval review of the new Imperial Japanese Navy, c. 1875. Anne S.K. Brown Military Collection, Brown University Library, Providence, USA.

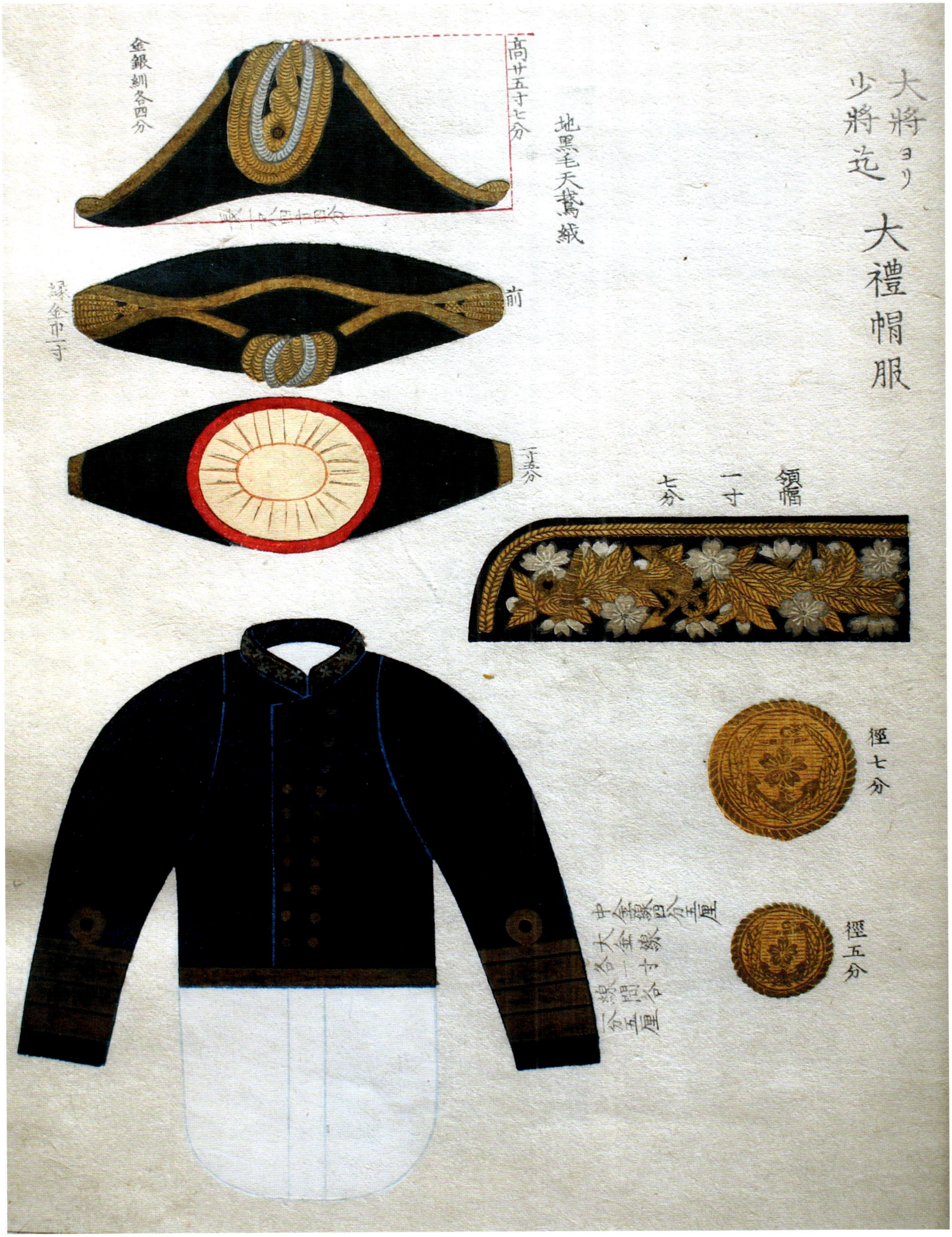

Navy officer's full dress hat, coat and buttons, 1873-1874 regulations. Note the embroidery detail on the collar. Anne S.K. Brown Military Collection, Brown University Library, Providence, USA.

Navy captain's frock coat, 1873-1874 regulations. Front and back view. Anne S.K. Brown Military Collection, Brown University Library, Providence, USA.

12-pounder cannons and 4-pounder mountain guns. By 1881, there were also two batteries armed with German Krupp cannons. Nine coast artillery companies were organized towards the end of the 1870s. From 1872, the second French mission helped set up arsenal employing some 600 workers at Tokyo and Osaka as well as a canon foundry at Oji. Black powder was made at Mito and Japan was determined to become self sufficient in "the manufacture of portable firearms, cannons and ammunition."

The Imperial Navy

When the Meiji imperial regime came to power in early 1868, the country had a number of modern steam powered warships bought abroad, either by regional clan navies or the shogun, but there was no national navy. A first step was the creation of a ministry of defense in January 1868 that would oversea both the army and the navy. Following the Boshin war, the imperial navy was formally created in July 1869 and it was decreed the following year that Britain's Royal Navy would be its model. In February 1872, the army and the naval services were separated and each now had their own ministry. In its early years, the new imperial navy was mainly a coast defense force. It also had an offensive capacity since it successfully carried out operations in Taiwan and Korea in 1874 and 1875. The government continued to strive for a powerful navy and, as the country's economy prospered, ordered cruisers from Britain and France while developing shipyards that could build modern warships in Japan. The British naval mission that was in Japan from 1873 to 1879 concentrated on the training and education of naval officers and one of its early naval cadets was the future Admiral Togo. Like the army, the navy was initially relatively small. In 1879, it had only 4,300 sailors manning twenty-nine steam warships that were armed with a total of 149 guns.

In 1882, an ambitious naval expansion program called for a force of forty-eight warships including twenty-two torpedo boats. These last were small vessels, but they potentially could attack larger warships according to the new French naval combat doctrine that favored fast and small warships. For a time, France's influence became predominant and the era's leading and most influential French naval engineer, Émile Bertin, spent four years in Japan supervising the construction of several cruisers and laid out the shipyards of Sasebo and Kure. By the early-1890s, the imperial navy was also obtaining fast cruisers from Britain and soon had, with China, one of the most powerful fleet in the Far East. The professionalism and training of Japan's naval personnel was, however, superior to that of the Chinese navy.

The first uniforms regulations for the officers and ratings of the new imperial Japanese navy were introduced in 1870. Until 1873-1874, the ratings did not have the usual sailor's jumper and cap with ribbon, but instead a dark blue single-breasted jacket with brass buttons and a blue cap without a visor. Successive dress regulations were issued in 1871, 1873-1874, 1883, 1887, 1896, 1900, 1914, 1919 and 1930. The models, especially from 1871, were the uniforms of Britain's Royal Navy, then the most modern and powerful maritime force in the world. In 1878, a British military observer noted that, "the officers of the Imperial gunboat Seiki, now at Portsmouth, whose dress is exactly like our own, even to the distinguishing rings of rank."

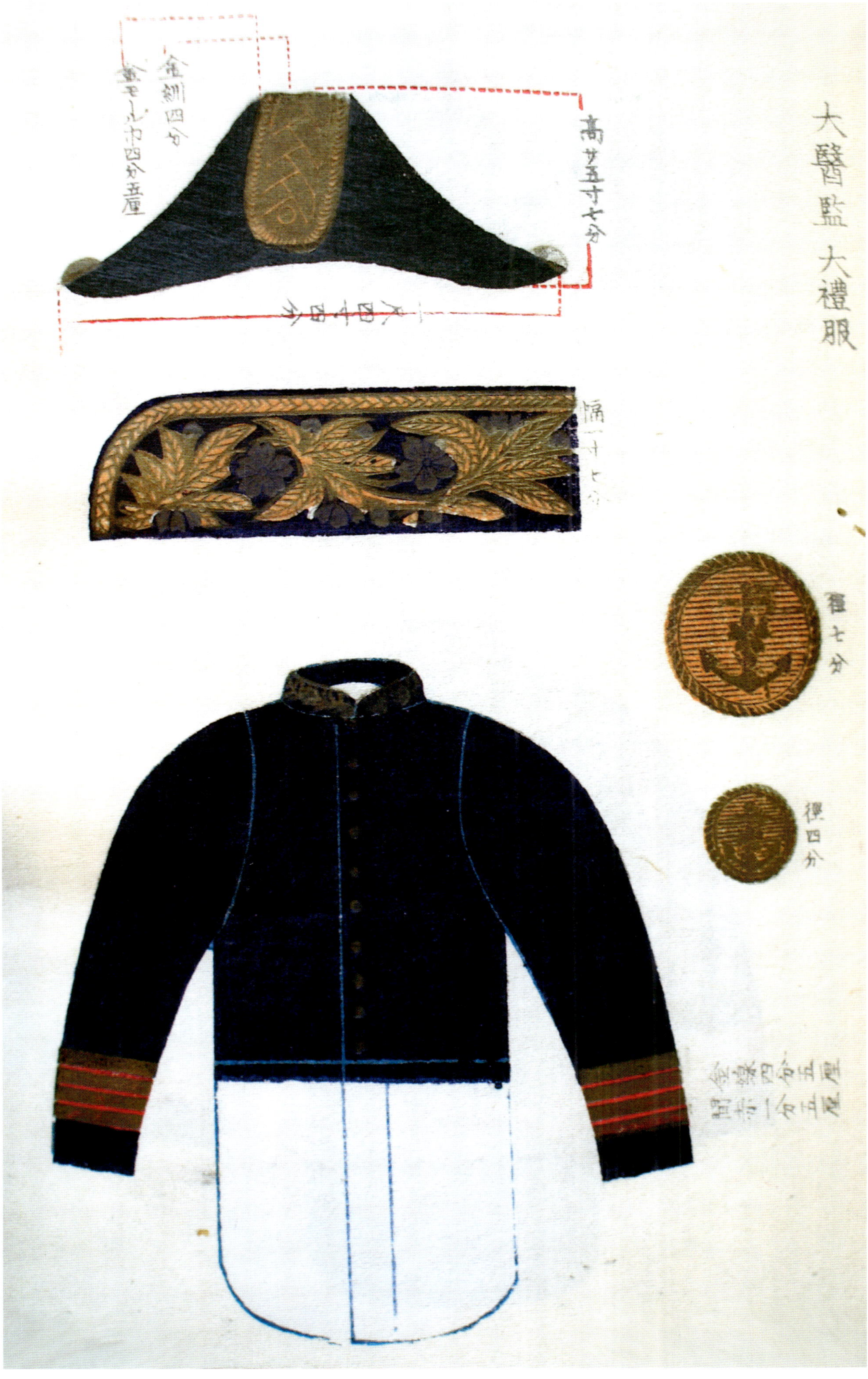

Navy medical captain full dress hat, coat and buttons, 1873-1874 regulations. Note the lack of the executive curl and the red lines of the naval medical staff between the lace bars. Anne S.K. Brown Military Collection, Brown University Library, Providence, USA.

Navy petty officer's summer service dress, 1873-1874 regulations. Anne S.K. Brown Military Collection, Brown University Library, Providence, USA.

Apart from a few changes on the badges such as replacing the British crown for Japan's gold chrysanthemum with sixteen petals (from October 1870), at a distance, the appearance of Japanese imperial naval personnel was indeed very much like its British model, but there were a few differences with some details. For instance, the white lace bordering the jumper's collar of ratings was made up of three narrow stripes in most navies, but there was only one wider bordering the collars of Japanese sailors. The other distinctive feature, which came in 1883, was the adoption by Japanese naval officers of the dark blue service jacket trimmed with black mohair. This garment was the Japanese officer's favorite uniform item. It was eventually widely worn for nearly all occasions and became the "trademark" of Japanese imperial navy officers by the early 20th century.

The main and rather curious feature that came with the first officer's uniform in 1870 was the executive curl on top of the cuff lace. Instead of being rounded, it had four pointed corners giving it something of a diamond look. Whatever its inspiration, the square curl must have raised some eyebrows and, in 1871, it was quickly replaced by

Navy sailor's summer service jumper, 1873-1874 regulations. The white service jumper has no blue cuffs with white lace. Anne S.K. Brown Military Collection, Brown University Library, Providence, USA.

the regular round curl as worn in Britain's Royal Navy. As can be seen by the plates illustrating this book, naval uniforms thereafter tended to be fairly standard. Apart from the usual changes due to the evolution of world military fashions – for instance the wider crown for peaked caps by 1914 – there were very few substantial changes. The rank badges adopted in 1870-1871 remained practically the same until the end of the Second World War although there were, of course, many trade badges that were adopted over the years because of technological progress.

The Marine Corps

In 1873, the Japanese imperial navy's corps of marines was created. It was closely patterned after the British Royal Marines and, like its model, consisted of marine infantry and of marine artillery. The marines were deployed in Korea during 1875 but, as it turned out, the corps did not prove to be extremely useful and the government abolished it 1878. Later on, temporary units of armed sailors that were trained as infantrymen to participate in shore landing parties were sufficient for most purposes. Army troops were also trained to conduct amphibious

Navy captain's full dress coat, waistcoat and trousers, 1883 regulations. Anne S.K. Brown Military Collection, Brown University Library, Providence, USA.

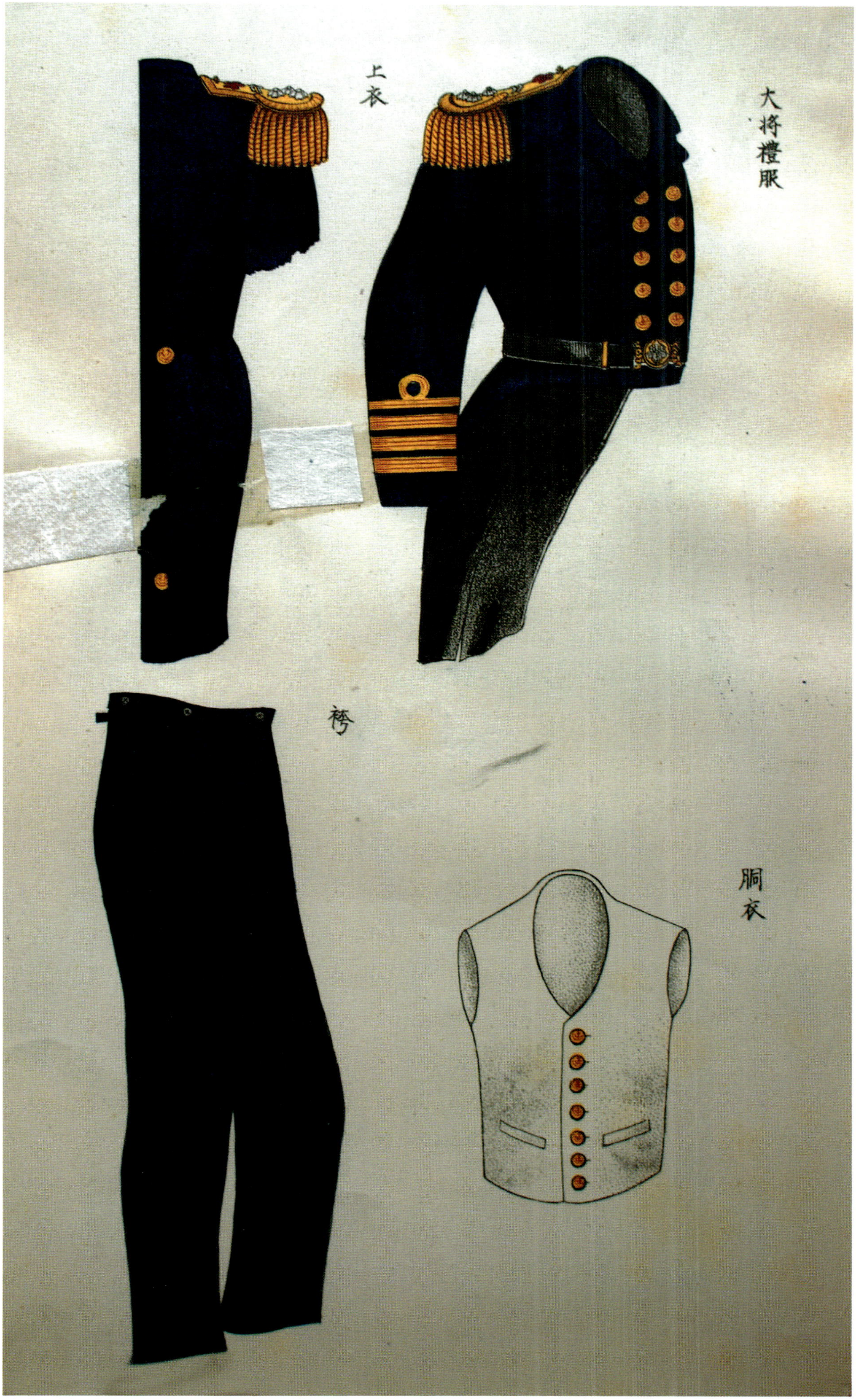

Navy captain's dress coat, waistcoat and trousers, 1883 regulations. Anne S.K. Brown Military Collection, Brown University Library, Providence, USA.

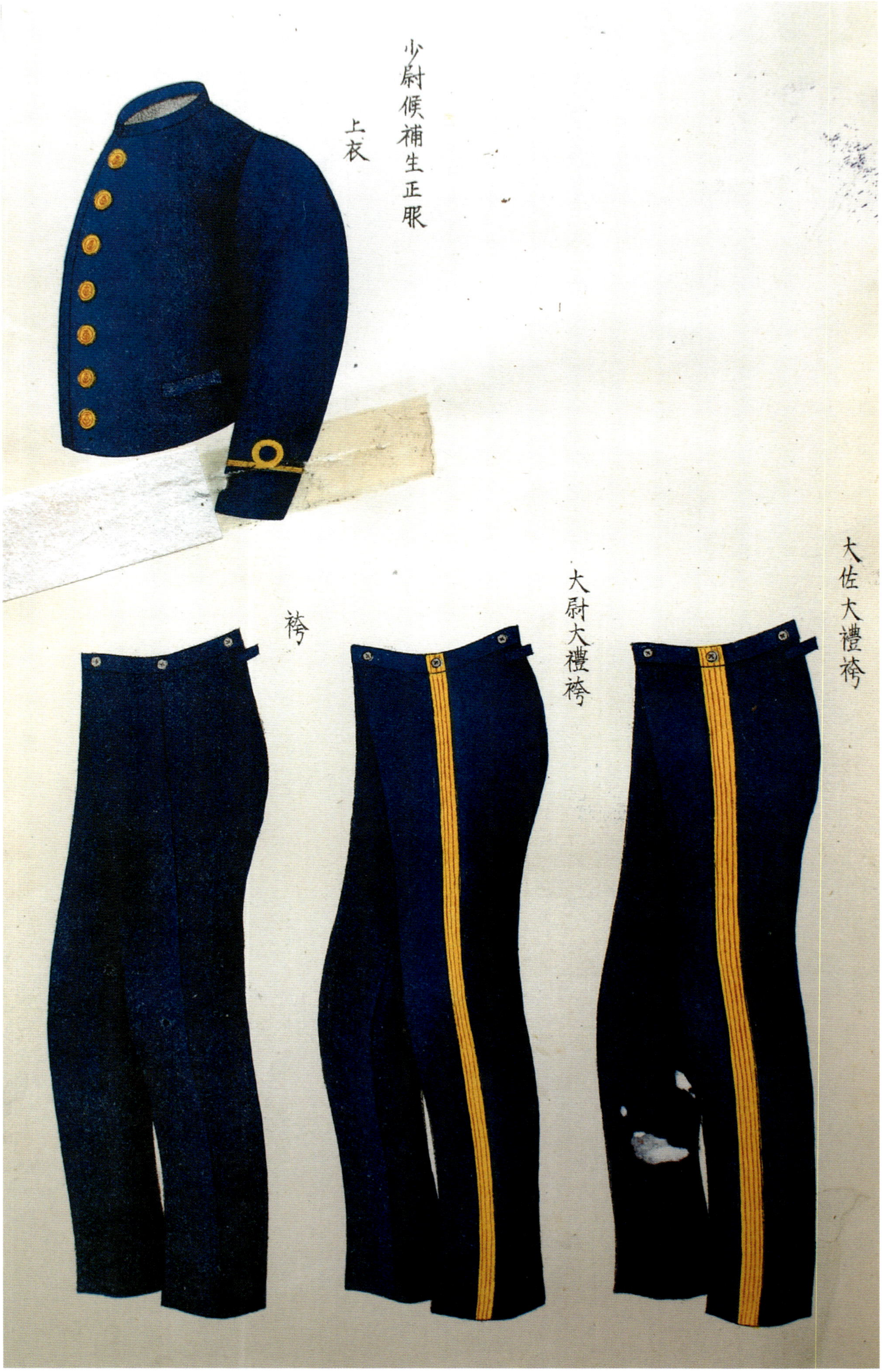

Navy midshipman's jacket and trousers, 1883 regulations. The trousers are for ordinary, dress and full dress occasions. Anne S.K. Brown Military Collection, Brown University Library, Providence, USA.

Navy captain's service uniforms, 1883 regulations. Top: frock coat. Bottom: service dress coat (dark blue with black lace). Anne S.K. Brown Military Collection, Brown University Library, Providence, USA.

Navy petty officer's dress coat and sword, 1883 regulations. Anne S.K. Brown Military Collection, Brown University Library, Providence, USA.

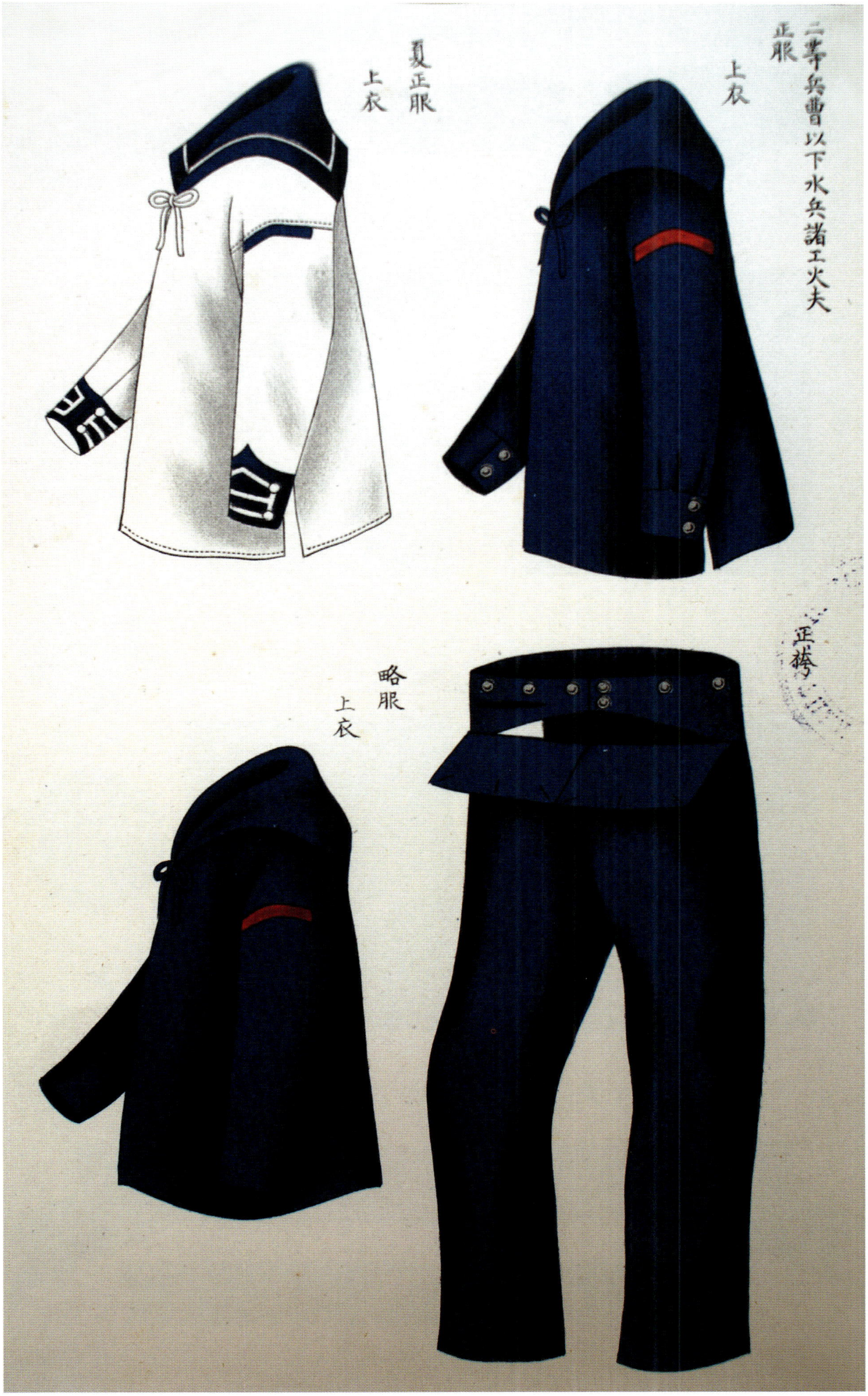

Navy sailor's jumpers and trousers, 1883 regulations. The white summer jumper is the dress garment. The blue jumpers are shown without the lighter blue collar edged with one white stripe. Anne S.K. Brown Military Collection, Brown University Library, Providence, USA.

Navy officer's overcoat and hood, 1883 regulations. Anne S.K. Brown Military Collection, Brown University Library, Providence, USA.

Navy foul weather clothing, 1883 regulations. Anne S.K. Brown Military Collection, Brown University Library, Providence, USA.

Marine artillery gunner's dress coat and shako, 1874 regulations. The cap badge has crossed cannons. Anne S.K. Brown Military Collection, Brown University Library, Providence, USA.

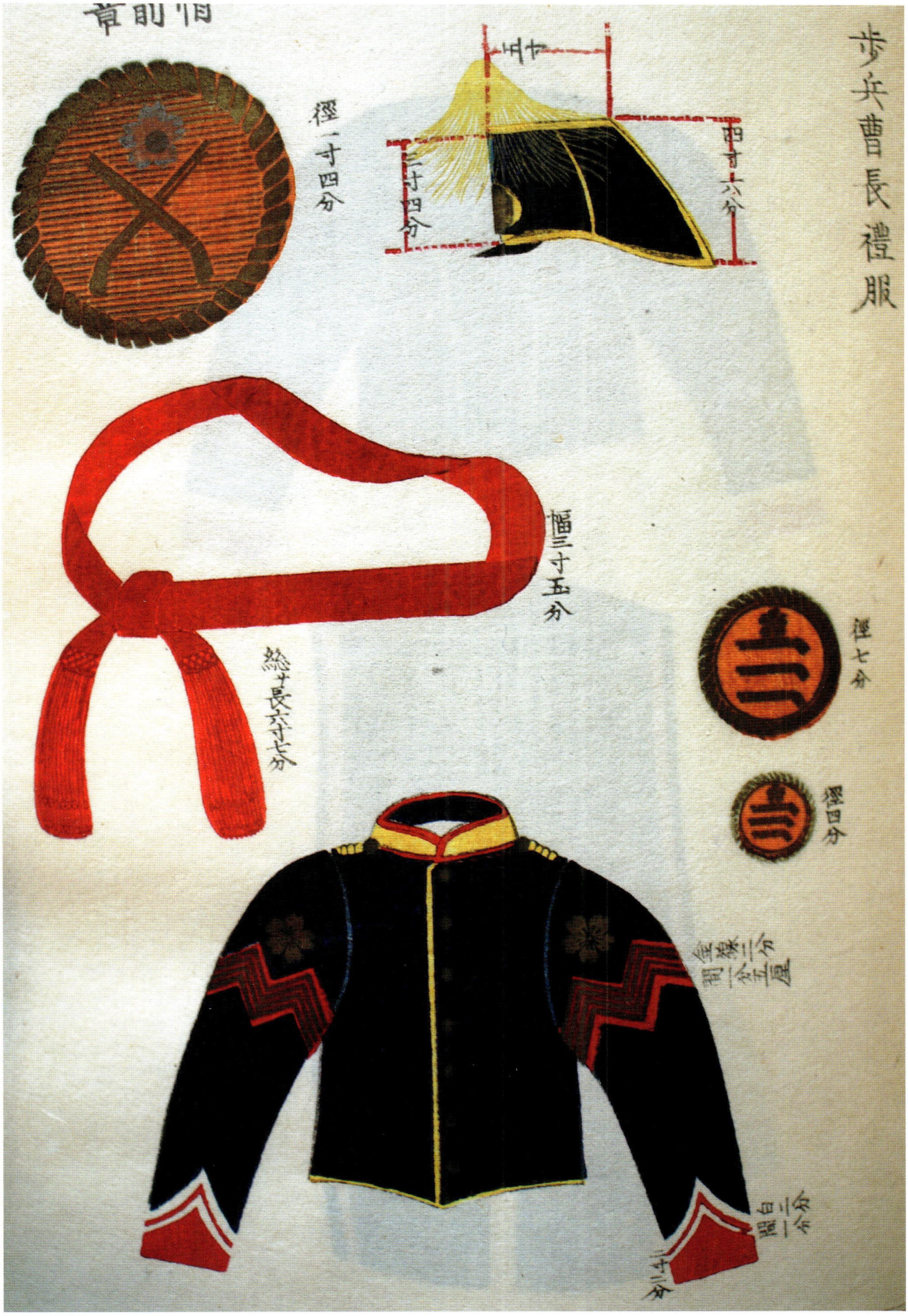

Marine infantry NCOs dress coat and shako, 1874 regulations. Marine sergeants wear a red sash, like the British Royal Marines. The cap badge has crossed rifles, the buttons have three rifles. Anne S.K. Brown Military Collection, Brown University Library, Providence, USA.

Marine infantry private's service dress coat and cap, 1874 regulations. The cuffs are plain. The marine artillery has a similar service dress coat to its color and the cap has a red pompon. Anne S.K. Brown Military Collection, Brown University Library, Providence, USA.

Marine band NCOs dress coat and shako, 1874 regulations. The trousers are dark blue with a red stripe. Anne S.K. Brown Military Collection, Brown University Library, Providence, USA.

A party of marine infantrymen fighting off a Korean attack on a Japanese navy gunboat making an hydrographic survey near Ganghwa Island when it was attacked in 1875. The officers are shown wearing a single breasted frock coat, the men wear the service dress short coat; all have the service dress cap. A NCO holds a marine battalion flag. Detail from a period print. Anne S.K. Brown Military Collection, Brown University Library, Providence, USA.

operations. It was only after the First World War that "Special Naval Landing Forces" were again organized in the navy from the late-1920s.

The 1873-1878 marine corps had uniform regulations that made up many plates in the extensive naval regulations of the time. Its dress was different from the one issued to army units. For marine infantry, it consisted of a dark blue skirtless jacket with a yellow collar edged with red piping, yellow shoulder straps and piping edging the front and the bottom, red pointed cuffs edged with two white laces; brass buttons bearing a small chrysanthemum over three rifles; dark blue trousers with a red stripe. For full dress, a British army style black shako edged with yellow lace, a brass badge bearing crossed rifles, and a yellow falling plume; for service dress, a dark blue peaked cap with a brass badge bearing crossed rifles and a small yellow pompon at top. The infantry's service dress jacket was the same as described above except that the cuffs were plain dark blue without any decorations.

For marine artillery, a dark blue skirtless jacket with a red collar edged with yellow piping, red shoulder straps and piping edging the front and the bottom, red pointed cuffs edged with two white laces; brass buttons bearing a chrysanthemum over three guns; dark blue trousers with a red stripe. For full dress, a British army style black shako edged with yellow lace, a brass badge bearing crossed cannons and a red falling plume; for service dress, a dark blue peaked cap with a brass badge bearing crossed cannons and a small red pompon at top. The infantry's service dress jacket was the same as described above except that the cuffs were plain dark blue without any decorations.

NCOs had, on the upper sleeves, yellow double chevron stripes that indicated rank. Senior NCOs had these chevrons in gold and also wore a red shoulder sash, like British sergeants. Their shako plates had a small chrysanthemum above the crossed rifles and guns. Officers had all dark blue fully skirted single-breasted tunics edged with red piping with gold lace on the collar and gold pointed chevrons above the cuffs, the senior rank having the collar covered with gold lace and four gold chevrons. They also had a plain dark blue service tunic with one to three gold chrysanthemums at each side of the collar as rank badges. They wore shakos in full dress and peaked caps in service dress. The chrysanthemum badge on their headdress plates were surrounded by gold wreaths like navy officers.

Marine musicians had the same type of uniform as the enlisted men, but in reversed colors for the jacket. It was red with dark blue collar and pointed cuffs, the two cuff laces being white at bottom and yellow at top. The brass buttons bore a stringed horn with a superimposed chrysanthemum. The shako had embroidered badges on red ground bearing a silver chrysanthemum surrounded by a gold wreath under a gold stringed horn and also had a white falling plume. When the marines were disbanded in 1878, the marine band was retained in the navy and its bandmasters continued to wear red uniforms and, eventually, caps with white falling plumes. They were reported as playing "Western music in a way that would not have disgraced a band of Europeans."

Marine officers wore, like army officers, a dark blue dress fully skirted tunic with two rows of gilt buttons on the chest, red collar and cuffs, yellow piping edging the collar and tunic's front, gold rank lace (no executive curl) at cuffs and gold epaulets with red strapa; dark blue trousers with a red stripe. They also had a service dress double-breasted navy style officer's jacket with lace at cuffs and a short single-breasted jacket with red shoulder cords and black rank cuff lace rank. They also had the dress shako and undress cap with gold rank stripes.

The Arts

As during the previous decades, the arts in Japan were profoundly influenced by the opening up of the nation to western influences. Once the Meiji regime was in firmly place, it was obvious that these influences were permanent and this was confirmed when the 1877 Satsuma rebellion was crushed. At the same time, it did not mean that the traditional art forms were banned; they now had competition from other cultures. In that sense, some of the most interesting items are the renderings of the 1873-1874 army and navy uniform regulations. They follow the organization of French and British dress regulations of the time, the items illustrated are European uniforms and weapons type, but the style, the spirit and the coloring of these plates are un-mistakenly Japanese! This is especially striking when one compares old photos to these uniform regulations: photos show oriental men dressed in western uniforms; the regulations show exquisitely rendered Japanese uniforms that are western in style.

The large prints, sometimes triptychs, continued to be produced and were obviously popular. Military events such as the incidents with Korea and the Satsuma rebellion were the subject of print publications, a few of which are reproduced here. As can be seen, a new perspective was rapidly being developed by artists to show new realities, such as steamships, guns and uniforms, put into scenes that were replete with Japanese aesthetic compositions and landscapes. The battle action and heroic postures are continued

The Child's Bath by Mary Cassatt, 1893. Although not concerned with military themes, this particular oil painting by eminent American artist Mary Cassat (1844-1926) epitomizes the growing influence of Japanese art in Europe and America. In 1890, Mary Cassat was very impressed by a large exhibition of Japanese prints while attending art school in Paris. Thereafter she produced a series of prints that were deeply influenced by Japan's sense of aesthetics. This painting is a culmination of Cassat's sensibilities, which emphasize decorative patterns. The subject resembles many Japanese prints, which often show intimate scenes of daily life. Chicago Art Institute.

much in the same style as in previous decades, but samurais were now replaced by uniformed officers and soldiers. All had the fiercely expressive faces typical of earlier samurai period art. The documentary aspect of the prints increased. Wars would be chronicled as formerly, but also notable military reviews and political events with the emperor's presence were seen. Prints with street scenes continued to be produced in the traditional style, but now also featured lampposts, trains, uniformed soldiers and carriages. Renditions of elegant ladies were as popular as ever and some of them were now dressed in western fashions while playing pianos or operating sewing machines.

Conversely, the influence of Japanese art was being felt in Europe and in the United States. Men and women who were destined to become amongst the most influential artists of their time were deeply impressed by the art they saw that came from Japan. It may not have been the very best examples of what Japanese artists and craftsmen could accomplish, but the art form shown was novel and extraordinary. Proponents of an art renewal such as Claude Monet and Vincent Van Gogh became avid collector of Japanese prints. Monet was so enthralled by all things Japanese that he had a small Japanese bridge built in his garden at Giverny and, in 1876, painted his wife Camille wearing a Japanese dress. Many of their works show links, obvious or more subtle, to Japanese art. Writing to his brother in 1886, Van Gogh stated prophetically that his work was, "constructed on the Japanese ... Japanese art is in decadence in its own country, but it is bringing new roots amongst the impressionists." Two years later, the magazine Le Japon Artistique appeared in Paris. The American artist Mary Cassatt was part of the impressionists group when she resided in France from the mid-1870s until the mid-1880s when she ceased to identify with any movement, preferring to experiment art forms on her own. She was certainly aware of Japanese prints, but seems to have been unimpressed by their quality until she saw an exhibition of prints by Japanese masters in Paris during 1890. She was much attracted by the designs and soft colors she saw and, in the following years, produced outstanding paintings as well as exquisite prints, even triptychs, that, according to art historian Adelyn Breeskin, "added a new chapter to the history of graphic arts" and these works "technically, as color prints ... have never been surpassed."

It is sometimes overlooked that academic artists in the West were also influenced by Japan's opening to the world, albeit not in the same way as impressionists. An early example is M.F. Girarg's 1873 "The Japanese Toilet" (not illustrated) that shows a naked young woman attended by two ladies dressed in elaborate Japanese costumes in a room filled by all sorts of Japanese objects including painted panels, many of them probably seen and noted six years earlier at the Paris World's Fair. Aimé Morot's "Nude with a Japanese umbrella" went in the same somewhat voyeur vein featuring an enormous umbrella as the background to a handsome young woman shedding her kimono (sold at Sotheby's, NY, in October 2003). These works too were manifestations of "Japonisme" in Europe. Insofar as prints of Japanese uniforms, one of the earliest Western rendition appears to have been Italian military artist Quinto Cenni's color plate published in Italy during the early-1880s.

The fascination of Japan also reached the British stage with Gilbert and Sullivan's "The Mikado" in 1885. This comic opera was an overwhelming world success and is still played today. This was due to Japan's promotion of its industries and its arts thanks to its official participation at the international fairs of Vienna in 1873 and Philadelphia three years later. In 1877, even as the Satsuma rebellion raged in southern Japan, the nation's first international trade fair was held for 102 days at Ueno. The emphasis of the fair was to show that Japan could make western industrial products, from ships to needles, as well as its more traditional goods such as prints and potteries. The fair was an outstanding success and more were held later on.

Chinese troops bearing flags, 1894. As can be seen, they wore China's traditional national dress consisting of sleeved or sleeveless surcoats, usually shown in various shades of blue, trimmed with black, red or other colors. These coats often had badges on the chest and the back. The flags were triangular and of many colors, their field bearing the figures of dragons or mottos. Detail from a triptych. Anne S.K. Brown Military Collection, Brown University Library, Providence, USA.

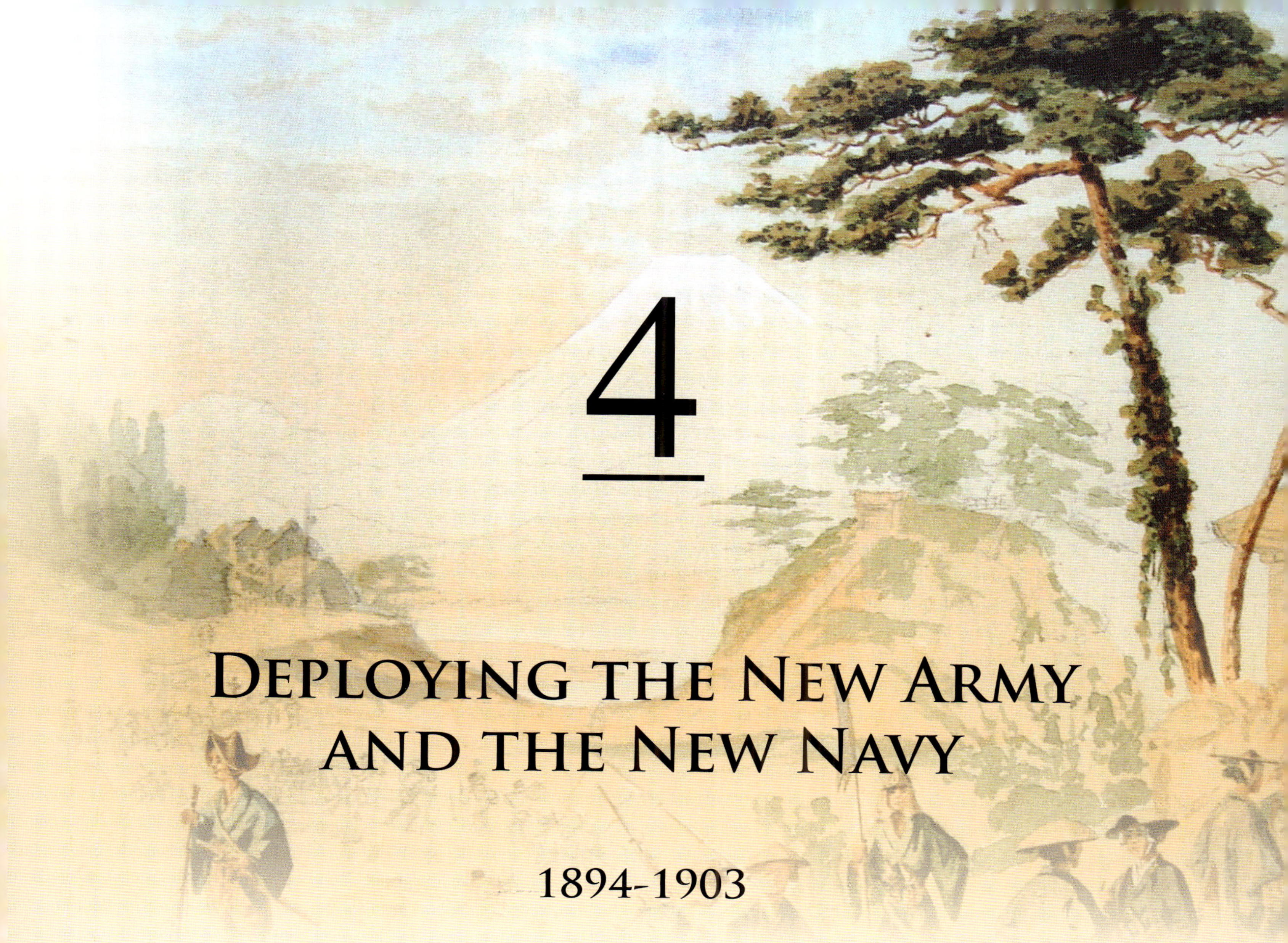

4

Deploying the New Army and the New Navy

1894-1903

War with China

Relations between China and Japan had never been very warm. From the early-1880s, they took a turn for the worse. As usual, Korea was the main bone of contention. At that time, the Korean government was backed by China which led some leading politicians in Japan to take the view that the peninsula's annexation was the only way to solve the issue. The Koreans were split as to whom they should support and all they really wished was to be left alone. Fate decided this was not to be. In 1882, the pro-Chinese Koreans initiated anti-Japanese riots in Seoul of such violence that many Japanese nationals were killed and Japan's ambassador and minister to the Korean court had to flee. This was sanctioned by China the following year when it reasserted that Korea was its tributary state. Japanese diplomats, accompanied by troops to guard them, were nevertheless back in Seoul by 1884, but the situation with China was in a stalemate. This was a very thorny issue for Japan. The temptation to declare war was great, but prudence prevailed. The Japanese imperial general staff warned the government that the armed forces were not yet large enough and properly prepared for a struggle against China. Therefore, by the 1885 treaty of Tientsin, both countries agreed to withdraw their troops from Korea. On its side, China too needed time: the French were bombarding southern Chinese forts and the Russians were trying to occupy the whole coastline between Siberia and Korea.

For Japan, a weakening China raised the specter that Korea might be taken over by a western power, probably Russia. It was thus crucial to expand and thoroughly prepare the imperial armed forces for a struggle that all knew would come, but no one knew when. By 1890, the maneuvers at Nagoya now showed a powerful and highly organized force that deployed quickly thanks to its use of railroads and, even more remarkable, its ability to mount major amphibious operations thanks to the close cooperation between the army and the navy. The obvious target to such an operation would be the Korean peninsula or the Chinese coast. Japan's national security was seen as increasingly threatened by China's persistent underlying attempts to erode its influence in Korea and by Russia's building the Trans-Siberian railway that would bring more troops to occupy the northern Chinese

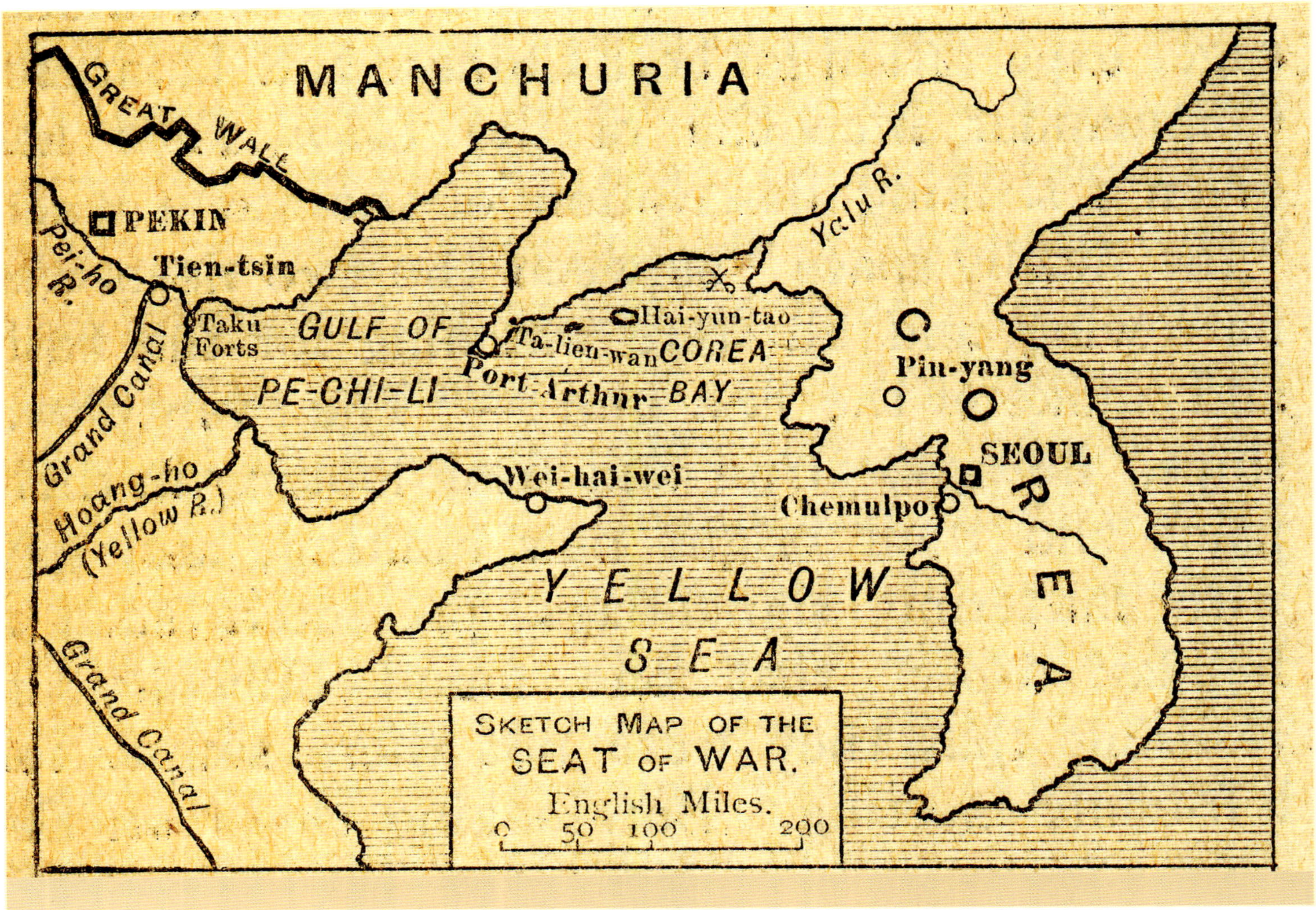

Sketch map of the seat of the Sino-Japanese War, 1894-1895. From Battles of the Nineteenth Century (c. 1900), Vol. 3.

coast. This would leave Japan without a buffer and was of course unacceptable to the island nation's government and people.

The spark that led to war with China came in Korea. In March 1894, a pro-Japanese Korean activist was assassinated in Shanghai and his body displayed in Korea by the Chinese as a warning to others who favored Japan. China then announced it was sending 2,800 troops into Korea to help suppress a local rebellion. Japan meanwhile had proposed to restructure the Korean government so as to modernize the country, but China sullenly refused to implement reforms. This time, Japan had enough of China's insults and disregard. The imperial general staff pronounced Japan's armed forces ready for war and mobilized reserves while a 4,500 men expeditionary force landed at Chemulpo (Inchon) in Korea to counter the Chinese in Korea.

By July, some of the Japanese troops were near Seoul to insure the security of some 10,000 Japanese citizens and diplomats in Korea so as to prevent a repeat of the 1882 murders. Meanwhile, the Korean government was caught in the middle of both China and Japan's pressures and was much torn with regards to reforms. Otori Keisuke, Japan's minister to Korea as well as commander of the expeditionary force, wished to see the King Li of Korea for decisions on these matters and an audience was set on 23 July. When he arrived under a strong escort, the Japanese soldiers were fired upon and fighting broke out at Seoul's palace gate between the Korean guards and Ambassador Otori's escort. To Japan, this was the final indignation. Negotiations were over and the war was on, if not officially declared. Japanese troops in Seoul lost no time, took over the royal palace and the city itself. Otori called for reinforcements and a pro-Japanese government was installed; some Korean troops now joined the Japanese. On 25 July, the Japanese fleet deployed in the Yellow Sea intercepted Chinese troopships escorted by cruisers that were heading for Korea near the island of Phungdo. Some 4,000 Japanese troops at Seoul then headed south and, on 28 July, met a 3,500 men Chinese force near the Korean port city of Asan. After a fierce fight, the Chinese force broke and fled to Pyongyang in the north. War between China and Japan was formally declared on 1 August 1894. The Sino-Japanese War was the first major conflict that pitted Japan against a foreign power since the 16th century and just like 300 years earlier Korea was the cause of the hostilities.

Skirmish at Seoul, Korea, 23 July 1894. On that date, the Japanese ambassador to Korea went to meet its king to demand government reforms and the withdrawal of Chinese troops in the country. At the palace gates, a skirmish broke out between the king's guard and the ambassador's military escort in which seventeen Koreans were killed and sixty were wounded while the Japanese troops had one killed and two wounded. The palace and the city were then taken over by the Japanese soldiers. This print shows the Japanese troops wearing the summer uniform. Ambassador Otori is shown at lower right in diplomatic uniform. Print on rice paper after Eiki Yamamoto from Jukichi Inouye's 1895 Scenes from the Japan-China War.

It should be noted that there was a Korean army of sorts numbering about 5,500 men. Some 3,500 of these troops were posted in Seoul and formed the most modern part of the force, being armed with American Remington rifle and trained by Americans. The artillery consisted of six guns at the royal palace that was guarded by a company of guard troops. The other troops serving elsewhere were armed with flintlock muskets and sabers. They barely could be called "soldiers" and were, "badly fed, badly paid, were employed sometimes as couriers, sometimes as policemen and sometimes personal as servants" to aristocratic officers who knew next to nothing about military matters. It seems none of the Korean troops had modern equipment and uniforms, except perhaps liveried palace guards. The navy amounted to a small gunboat. Needless to add that neither China nor Japan took the Korean forces seriously and everyone knew they would have no importance in the conflict.

The Chinese and Japanese forces would be the two contestants. The armies facing each other were totally different. Numerous as it may have been, the Chinese army was really a collection of several semi-provincial forces that, on the whole, had not progressed a great deal since the 16th century. Chinese soldiers were nevertheless brave and resilient and could put up quite a stubborn fight. But there was no general staff, no effective central command, no quartermaster or logistical services or anything else that one would expect in a 19th century army. Officer quality was often abysmal, soldier training poor and steeped in outdated warrior traditions. There were several types of armies in China: the regular imperial Manchu (or "of the eight banners") troops, the regular provincial (or "green banner") troops, the irregular (or "braves") troops and the frontier troops of Turkestan and Mongolia. The latter could not be deployed so the war would be fought by the three other categories.

The Japanese enter Seoul, 23 July 1894. Although the pro-Japanese Korean prince Taewogon (or Tai-in-Kun) is shown riding next to ambassador Otori's carriage, Taewogon had actually entered the palace with troops hours earlier. The print shows the Japanese troops having secured the city's gates and dispersing the remaining opponents in a "moping up" operation in the background. The Japanese troops are shown in the summer white uniforms with red trim. Triptych after Watanabe Nobukazu. Anne S.K. Brown Military Collection, Brown University Library, Providence, USA.

Chinese troops are charged by Japanese infantry near Asan, Korea, 28 July 1894. After a fierce fight, the Chinese force broke and fled. The contrast between the traditional dress of the Chinese soldiers and efficient-looking Japanese white summer uniforms is striking. Anne S.K. Brown Military Collection, Brown University Library, Providence, USA.

Japanese ships intercept and sink a Chinese troop convoy near the island of Phungdo, 25 July 1894. After defeating two Chinese escort cruisers, three Japanese cruisers summoned the two Chinese troopships to surrender. Both did, but the troops on board one of them, the transport Kowshing, mutinied against the ship's officers and crew. The Japanese cruiser Naniwa signaled to the crew to save themselves by jumping into the sea. The Chinese troops meanwhile opened fire on the cruiser, but their guns were no match against naval cannons and the transport was sunk with an estimated loss of over a thousand men including two generals. The print shows the European ship's captain and quartermaster being rescued by a Japanese longboat. Print on rice paper after Eiki Yamamoto from Jukichi Inouye's 1895 Scenes from the Japan-China War.

The first and most modern force was the imperial Manchu army that numbered from 70,000 to 100,000 men most of whom were armed with firearms. Some 5,000 had been trained in the use of German Mauser rifles and were used as instructors so that, "only perhaps half of that force knows how to handle rapid fire rifles", noted a French observer. The imperial Manchu army also had some 80mm and 90mm Krupp artillery. The second force, but the most important in numbers, consisted of the regular provincial troops were the responsibility of the local governor of a province and, throughout China, may have amounted to about half a million men. But they were somewhat autonomous from each other and seemed to have been most useful as a sort of internal constabulary force. Many provincial soldiers were still only armed with edged weapons. They were led by 6,000 officers whose knowledge of modern military sciences was usually abysmal. These troops were not renowned for their discipline and were often seen as bullies by the very people they were supposed to protect. The third force consisted of irregulars temporarily hired during an emergency. They were seen as a gathering of turbulent and undisciplined ruffians of little military value. There was no conscription in China. Thus, in spite of its huge population of over three-hundred million souls, China could perhaps send about 300,000 men "that could be called soldiers" to fight the Japanese army. And unlike its opponent, the Chinese army had no logistical, administrative or medical corps to feed, arm, pay and care for its soldiers. Uniforms were really traditional liveries when they could be had. Intelligence services as to its enemy's force and capacity were next to nil. China had no modern arms industry and had even stopped buying ammunition from abroad in 1891.

By comparison, it was astounding to see Japan's army. One foreign observer felt the Chinese troops were like a

Engagement between Chinese and Japanese troops, Korea, August 1894. The Chinese soldiers are shown in the foreground dressed in green livery coats and armed with spears, the Japanese troops in white summer dress except for the officer dressed in a black Attila jacket. Triptych after Shinitschi. Anne S.K. Brown Military Collection, Brown University Library, Providence, USA.

Japanese troops capture weapons from the fleeing Chinese in Korea, August 1894. After the battle of Asan, the captured supplies proved very valuable to the Japanese armies on campaign. Triptych after Nosai Nabukazu. Anne S.K. Brown Military Collection, Brown University Library, Providence, USA.

Capture by infantryman Harada Jukichi of the rampart above the Genbumon Gate at Pyongyang, 15 September 1894. Jukichi was the first, and for a time the only soldier, to succeed in climbing the wall unscathed despite "a shower of bullets" and overcome the Chinese on the parapet. The artist has given this print much atmosphere by his skillful use of color washes in the landscape. Triptych print after Kobayashi Kiyochika. Anne S.K. Brown Military Collection, Brown University Library, Providence, USA.

Assault of Pyongyang, Korea, 15 September 1894. Following the defeat of the Chinese army, the Japanese troops moved north to take Pyongyang on the Taidong River. On the morning of 15 September, columns of Japanese troops attacked the walled city with artillery support. The soldiers climbing the walls at right allude to a dozen soldiers who "succeeded in climbing the castle wall and, falling upon the Chinese, opened the gate to their comrades." The city fell shortly thereafter. Print on rice paper after Eiki Yamamoto from Jukichi Inouye's 1895 Scenes from the Japan-China War.

force out of Ancient Greece while their Japanese opponents were the Asian emulation of the imperial German army, which then was seen as the world's best and most powerful. Added to that were some of the French army's best features. Here then was an Asian army with all the strategic and tactical staff corps, educated officers, trained soldiers, good uniforms, modern weapons and all the service and support units seen in European armies. The same could be said for the navy, obviously far better trained than its Chinese rival. Furthermore, Japan now had a modern arms industry and was gradually attaining self-sufficiency in weapons and ammunition production. Its manufactures produced quantities of Murata repeating rifles, quick-firing field guns, smokeless powder for ammunition, range finders and even binoculars for officers.

From the outset, it did not look good for the imperial Chinese forces. Japan's strategic aim was to fight the war in Korea and north China. The imperial general staff had good intelligence and the army structure was set up to carry out instructions quickly and efficiently with all the support services thanks to state-of-the-art communications networks. The Japanese could field 120,000 men in China divided into two armies, the 1st Army having the 3rd and 5th divisions and the 2nd Army being made up of the 1st, 2nd and 6th divisions. The 4th division acted as a reserve. The imperial guard division also did, but it was eventually tasked with the invasion of Taiwan. The standing army was about 85,000 men to which were added 105,000 reservists that were called up. When the territorial force was added, the whole army numbered up to 300,000 men that were all trained, uniformed and armed with modern weapons. Japan then had a population of forty million people.

The campaign got under way quickly, the Japanese keeping the initiative thanks to good planning and efficient deployment of land and sea forces. By 16 September, Japanese troops of the 1st Army led by Marshal Yamagata had reached, attacked and taken Pyongyang, which was a decisive victory. The Chinese troops retreated towards China. The next day, 17 September, the Japanese fleet under Admiral Ito almost annihilated the Chinese fleet at

Although wounded, infantryman Harada Jukichi managed to fight off Chinese soldiers and open the Genbumon gate at Pyongyang, 15 September 1894. Triptych print after Kobayashi Kiyochika. Anne S.K. Brown Military Collection, Brown University Library, Providence, USA.

Japanese soldiers triumphant at the capture of Pyongyang, 15 September 1894. A mounted field officer of infantry is at the center with buglers near him. On each side, two columns of overjoyed Japanese infantryman. The flag at the left indicates a regiment's second battalion. At the center are heaps of Chinese dead soldiers, flags and captured cannons. Triptych print after Kobayashi Kiyochika. Anne S.K. Brown Military Collection, Brown University Library, Providence, USA.

Naval battle of the Yellow Sea (or Yalu or Haiyang, off Korea), 17 September 1894. Two days after the fall of Phyongyang to the Japanese, a Chinese fleet of thirteen warships escorting reinforcements for its garrison appeared off the Korean coast. It was met and defeated near the island of Haiyang by a Japanese fleet of eleven ships, the Chinese loosing four warships. It was the world's first naval battle that opposed modern warships and proved the superiority of the quick-firing guns used by the Japanese. Thereafter, the Japanese were masters of the Yellow sea and were now able to safely transport troops to attack China itself. Print on rice paper after Eiki Yamamoto from Jukichi Inouye's 1895 Scenes from the Japan-China War.

the battle of the Yellow Sea near the mouth of the Yalu River, another decisive victory. Japan had now naval control over the Korean peninsula and the last Chinese soldiers left Korea on 9 October. The 1st Japanese Army was not far behind and, on 24 October, crossed the Yalu River into Manchuria. For the first time ever, the heirs of the samurai warriors were marching into China.

They were joined in China by the 2nd Japanese Army under Marshal Omaya at the end of October when it landed on the Liaotung Peninsula in the middle of its southern coast. The 2nd Army marched southwest towards the vital ports of Dairen (Talienwan) and Port Arthur (Lushunkou, Ryojun). Dairen was taken on 6 November and the ultimate prize, Port Arthur, fell to the Japanese forces on 21 November. This victory was marred by lapses in the troop's discipline that resulted in the massacre of hundreds (or thousands – this incident is still very much debated) of the inhabitants as well as widespread looting and rampage. Certainly, it was a negative blur to the Japanese troops that was eagerly reported by American and European correspondents, often with rather smug racism. It seemed that Wellington's British troops' outrages at Badajos and San Sebastian had never occurred... Not to mention similar excesses by all other western armies. The disorders in Port Arthur had apparently been sparked by the discovery of Japanese corpses beheaded and horribly mutilated by Chinese soldiers. Nevertheless, it was unacceptable and while the allegations were denied, it was made clear that no such behavior was to occur.

Meanwhile, the 1st Army advanced into Manchuria now separated into two columns, the 3rd division pursuing Chinese troops north and capturing towns along the way, the 5th division heading towards Mukden (Shenyang) to the northeast. Marshal Yamagata was now contemplating marching on Peking (Beijing) itself by reuniting his two divisions. Prime minister Ito did not see it that way. That could be too much of a victory that would backfire diplomatically with other powers. The marshal had

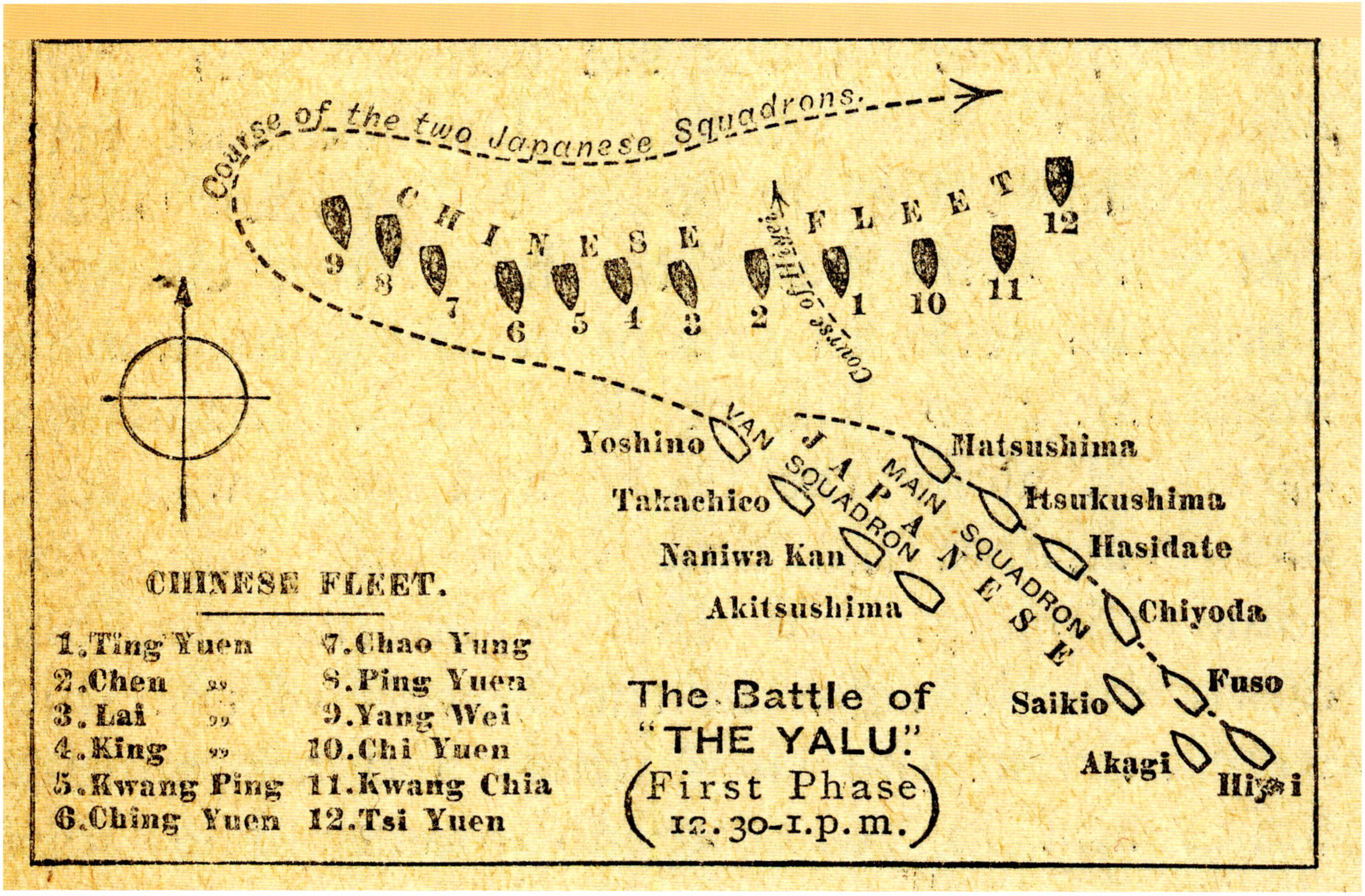

Map of the naval battle of the Yellow Sea or of the Yalu on 17 September 1894. The ships are shown in their positions at 12:30-1:00 pm. From Battles of the Nineteenth Century (c. 1900), Vol. 3.

previously asked to be relieved for stomach ailment and Ito now granted his request. The 1st Army stayed south of the Liao River in Manchuria.

The remains of the Chinese fleet had retreated across the Yellow Sea to Weihaiwei at the tip of the Shangdong Peninsula. Marshal Omaya's 2nd Army landed there without opposition from 20 to 24 January 1895 and marched towards Weihaiwei. The Chinese Beiyang army troops put up a fierce resistance and General Odera was one of those killed during the assaults on the outlying forts on 1 February. The forts fell and the deserted city was occupied the following day. Blockading the harbor were forty-one Japanese navy ships poised to destroy the fifteen Chinese ships within. Japanese ships made repeated and successful attacks between 7 and 9 February that sank or led to the capture of nearly all the Chinese ships. On 12 February, Chinese Admiral Ting surrendered.

Following the fall of Port Arthur and Weihaiwei, negotiations started that culminated in the signature of peace preliminaries on 17 April 1895, which were ratified on 8 May 1895. By the terms of the peace treaty, China recognized the independence of Korea, paid a large sum as indemnity and ceded Taiwan and the Pescadores Islands to Japan. The Liaotung Peninsula had originally been included, but Russia, Germany and France intervened in China's favor and Japan deferred. Nevertheless, this victorious war elevated Japan to world power status. It was now undeniably Asia's most militarily powerful nation and it suddenly found itself in the midst of international power balance brokering.

However, the war was not quite over for some Chinese and some Japanese soldiers. The cession of Taiwan to Japan was not greeted with joy on the island and, when the first Japanese arrived at the end of May 1895, they met open resistance from Chinese troops who were joined by many Taiwanese volunteers. The main cities were occupied by Japanese troops while opponents retreated to the mountains and jungles. Four months of guerrilla style fighting ensued largely in countryside hills and bamboo jungles, but the 50,000 Japanese troops prevailed, their "splendid discipline and unequalled bravery" being reported by American correspondents. The remaining Chinese forces finally surrendered on 15 October.

In all, the Japanese lost over 1,000 men in action and some 17,000 to sickness during the conflict. Many Japanese were disappointed with the skimpy gains of the war, but, at the moment, the nation was too weak to face

Battle at the Yellow Sea (or Yalu or Haiyang, off Korea), between the imperial navy's ship Akagi against a Chinese battleship, 17 September 1894. The small upper right panel a a few words in English: "Terrible war of General [Commander] Sakamoto, Leader of Imperial Warship Akagi." The Akagi was severely damaged, but the Chinese lost three cruisers and another warship in the battle. Commander Hachirota Sakamoto was killed in the engagement. Print after Mezuno Toshikata. Anne S.K. Brown Military Collection, Brown University Library, Providence, USA.

Undersea combat, Sino-Japanese War, 17 September 1894. This extraordinary triptych shows an unrecorded underwater combat between Chinese (at left) and Japanese (at right) divers. This print may be one of the earliest to show undersea combat. It proved to be immensely popular. Triptych after Kuniyoshi published in October 1894. Anne S.K. Brown Military Collection, Brown University Library, Providence, USA.

Navy sailors serving a cannon, possibly at the battle of the Yellow Sea or of the Yalu on 17 September 1894. The sailors and officers wear summer uniforms. Some officers are shown in the white service jacket trimmed with black lace rather than the regulation white. Print after Mezumo Toshikata. Anne S.K. Brown Military Collection, Brown University Library, Providence, USA.

A Japanese navy warship overcomes a Chinese gunboat, possibly at the battle of the Yellow Sea (or Haiyang, off Korea), 17 September 1894. Anne S.K. Brown Military Collection, Brown University Library, Providence, USA.

General attack by Japanese troops on Chiu-lien-cheng, China, on 25 October 1894. This action-packed large triptych print show General Katsura Taro with infantry at left, cavalry at center and more infantry with artillery at right. The Chinese troops were defeated and fled leaving behind seventy-four field guns, four machineguns and over 4,000 rifles with a vast supply of ammunition. With the fall of this important city on the Chinese side of the Yalu River, the Japanese could now advance into Manchuria. Triptych after Adachi Ginko. Anne S.K. Brown Military Collection, Brown University Library, Providence, USA.

Japanese scout along the Yalu River, northern Korea, late 1894. In what is an exceptionally peaceful scene in the midst of nature, the scout observes Chinese army campfires across the river. Detail of a triptych print by Kobayashi Kiyochika printed in 1894. Anne S.K. Brown Military Collection, Brown University Library, Providence, USA.

Lieutenant general Yamaji, division commander in the Second Army, lands with his staff on the Liaotung Peninsula, China, on 24 October 1894. The landing was skillfully executed and remained undetected by the Chinese. General Yamaji, nicknamed the One-Eyed-Dragon General because he was blind in one eye, is greeted by a senior field officer with a bugler. Detail of a triptych print by Kobayashi Kiyochika printed in January 1895. Anne S.K. Brown Military Collection, Brown University Library, Providence, USA.

a major western power. The armed forces needed to be much larger. In 1896, the army increased in size to twelve divisions and the navy entered into a major expansion. Japan's control of Korea became increasingly difficult when China leased Port Arthur to Russia in 1897, in effect turning over the Liaotung Peninsula and part of Manchuria to that nation's influence. On the other side of the Yellow Sea, Tsingtau was leased to Germany, which gave control over the Shangtung Peninsula from 1898 to one of Europe's most powerful nations.

A result of the Sino-Japanese War was the beneficial and rapid expansion of the Japanese Red Cross during and after the war. Founded in 1875, it had its origin in 1866 when a committee "of volunteer help to [wounded or sick] soldiers" was organized under the patronage of Princess Komatzu and this gave consideration and prestige to the nursing profession during the Meiji era. The empress-mother was seen making bandages and other female members of the imperial family visited hospitals and took part in Red Cross work. Nursing courses were given in the hospitals to young ladies following the European systems and those who graduated became registered nurses. This was an important era in the

Imperial guard infantry manning a field piece, c. 1894. All wear the white summer cap cover and trousers. Note the electric spotlight in the background. Anne S.K. Brown Military Collection, Brown University Library, Providence, USA.

Japanese infantrymen being ferried to shore by a longboat manned by navy personnel, January 1895. Some fifty ships landed troops at Rongcheng Bay on the northeast end of the Shangdong Peninsula for the advance on Weihaiwei. The army officer standing wears a service dress Attila jacket. Detail of a triptych print by Kobayashi Kiyochika printed in January 1895. Anne S.K. Brown Military Collection, Brown University Library, Providence, USA.

Japanese troops take possession of Port Arthur, 1 December 1894. Following the fall of most forts guarding the city on 21 November, a Chinese relief force was defeated at Kinchow and the doomed garrison of Port Arthur finally surrendered. The print shows infantrymen raising their color over the town. Regrettably, discipline broke down within some of the Japanese units and some soldiers went on a murderous rampage in the town, even killing some of their officers who tried to stop them before order was restored. Print on rice paper after Eiki Yamamoto from Jukichi Inouye's 1895 Scenes from the Japan-China War.

Japanese troops wearing winter uniforms in China, early-1895. This included a substantial greatcoat with its hood featuring attachable flaps to cover the lower head. Officers had fur trim edging the greatcoat's collar, cuffs, front and skirts. In this instance, the field officer's horse is also well covered against the elements. Print after Kobayashi Kiyochika. Anne S.K. Brown Military Collection, Brown University Library, Providence, USA.

Japanese troops advance on the ice towards Weihaiwei, January 1895. Following its successful campaign in northern China's Liaotung Peninsula, the 2nd Army was carried over by the imperial navy to the Shangdong Peninsula at the end of January 1895. The target was Weihaiwei and the two parts of the triptych shown portray a field officer, possibly of artillery, watching a field artillery battery traveling over the ice of a frozen river. He wears the officer's dark blue overcoat trimmed with fur, its turned down hood showing its red lining. Note the winter padded blanketing for the horse. Print after Kobayashi Kiyochika. Anne S.K. Brown Military Collection, Brown University Library, Providence, USA.

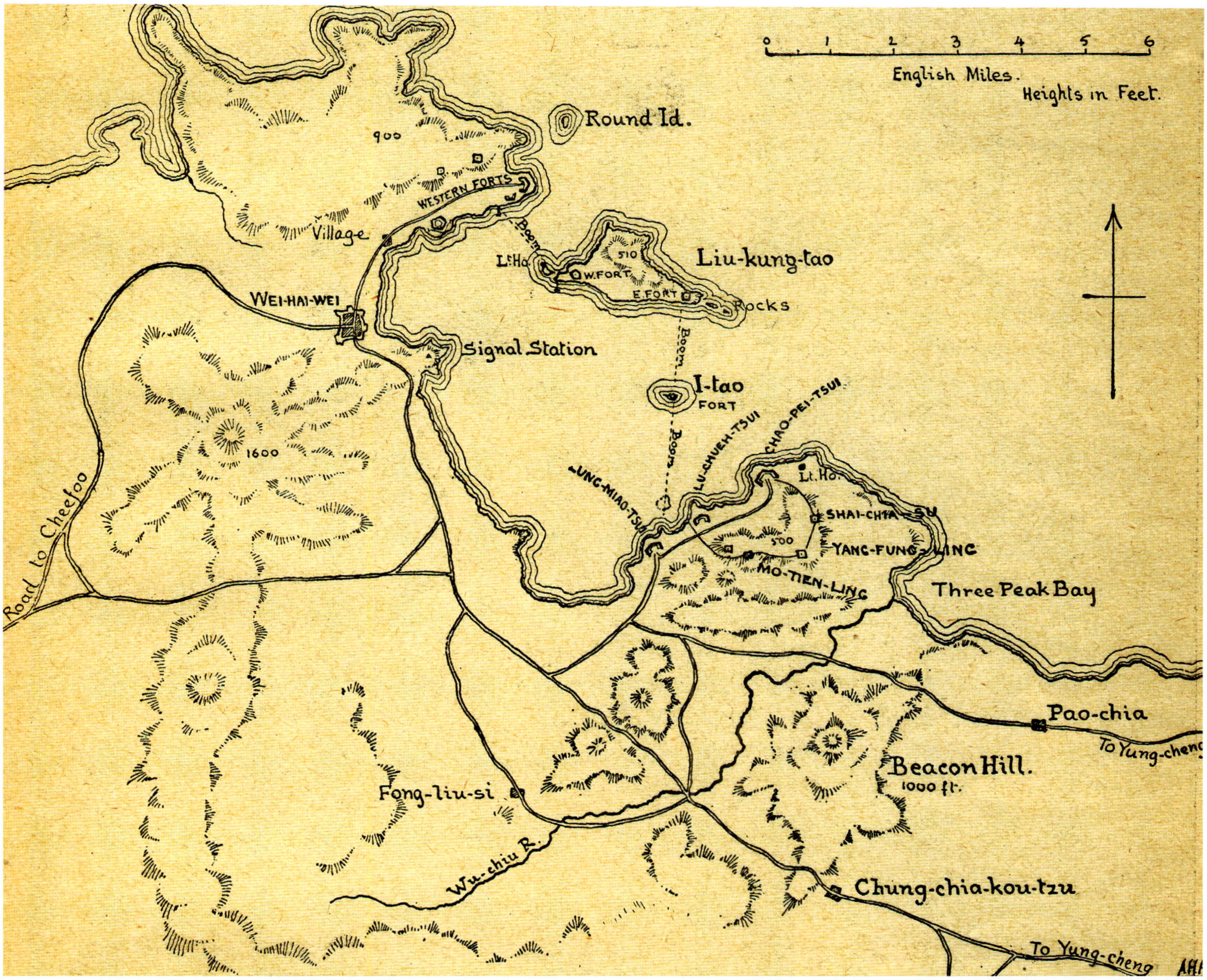

Map of Weihaiwei Bay and its surroundings. The Chinese retreated to the island of Liukung until compelled to surrender on 12 February 1895. Map from Battles of the Nineteenth Century (c. 1900), Vol. 5.

nation's health care, which was transformed by keen young doctors that had often been schooled in Europe or in the United States and by a professional approach to nursing and to pharmacy. As with schools, setting up a medical system was seen as patriotic work by the Japanese people. Efficient health services were seen not only in the armed forces, but throughout the nation. Nearly 200,000 people were active in the Japanese Red Cross Society by the early-1890s. Insofar as military medical services were concerned, the large number of soldiers that had died of sickness during Sino-Japanese War revealed that more resources were needed in the field to keep the troops healthier. This was largely accomplished by 1900 when the Boxer Rebellion broke out. By then, the military arm of the Japanese Red Cross even included two hospital ships and "the excellence of its organization" was lauded by the other allied contingents.

Boxer Rebellion

Within China, foreign influences and encroachments were increasingly resented during the later-1890s. These feelings gave rise to the "Boxer" movement that strove to rid China of all foreigners by violent means. The Chinese imperial government of the Qing dynasty initially tried to suppress the Boxers, but then reversed its stand and allowed the movement discreet and, in some cases, public military support. The imperial government's policy under dowager empress Cixi also sought to reduce foreign influence in China. From early-1900, groups of armed Boxers started attacking European, American and Japanese missionaries, businessmen and diplomats as well as Chinese Christians in northeastern China. Hundreds of foreign families were killed as well as over 20,000 Chinese Christians. In the imperial capital of Peking (now Beijing), the foreign diplomats were all housed in the same area and they fortified themselves in a

Skirmish between Chinese troops, probably in late January 1895. This is likely an incident during the Weihaiwei campaign when the Japanese army approached that port town. Chinese soldiers are in the foreground being overrun by Japanese troops climbing up the hill they defend. The whole action is during a snow fall and the snowflakes speckled on the evening sky give an odd "Christmas card" look to this attractive triptych print. Anne S.K. Brown Military Collection, Brown University Library, Providence, USA.

A huge explosion in a Chinese fort is the backdrop for this print showing the Japanese assault on the coastal forts at Pohchihyaisu near Weihaiwei, in late January 1895. The foreground shows Japanese infantrymen firing on Chinese soldiers shown as shadows with triangular flags over them. The print itself, probably after Kobayashi Kiyochika, is a masterpiece insofar as its composition and coloring. Anne S.K. Brown Military Collection, Brown University Library, Providence, USA.

Line cavalry charging at the battle of Ikaeiei, near Weihaiwei, 30 January 1895. The artist has rendered a snowstorm and smoke effects, putting the troopers in an almost groundless and surrealist setting. Print after Kobayashi Kiyochika. Anne S.K. Brown Military Collection, Brown University Library, Providence, USA.

Major general Odera at the battle of Ikaeiei, near Weihaiwei, 30 January 1895. He is shown in service dress highlighted with snow. Just behind him is the journalist Kubota Beisen. A soldier of the engineers (note the shovel fixed to his knapsack) and a line infantryman are nearby. Detail of a print after Kobayashi Kiyochika. Anne S.K. Brown Military Collection, Brown University Library, Providence, USA.

Japanese field artillery in action during a snowstorm, early 1895. Detail from a triptych. The officer wears the officer's fur trimmed overcoat. The men have the artillery uniform with yellow collar, shoulder straps, cuff and trouser stripes. A dead Chinese soldier lies half buried in the snow. Print after Kobayashi Kiyochika. Anne S.K. Brown Military Collection, Brown University Library, Providence, USA.

Japanese troops firing at the enemy from a trench during a heavy snowstorm near Ikaeiei and Pohchihyaisu, near Weihaiwei, China, in late January 1895. They are shown covered in snow, a favorite feature in Japanese art prints. At right, one of the soldiers is shoveling snow. Print probably after Kobayashi Kiyochika. Anne S.K. Brown Military Collection, Brown University Library, Providence, USA.

Capture of Pohchihyaisu, 30 January 1895. The remnants of the Chinese fleet took refuge at Weihaiwei, which the Japanese blockaded. On 25 January 1895, a Japanese army landed at Yungehing which it immediately took and marched towards the east coast forts at Pohchihyaisu. The town was defended by landward forts that were taken. The print shows the death of Major General Odera and Tokyo newspaper correspondent Kubota Beisen during the assault at Ikaeiei. The band on the general's cap should be red. Print on rice paper after Eiki Yamamoto from Jukichi Inouye's 1895 Scenes from the Japan-China War.

Japanese troops capture a Chinese fort at Pohchihyaisu, near Weihaiwei, in a snowstorm, late January 1895. An officer plants a Japanese regimental color over the large Chinese coastal gun; the men are overjoyed at their success and signal to the Japanese fleet that the position is secured. Triptych after Kobayashi Kiyochika. Anne S.K. Brown Military Collection, Brown University Library, Providence, USA.

defense perimeter to avoid being massacred. There were, besides 844 soldiers and sailors from eight nations, 473 foreign civilians and diplomats and some 3,000 Chinese Christians in the legation quarter, which was besieged by the Boxers from June 1900. Colonel Shiba with another officer and twenty-four sailors of the Japanese imperial navy were especially noted for their most distinguished behavior in battle. In the city of Tianjin, foreigners (including young mining engineer Herbert Hoover who would later become the 31st U.S. president) and Chinese Christians also barricaded themselves successfully. All hoped for relief from certain death at the hand of the Boxers.

As the situation in China worsened, an alliance of eight nations (by importance of military contribution: Japan, Russia, United Kingdom, France, United States, Germany, Italy and Austria-Hungary) was quickly formed to rescue the Peking embassies and defeat the Boxers. A first attempt with only 2,000 troops failed in early June, but a much larger force of 55,000 men was assembling. Japan contributed by far the largest contingent committing some 21,000 troops as well as the largest naval force: eighteen warships. Russia came next with 13,000 troops and ten warships, Great Britain 12,000 troops and eight warships, France 3,500 troops and five warships, the United States 3,500 troops and two warships, Germany with only 300 troops but five warships, Italy two warships and Austria-Hungary one. On 16 June, the expeditionary force appeared off the China coast and the Chinese Taku coastal forts fell after an allied bombardment and an assault the following day. Once assembled, the force moved into the interior towards Peking. On 14 July, Japanese troops broke into Tianjin's southern gate and the city was taken, its foreign legation quarter having sustained a month long siege. Peking was eighty miles away, but a 70,000 strong Chinese army was in the way to stop the relief expedition. Nevertheless, a 20,000 man allied force defeated the Chinese army and reached Peking on 14 August while the Boxers and Chinese imperial soldiers abandoned the city.

For China, the consequences were tragic. Foreign troops occupied the main cities in northern China for over a year and led punitive expeditions to round up and kill Boxers or suspected Boxers. Revenge was the order of the day and the country was subject to widespread looting and mass executions of mostly innocent people. China was condemned to pay an enormous sum in reparations, which it did until 1939. However, the Boxer Rebellion did put a damper to foreign colonial ambitions in China.

For Japan, its participation was the nation's first large scale deployment of troops and warships within an international alliance gathering the world's major powers. When one considers that twenty-three years before, the Satsuma samurais had revolted in Japan with roughly the same aims as the Boxers, the enormous and successful change in Japanese society during the last quarter of the 19th century becomes apparent. The

Torpedo boat attack on the Chinese warships at Weihaiwei, February 1895. Following the capture of the coastal forts, four small Japanese torpedo boats attacked the still potentially dangerous Chinese warships at Weihaiwei harbor and sank five out of six Chinese ships without loosing any boats. Weihaiwei surrendered thereafter. Print on rice paper after Eiki Yamamoto from Jukichi Inouye's 1895 Scenes from the Japan-China War.

The fall of Liukung Island, 7-14 February 1895. After the capture of Weihaiwei and all its coastal forts, the Japanese forces besieged nearby Liukung Island which surrendered on 14 February. Print on rice paper after Eiki Yamamoto from Jukichi Inouye's 1895 Scenes from the Japan-China War.

country had succeeded in its gamble to westernize its institutions, economy and armed forces and become the most powerful independent Asian nation. In 1900, western nations did not take Japan too seriously yet as a world power, but they would have to within a few years...

Uniforms

The dress of the army during the 1890s and early-1900s followed the regulations of 1886. As seen in the preceding chapter, they were quite comprehensive and had practically no changes until the introduction of khaki during the Russo-Japanese War. In the Sino-Japanese War and the Boxer Rebellion in China, the dress worn in the field by the army was the dark blue uniform worn except for the white summer dress. In a few prints showing troops in battles of the war with China, the white uniform is shown with red trim, possibly decorative highlights added by the units or "improvements" by the artists for visual effect. In 1900, officers were assigned a simplified field uniform in the form of a five-button frock, both in white and dark

An officer on reconnaissance in Manchuria during a snowy night in early 1895. He wears the overcoat with its hood. Detail from a triptych after Kobayashi Kiyochika. Anne S.K. Brown Military Collection, Brown University Library, Providence, USA.

On 23 March 1895, a Japanese force landed on the Pescadores (Penghu) Islands west of Taiwan and quickly overcame the small Chinese garrison. This work showing a Japanese officer slaying a Chinese soldier is especially notable as it portrays all the elements of typical samurai combat prints. The main difference is that the Japanese officer and soldiers (in the background) wear uniforms rather than traditional liveries like the Chinese soldiers. Anne S.K. Brown Military Collection, Brown University Library, Providence, USA.

Imperial guard cavalry, April 1895. The troopers are part of a squad escorting the emperor's carriage at the victory celebrations at the end of the war with China. One holds the imperial standard. The troopers have, curiously, Attilas with medium green cuffs and piping in front rather than the blue piped red associated with guard cavalry units. Print after Nobukazu. Anne S.K. Brown Military Collection, Brown University Library, Providence, USA.

blue versions. The field service blue-black Attila also continued to be worn by most officers.

Winter clothing became quite important since the Sino-Japanese War was fought in northern China and partly during the late fall and winter of 1894-1895. Greatcoats had been part of the uniform since the 1873-1874 regulations and refined in the 1886 regulations. A rather unique item, part of the winter equipment since 1873-1874, was the detachable hood that buttoned around the neck. The officer's greatcoat was dark blue with brown fur trim at the collar and cuffs as well as edging the front and the skirt. The top of the cuff had piping of the corps color although this is not always shown in prints (generals and staff officers having dark blue, theirs' would not show). The enlisted men initially had grey greatcoats, but the color is shown as a brown hue by the 1890s. American observers were quite impressed by the Japanese army's winter dress: "The cold-proof winter overcoat is made of thick woolen cloth. It has a large collar covered with fur, which is of course inside when the collar is raised. From the middle of the edge of this collar a cotton cap or hood can be pulled out so as to cover the head, and over this can be worn the ample detached woolen 'cold-proof' hood. Hanging by cords from the neck are large gloves or mittens – one division for all the fingers and one for the thumbs… A sheepskin coat with the wool outside is also issued for severe weather; it fastens at one side …"

As photographs show, foreign correspondents and observers were impressed by the efficient and smart looking Japanese uniforms. Prejudices towards non-Westerners were high in those days and centered partly on the "quaint" or "savage" features of Asian or African costumes and hairstyles. In that context, it was impossible to compare the appearance of a Boxer warrior with that of a Japanese soldier, which was puzzling to many racist Westerners. Not only did the Japanese army look very good in its attractive and sober uniforms, but its excellent battle record in China proved that Asians could be outstanding on the battlefield.

Imperial guard cavalry at the victory celebrations, April 1895. They are part of a detachment escorting the emperor's carriage and one trooper bears the imperial standard. The uniforms shown are generally correct except that the collar on the coats should be medium green. Anne S.K. Brown Military Collection, Brown University Library, Providence, USA.

Weapons

The Murata 8mm Type 22 (M. 1889) was the standard rifle used in the Sino-Japanese War of 1894-1895 with its carbine version for mounted troops introduced during 1894. Three years later, the new Arisaka Type 30 (M. 1897) was the first box-magazine infantry rifle in Japanese service. Designed by Nariaki Arisaka, it generally followed the German Mauser-Mannlicher rifles and gradually replaced the Murata rifles. A version for the navy, the Arisaka Type 35 (M. 1902) was also made.

With regards to swords, Western type continued to be the regulation patterns for officers and enlisted men. However, it seems that some officers used samurai type sword blades mounted with elongated Western style hilts that included a long "D" guard and that some even used the traditional "buke-zukuri" mountings.

The Imperial Navy

In the early-1890s, the Japanese navy's main rival was the Chinese navy that was built up with German help. An important step in the evolution of the Japanese navy was the creation of its naval general staff in 1893 showing that it was now large enough to play a role in East Asian naval strategy. The 1894-1895 Sino-Japanese War established the superiority of the Japanese navy. It easily managed to protect its sea links to Korea and northern China and sink eight of the twelve major Chinese warships. However, for all their heroism, the lighter Japanese torpedo boats, destroyers and light cruisers could not subdue the two German-made battleships of the Chinese navy. This lack of capacity was immediately recognized in Tokyo and several battleships were ordered at once from Britain while Japan's military shipyards laid new keels for large warships. The navy was greatly expanded during the next decade. Its strength went from 10,000 officers and men in 1893 to nearly 41,000 by 1904 while over a hundred new ships were commissioned during that period. The benefit of such a policy, expensive as it may have been, was soon apparent. By the turn of the century, the imperial Japanese navy was the most powerful in Asia and one of the key attractions for Great Britain when it signed the 1902 alliance treaty with Japan.

Japanese troops landing in Taiwan, May 1895. The enlisted men would appear to be imperial guard infantrymen from the red band on their caps, but the officers seem to have the line's yellow band or dark blue kepis. The imperial guard division was assigned the occupation of the island. The flag identifies the 2nd battalion of a regiment. Anne S.K. Brown Military Collection, Brown University Library, Providence, USA.

The Japanese imperial guard attacks a Chinese position in central Taiwan, summer of 1895. The troops are shown wearing the white tropical dress. The enlisted men wear the distinctive imperial guard red headband on the Havelocks covering their caps; the officers in the foreground have British-style white colonial pattern helmets. Anne S.K. Brown Military Collection, Brown University Library, Providence, USA.

Chinese troops are surrounded and defeated by the Japanese army, Korea, summer 1895. This large triptych print may show an incident of the campaign in central Taiwan. The Japanese troops are of the imperial guard infantry in summer dress and the print shows their disciplined firepower. Anne S.K. Brown Military Collection, Brown University Library, Providence, USA.

Japanese troops fighting in Taiwan, summer of 1895. Although China ceded Taiwan, many Chinese troops and resistance fighters of various types did not accept the cession and fought the Japanese troops that arrived on the island from late May. This print shows Japanese imperial guard troops, distinguished by their red cap bands, in the distance moving forward to attack the rather ragged-looking Chinese resistance fighters in a bamboo thicket. It is a remarkable union of the highly bucolic qualities of Japanese nature prints with the action-packed warrior prints. Anne S.K. Brown Military Collection, Brown University Libvary, Providence, USA.

Imperial guard band, 1897. These bandsmen are shown with light green cap bands, coat collars, cuffs and trouser stripes. The uniform is otherwise standard for army bands. Print after Nobukazu. Anne S.K. Brown Military Collection, Brown University Library, Providence, USA.

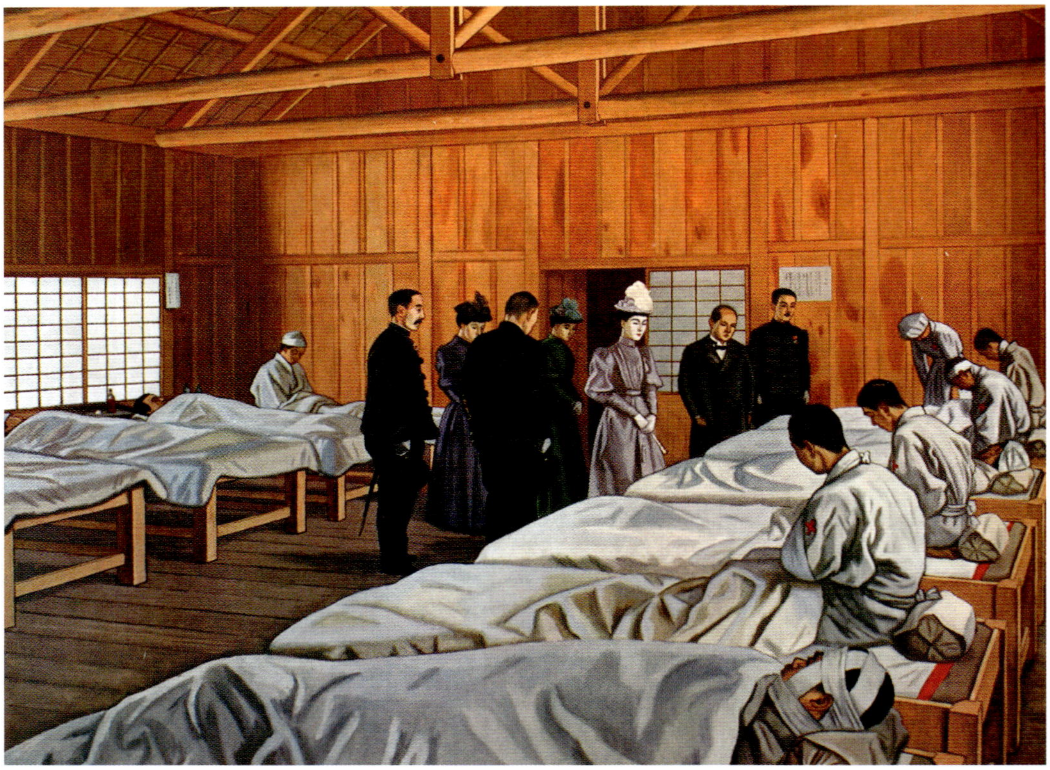

The empress visiting a military hospital, c. 1894-1895. This remarkable print mixes western type illustration technique with the Japanese sense of symmetry. The empress and her retainers all wear western style fashions and uniforms; the patients who can all respectfully bow. Anonymous print. Anne S.K. Brown Military Collection, Brown University Library, Providence, USA.

The Arts

Japan had not been at war with a foreign power in three centuries so that much of the war art produced since the 17th century portrayed previous ancient wars apart from a moderate production on recent and mainly internal conflicts such as the Satsuma rebellion. Now artists and printmakers had the opportunity to show the feats of the new army and its new heroes. Quite a lot of prints were produced, indeed many more than those printed here, which shows a sizeable consumer interest in this type of art.

The style of the great majority of the prints seen resolutely followed the traditional depictions. Again, the heroic postures and the fierce facial expressions were usually the central features of uniformed figures in action prints. The Chinese enemies were depicted with expressions of fright and wearing their slovenly Asian costumes. By contrast, Japanese soldiers and sailors were shown neatly dressed in uniform, which gave them an air of efficiency. The figures themselves were reminiscent of samurais, but wearing modern uniforms. The print's backgrounds were very much in the style of traditional Japanese art. They were filled with trees, plants, flowers and mountains typical of the finest renderings of Japanese landscape art. These peaceful-looking perspective backgrounds contrasted with the action figures in the foreground, sometime achieving a sort of balance between the tension of battle and the calm of peace. In some prints, clouds or smoke could give them an abstract quality. The skies were often depicted somber and solemn or else in exceptionally fine and vivid colors.

By the 1890s, color prints made from lithographic presses were gaining public acceptance in Japan as elsewhere in the world. These totally mechanically produced plates were far cheaper and, although they certainly did not have the same subtle tones, they did convey action and information at a price that the majority of the public could afford. It must not be forgotten that the hand made prints, while enjoying favor, always had a smaller following mainly recruited amongst art connoisseurs. Now, even magazines and newspapers were occasionally including in color pages on a variety of subjects to attract buyers. This was not particular to Japan; it was occurring in all countries that had a substantial printing industry and an educated population that could read and write.

In Japan, traditional art was being challenged by the Western way of illustrating themes that fully exploited the possibilities of lithographic printing. When one compares the plates in our pages reproduced from the traditionally illustrated "Book of Customs" and the history of the Sino-Japanese War (printed on rice paper with text in English) with the prints of the Boxer Rebellion, the differences are evident and striking, the latter print having a standard composition and very bold primary colors. Another remarkable lithograph of that period shows the empress visiting a military hospital; in spite of its very documentary style, the composition and bareness of the interior points to its Japanese origin.

The Red Cross Society and the medical corps, 1894-1895. Founded in 1875, the Red Cross Society was patronized by the empress and was the leading medical care society in Japan. In 1894, nearly all its 190,000 members were women who provided medical supplies and money for nursing services and hospitals. The Japanese medical corps tended to both the Chinese as well as the Japanese wounded, a somewhat novel practice in Asian conflicts. The corps' green facing color has taken a light blue hue in this print. Print on rice paper after Eiki Yamamoto from Jukichi Inouye's 1895 Scenes from the Japan-China War.

Navy landing party during the war with China, 1895. The sailors wear gaiters and carry rifles. The officer seems to only have a sword. Anne S.K. Brown Military Collection, Brown University Library, Providence, USA.

Sailor and officer, 1890s. The sailor is in dress uniform and wearing accouterments for sentry duty. He holds the envelope that apparently held the long message given to the officer. The officer wears service dress, but his sub-lieutenant's rank stripes are shown in gold rather than the regulation black lace. Anne S.K. Brown Military Collection, Brown University Library, Providence, USA.

Generals and staff officers, 1894. Artillery, 1894. The uniform are those prescribed by the 1886 regulations. From left to right: generals in full dress, dress and service uniforms; staff officers of infantry and cavalry (second from right) in service dress. Print after Moritz Rhul.

Cavalry and gendarmerie, 1894. The uniform are those prescribed by the 1886 regulations. From left to right: imperial guard cavalry officer and trooper; line cavalry officer and trooper; gendarmerie officer and trooper. The green collar and stripes and the yellow braid has been electronically added because some areas were left blank or were erroneously colored. Print after Moritz Rhul.

Artillery, 1894. The uniform are those prescribed by the 1886 regulations. From left to right: imperial guard artillery NCO, officer and gunner; line artillery officers and gunner. The yellow facings and gold lace have been electronically added because some areas were left blank or were erroneously colored. Print after Moritz Rhul.

Infantry, 1894. The uniform are those prescribed by the 1886 regulations. From left to right: imperial guard infantry NCO, officer and private; line infantry officers and private. Print after Moritz Rhul.

Medical and service corps, 1894. The uniform are those prescribed by the 1886 regulations. From left to right: officers and enlisted man of the medical corps; finance officer; intendance corps officer and enlisted man. Print after Moritz Rhul.

Allied capture of the Taku forts on the coast of China, early-June 1900. The print shows a joint assault of British troops and Japanese navy personnel on a Chinese battery. A Japanese navy officer with a party of sailors save a British flag. The art style of this print by a Japanese illustrator shows heavy influence from illustrations of battle art as seen in the popular press produced in Europe and America. Anne S.K. Brown Military Collection, Brown University Library, Providence, USA.

Japanese troops attack the Boxers at T'ien-chin (Tianjin), China, 14 June 1900. Japanese colonel Kuriya was in command and is shown mounted with some of his officers at right. Print after Yasutaka Utagawa. Library of Congress, Washington.

Japanese and British troops assault the machine works defended by what appears to be imperial Chinese soldiers at T'ien-chin (Tianjin), China, 14 June 1900. The British troops are shown in red coats, but actually wore khaki on campaign since 1886. Print after Torajiro Kasai. Library of Congress, Washington.

Joint attack of British and Japanese infantry on the outskirts of Peking (Beijing), China, 14 August 1900. The Japanese infantrymen are shown in summer uniforms. The British troops are shown with red coats, but really wore khaki. The last time red coats were used by British troops on campaign was in 1885. Print after Torajiro Kasai. Library of Congress, Washington.

Men of the 2nd Japanese Infantry Regiment break through the southern gate of the city of T'ien-chin on 14 June 1900. Print after Torajiro Kasai. Library of Congress, Washington.

NCO and enlisted men of the 5th Regiment of Cavalry, Peking (Beijing), China, 1900. Photographed in marching order. Dark blue attila with green collar and yellow cords and lace (the film of the period shows yellow as being dark), red trousers with green stripe, dark blue cap with yellow band and piping, black leather equipment. U.S. Army photo.

Officers of the 21st Infantry Regiment, Peking (Beijing), China, 1900. Photographed in marching order. From left to right: two second lieutenants and a lieutenant. The second lieutenant at left wears a new dark blue five-button frock. The other have the all dark blue-black Attila coat with black cords, dark blue trousers with red piping, dark blue cap with yellow band and piping (the film of the period shows yellow as being dark), black leather equipment. U.S. Army photo.

NCO and enlisted men of the 5th Artillery Regiment, Peking (Beijing), China, 1900. Photographed in marching order. From left to right: a sergeant first class and four privates first class. Dark blue coat with yellow collar, shoulder straps and lace, dark blue trousers with yellow stripe, dark blue cap with yellow band and piping (the film of the period shows yellow as being dark), black leather equipment. U.S. Army photo.

Enlisted men of the 21st Infantry Regiment, Peking (Beijing), China, 1900. Photographed in marching order. Dark blue coat with red collar, shoulder straps and lace, dark blue trousers with red stripe, dark blue cap with yellow band and piping (the film of the period shows yellow as being dark), black leather equipment. U.S. Army photo.

NCO and enlisted men of the 5th Pioneer Battalion, Peking (Beijing), China, 1900. Photographed in marching order. From left to right: Back view of a pioneer. NCO at center. Back view of a pioneer with shovel attached to his knapsack. Dark blue coat with crimson collar, shoulder straps and lace, dark blue trousers with crimson stripe, dark blue cap with crimson band and piping, and black leather equipment. U.S. Army photo.

General officer, c. 1900. Service dress.

Imperial Guard infantry officer, c. 1900. Campaign dress.

Line cavalry officer, c. 1900. Service dress.

Gendarmerie major, c. 1900. Dress uniform.

Medical corps general, c. 1900. Service dress.

Train officer, c. 1900. Dress uniform.

Intendance officer, c. 1900. Dress uniform.

Accounting officer, c. 1900. Dress uniform.

Imperial Guard artillery officer, c. 1900. Campaign dress.

This page: Original watercolor and ink caricatures by J. Rony. Anne S.K. Brown Military Collection, Brown University Library, Providence, USA.

Navy uniforms, 1890s. Top row: sea officers in various orders of dress. The admiral at right is in full dress. Middle row: at left a senior petty officer, an officer in summer dress and various non-combatant officers. Bottom row: sailors and petty officers. The figure wearing the red jacket and the plumed shako is a bandmaster. This contemporary uniform print appears to have first been published during the 1890s. Later and somewhat altered versions were published up to the 1930s. Anne S.K. Brown Military Collection, Brown University Library, Providence, USA.

Cartoon of Japanese sailors shutting up Port Arthur, pictured as a Russian soldier's head, with nail-like warships, 1904. This is one of many caricature prints by Kiyochika Kobayashi (1847-1915). Library of Congress, Washington.

5

The Russo-Japanese War: Japan Becomes a World Power

1904-1905

Following the end of the war with China, it became quickly apparent to Japan that Russia was especially interested in carving out a fair domain south of Siberia. It had obtained part of Manchuria and the Liaotung Peninsula with its prize harbor, Port Arthur, which was immediately heavily fortified. Thus, the northern Chinese coast became Russian from Siberia to the Yellow Sea and Russian agents worked hard to minimize Japan's influence in Korea. Germany had also obtained concessions on the southern part of the Shangtung Peninsula. It looked as if the fruits of the Japanese army's conquests had benefited other countries. In any event, the control of Korea remained the key issue and, at this point, the Russians were vying to dominate the area that Japan felt vital to its security. As early as 1896, it therefore embarked in major expansion programs for its army and its navy.

The Japanese government felt that, sooner or later, war with Russia would break out. Thousands of Russian troops sent to participate in the suppression of the Boxer rebellion stayed in Manchuria. Japan pressed for withdrawal and Russia diplomatically agreed, but most of the troops actually stayed in China. Indeed, the Russians grew increasingly arrogant towards both the Chinese and the Japanese officials. However, in early-1902, a great diplomatic success for Japan ensued by its treaty of alliance and friendship with Great Britain. It insured Britain and Japan's mutual benevolent neutrality in case of war with another power and support if there was more than one enemy. Thus, Russia's ally, France, could find itself at war with Great Britain if it intervened in a Russo-Japanese conflict, something no one in Paris or London wanted. The treaty also spawned positive industrial and cultural relations between Britain and Japan.

Meanwhile, Russian troops were in Manchuria with reinforcements arriving by the nearly finished Trans-Siberian Railway. Korea was slipping more towards Russia. In Tokyo, the staff considered the armed forces ready by late-1903 and, while diplomats continued to press for Russian withdrawals, a supreme war council was established on 28 December. The forces were now discretely deployed. Diplomatic relations went from bad to worse and they were severed on 6 February 1904. War was practically the only option left and the

The Japanese navy's surprise attack on the Russian warships at Port Arthur, night of 8-9 February 1904. Print after Sadajiro Ariyama . Library of Congress, Washington.

The Japanese warships at the naval battle of Port Arthur, morning of 9 February 1904. This view shows the Japanese ships moving in and firing at the Russians ships that are badly hit. Print after Torajir Kasai. Library of Congress, Washington.

The emperor Meiji with his staff at a military review, 1904. At left, a guard cavalryman holds the emperor's personal standard. The staff officers behind him all wear general's or general staff uniforms. At right, a file of imperial guard infantry recognizable by the red shako. Print in: Pictorial Reports of the Russo-Japanese War (Tokyo, 1904-1905).

The Japanese "Sazanami" torpedo ship attacks a Russian warship near Port Arthur on 10 March 1904. Both ships shown in the foreground are shown very close to each other, which was actually the case. It was not an effect given by the artist to increase the scene's drama to the maximum. During the engagement, a Japanese sailor jumped on the deck of the Russian ship, "cut at the enemy captain and kicked him into the water." Detail from a triptych print after Kokyo published in Tokyo only eighteen days after the event. Anne S.K. Brown Military Collection, Brown University Library, Providence, USA.

The Russian warships at the naval battle of Port Arthur, morning of 9 February 1904. The Japanese prints show the Russian ships as being badly hit. The battle was actually inconclusive although the Russians had seven ships damaged compared to slight damage for the Japanese. Print after Torajir Kasai. Library of Congress, Washington.

The Japanese sailor from the "Sazanami" torpedo ship who jumped on the deck of the Russian warship in the attack of 10 March 1904 kicks the enemy captain overboard. Detail from a triptych print. Anne S.K. Brown Military Collection, Brown University Library, Providence, USA.

Japanese sailors and infantry officers in a longboat, March 1904. A night engagement is shown with Russian spotlights trying to light up the boats for their gunners to sink the seventy-seven stranded Japanese that tried to reach their transport vessels. The whole composition portrays tension by the rendering of the waves, the explosions and the masterly combination of dark and light hues. Detail from a triptych print. Anne S.K. Brown Military Collection, Brown University Library, Providence, USA.

Japanese torpedo boats put out of action Russian torpedo boats at Port Arthur, 10 March 1904. Library of Congress, Washington.

A Japanese longboat spotted and fired upon by Russians, March 1904. According to the print's captions, this was a heroic action by seventy-seven stranded Japanese that decided to rally their transport vessels or sink and die rather than surrender to the enemy. The event occurred near Port Arthur. Print after Kuroki Hannosuke. Library of Congress, Washington.

Japanese imperial guard troops guarding Russian prisoners at Chemulpo, Korea, February 1904. The 700 Russians, most of whom appear to have been sailors, were taken at the surrender of Chemulpo (now Inch'on), Korea in February. Library of Congress, Washington.

favored option of Tsar Nicholas II. Many Russians felt the Japanese would back down and not dare to fight the Russian Empire.

In 1904, the Japanese navy had six battleships, eight armored cruisers, nine cruisers, twenty-four destroyers and sixty-three torpedo boats. It was one of the most modern fleets afloat. The Russian fleet was much larger, but it was divided into a Baltic fleet, a Far East fleet and its Black Sea fleet. This last fleet could not be deployed outside of the Black sea so that the Far East fleet was the one that would first have to face the Japanese navy and could only be reinforced many months later by ships from the Baltic fleet. The Russian Pacific fleet had seven battleships, eleven cruisers, two torpedo-cruisers, twenty-five destroyers, six gunboats, ten torpedo boats and nineteen auxiliary vessels. Most were based in Port Arthur except for three cruisers with a few torpedo boats at Vladivostock. Naturally, the Japanese navy's agenda was to destroy both the Far Eastern and the Baltic fleets one after the other.

The spark that started the hostilities occurred on 8 February 1894 when a Russian gunboat fired a couple of rounds at a Japanese warship off Chemulpo, the port of Seoul, Korea's capital. The Japanese responded and Admiral Uryu Sotokichi powerful squadron soon put the two Russian warships out of action. Nevertheless, for the Japanese, that this would occur without warning in Korea was the supreme indignity. If being fired upon was not immediately countered, the Japanese felt that Russian forces would just walk in and take over the Korean peninsula.

As it turned out, a substantial part of the Japanese fleet under Admiral Heihachiro Togo was on maneuvers in the Yellow Sea. At about 10:30 pm, his fleet arrived off Port Arthur and immediately attacked the Russian naval squadron there with torpedo boats and three Russian ships were badly hit including the powerful battleship Tsesarevich. The battle continued the next day, but was inconclusive and no ships were lost although some were damaged. Repairs were easier for the Japanese at the fully equipped shipyard of Sasebo while the Russians only had limited facilities at Port Arthur. It was a surprise attack, but the Russian fleet was caught unprepared in spite of being in a potential war zone. Admiral Togo's next actions were all aimed at blocking the Russian fleet in the harbor. A first attempt failed on 24 February, another on 10 March succeeded in laying mines at the harbor's entrance. On

A Japanese artillery unit enters Seoul, Korea, on 11 February 1904. Le Petit Parisien, 28 February 1904.

13 April, the Russian flagship Petropavlovsk blew up on a Japanese mine attempting a sortie, but on 3 May, two Japanese battleships were sunk by Russian mines – it was the worst day of the war for the Japanese navy. Later attempts to break out also failed and more ships were lost on both sides, but the Russian ships were basically stuck in Port Arthur.

Shortly after the battle of Chemulpo in February 1904, the 42,000 strong Japanese 1st Army landed in Korea under General Kuroki Tamemoto and went after General M.I. Zasulitch's 25,000 men Russian army in the country reaching the southern bank of the Yalu River in late April. The Russians were dug in on the north side of the river. From 27 to 30

April, the Japanese assaulted and defeated the Russians who suffered some 2,700 casualties against over a 1,000 for the Japanese who maneuvered in a brilliant pincer movement. The news of this defeat came as a surprise to the Russians who now realized that the Japanese army was a match and that the war might be tougher than anticipated.

On 25-26 May, the 35,000 men Japanese 2nd Army then landed on the Liaotung Peninsula and drove the Russians back into Port Arthur although it suffered some 4,300 casualties at the battle of Nashan, north of Port Arthur. By 30 July, the Japanese army invested Port Arthur and siege operations began. The besieging Japanese army under Maresuke Nogi was about 80,000 strong and would grow to some 150,000 men during this long siege. The 50,000 Russians in Port Arthur were led General Anatoly Stoessel. There were several battles during the siege, notably those of Orphans Hills (7-9 August), 174 Hill (19-24 August) and 203 Meter Hill (28 November-5 December) in which Japanese assault troops took tremendous casualties before taking the positions after truly desperate fighting. Tactics changed and the Japanese finally opted to pound the place into surrender. In December, Japanese sappers placed mines that blew up several Russian forts, the last of which was destroyed on 31 December. The place was hardly tenable and Port Arthur finally surrendered on 5 January 1905.

Japanese imperial guard cavalry battling Russian cavalry. This action took place near the Seven-Star gate at Pyongyang (Korea) on 28 February 1904. According to the Japanese, six cavalrymen encountered "several scores of Russian cavalry" and drove them off "without any difficulty." Detail from a triptych print after Yoshikuni published on 4 April 1904. Anne S.K. Brown Military Collection, Brown University Library, Providence, USA.

Japanese imperial guard cavalry fighting Russian Cossaks near Chongju in northern Korea during March 1904. Print after Kuroki Hannosuke. Library of Congress, Washington.

Japanese imperial guard cavalry skirmishing, probably in northern Korea during the spring of 1904. Detail from a triptych print. Anne S.K. Brown Military Collection, Brown University Library, Providence, USA.

The casualties were extraordinarily high at the siege of Port Arthur. For the Japanese, some 90,000 killed, wounded and sick while the Russians had over 31,300 killed, wounded or missing. The causes of this bloodbath appear to have been multiple. The doctrine of massive frontal assaults taught by German army advisers is said to have been one factor because this tactic tested many technological novelties that were first used at the siege of Port Arthur. In what was a prelude to the battlefield slaughters of the First World War, both sides used machineguns, hand grenades, barbed wire, electrified wire fences, land mines, magazine rifles, rapid fire light howitzers, mortars capable of firing 500kg shells, electric searchlights and even radio signals.

With Port Arthur taken, General Nogi marched north with 120,000 men to join Marshal Oyama's 2nd Army that was holding a 200 mile front near Mudken (Shenyang). The 1st, the 4th and the under strength and newly formed 5th Army were also part of the combined Japanese army that may have numbered as many as 270,000 men. The Russians had up to 276,000 men under General Alexei Kuropatkin at Mudken and along its front. There had been several previous battles along this front.

Landing of the 2nd Japanese army on the Liandong Peninsula in China on 5 May 1904. The Russian forces occupying the area were compelled to withdraw. Print after Hannosuke Kuroki. Library of Congress, Washington.

Line cavalry charging led by a general officer, 1904. This print after Kikuzo is notably more westernized in its style. Anne S.K. Brown Military Collection, Brown University Library, Providence, USA.

Japanese imperial guard infantry charges across a pontoon bridge at the battle of the Yalu River, on the border of Korea and China from 25 April to 1 May 1904. Detail from a triptych print. Anne S.K. Brown Military Collection, Brown University Library, Providence, USA.

Line infantrymen of the 2nd Army attack the gates of the walled town of Chinchou (Jinzhou), 24-25 May 1904. The small Russian garrison put up a valiant resistance but the town was taken. It was the first phase of the larger battle of Nashan, which the Japanese won. Note the regimental colors at the foreground and the 2nd battalion flag with the troops at the middle ground. Triptych print. Anne S.K. Brown Military Collection, Brown University Library, Providence, USA.

A Japanese infantry assault column captures a Russian fortified position at the Battle of Nashan, 26 May 1904. Apart from the men in uniform, the action is skillfully shown in grey smoke with the background orange glow of explosions. Bits of barbed wire in the right foreground. Detail from a triptych print after Getsuzo published on 20 August 1904. Anne S.K. Brown Military Collection, Brown University Library, Providence, USA.

Line infantry of the 2nd Army move towards the gate of the walled town of Chinchou (Jinzhou), 24-25 May 1904. Triptych print. Anne S.K. Brown Military Collection, Brown University Library, Providence, USA.

A blindfolded Japanese cavalry staff officer holding a message for the Russian commander accompanied by a bugler bearing a white flag is inside the Russian fortifications at Port Arthur in 1904. A Russian officer removes the blindfold so the message may be formally given. This unsigned illustration shows the contrast between the French inspired Japanese officer's uniform and Russian military dress. Russian men at that time much favored growing a beard, a fashion that Japanese men seldom followed. Detail from a lithograph in Le Petit Parisien, 4 September 1904.

Napoleon III and his staff at the battle of Solferino (Italy), 1859. This detail of the large and widely printed work by Ernest Meissonnier (1815-1891) shows the inspiration for some of the figures on the print of the Japanese attack near Hsimucheng, Manchuria, on 31 August 1904. Private collection.

Japanese attack on a Russian army near Hsimucheng, Manchuria, on 31 August 1904. The print shows General Nozu Michitsura with his staff leading 34,000 men of the 5th and 10th divisions of the Fourth Japanese Army that engaged the 33,000 strong Russian Second Siberian Corps. The Russians withdrew when the Japanese advance threatened to encircle them. This print follows closely the battle art seen in European countries. Library of Congress, Washington.

A view of the assault on the Russian fortified position, possibly that of Takushanm on 9 August 1904. Note the barbed wire in the foreground. The style of this print follows western battle illustrations. Anne S.K. Brown Military Collection, Brown University Library, Providence, USA.

Japanese infantry struggling through barbed wire during an attack on the fortifications of Port Arthur, 1904. Note the anguished soldier with the wire cutter in the foreground. This dramatic view was the work of French illustrator Louis Malespine. It was largely through prints like these made by military and historical illustrators such as Malespine or Louis Bombled that many Europeans saw Japanese troops in the war. From M. Galli's profusely illustrated La Guerre en Extrême-Orient (Paris, c. 1905).

From 20 February to 11 March, the combined Japanese army attacked on various parts of the front in the middle of winter. The cold weather proved to be an advantage to the Japanese since the Hun River as well as others were frozen. Japanese generalship proved more talented and, by early March, the Russian troops were on the verge of being surrounded. On 7 March, General Kuropatkin started to withdraw and Marshal Oyama instructed his troops to pursue and destroy the enemy. The Russians panicked and fled north, leaving many wounded in their wake. On 10 March, the Japanese army entered the city of Mudken. Again the casualties were horrendous. Some 85,000 Japanes killed or wounded and up to 88,000 Russians including 28,000 missing in action. Both sides were now exhausted.

Meanwhile, the Russian Baltic fleet (renamed 2nd Pacific Squadron) consisting of seven battleships, an armored cruiser, seven cruisers, nine destroyers and fourteen auxiliary ships under the command of Vice Admiral Zinovi Rojhestvenski left the Baltic Sea and arrived off Madagascar in late December 1904. There it was joined by ships of the 3rd Pacific Squadron and headed for Korea. The fleet now had twenty-seven ships including eight battleships. Port Arthur and Mudken had fallen and what remained of the Russian East Asian fleet was blockaded in Vladivostock. Admiral Togo correctly deducted that Rozhestvensky would try to slip past the strait of Tsushima to reach Vladivostock and attacked the Russian fleet on 27 May. The Japanese had eighty-nine ships, but only four battleships. This was compensated by twenty-seven cruisers. The ensuing battle showed the outstanding superiority of Togo and his officers regarding naval tactics and this was followed by night attacks early on 28 May. It was a disaster for the Russian fleet, which lost twenty-one ships sunk (including seven battleships) and seven captured. The Japanese imperial navy achieved a crushing victory. The Russian lost 4,380 sailors killed while the Japanese had only three torpedo boats sunk and lost 117 sailors. Barely thirty-five years after its creation, the imperial navy of Japan was recognized as one of the best in the world. Admiral Togo was hailed as the Japanese Nelson.

After the battle of Tsushima, a Japanese squadron landed troops on the Russian Sakhalin Islands north of Japan who surrendered without resistance. Amidst the victory celebrations, Japanese generals and politicians were now anxious to stop a war that had been very costly. Industrial production could not keep up with the demands in ammunition and war products in what was really the first "modern" war of the 20th century. The Japanese

Marshal Omaya and his staff entering Mudken on 10 March 1905. This print of a painting after Takeshiro Kanokogi shown the remarkable evolution of some Japanese artists towards western academic documentary painting. The figures, uniforms and architectural features are given with accuracy and obviously based on photographs. Anne S.K. Brown Military Collection, Brown University Library, Providence, USA.

Japanese imperial guard infantrymen take a Russian field battery at the battle of Shaho, 5 to 17 October 1904. Note that the Russian gunners are shown with blue uniforms, but they were actually dark green. Detail from a triptych print after Yoshikuni published on 12 November 1904. Anne S.K. Brown Military Collection, Brown University Library, Providence, USA.

Japanese infantry charges Russian troops over a bridge near Fort Dashiqiao, August 1904. The Japanese enlisted men wear the new khaki campaign uniform, but their officer has the older Attila. Detail from a triptych print after Yoshikuni published on 10 August 1904. Anne S.K. Brown Military Collection, Brown University Library, Providence, USA.

A general with a group of staff officers at the battle of Liaoyang, October 1904. All wear either the new khaki uniform or the white summer dress. The officer peering through his binoculars may be General (later Marshal) Oyama. Detail from a triptych print after Yoshikuni published on 12 October 1904. Anne S.K. Brown Military Collection, Brown University Library, Providence, USA.

Japanese gunners serving a 28cm (11-inch) caliber howitzer at the siege of Port Arthur, late-1904 or early-1905. Eighteen of these large guns fired 16,940 shells during the siege. The gunners all wear the dark blue uniform with yellow facings. Illustrated London News, 11 February 1905.

asked U.S. President Theodore Roosevelt to mediate and on 5 September 1905, the Treaty of Portsmouth (New Hampshire, USA) ended the conflict. This time, the Liaotung Peninsula with Port Arthur, half of the Sakhalin Peninsula, Korea (which would be annexed five years later) and the Manchurian railway lines went to Japan. Still, the Japanese nationalists were not content considering the sacrifice given and many felt that, once again, the diplomats had squandered the armed forces' victories. But it was a happier time for the Japanese compared to the deeply humiliated Russians who now found themselves without a fleet and with a catastrophic loss of prestige as a credible power. Japan's outstanding victory against such a power as the Russian Empire definitely established it as one of the leading world powers. All the others were European or, in the case of the United States, of European origin. Japan was the first Asian nation to achieve world power status, less than forty years after the instauration of Meiji's enlightened rule. Some Westerners mused about a "Yellow Peril" should China wake up one day. For now, even the most racist westerners had to acknowledge that, both on land

Admiral Togo with his officers on the bridge of the battleship Mikasa, just before the battle of Tsushima fought on the morning of 27 May 1905. Note the "Z" signal flag being hoisted on the upper left; Togo used it to order the attack to his fleet. Print after Shotaro Tojo (1865-1929). Anne S.K. Brown Military Collection, Brown University Library, Providence, USA.

Naval battle, probably that of Tsushima, that went into the night of 27 May 1905. The Japanese flagship Mikasa leads the line while many Russian ships are seen in flames. In was indeed a disaster for the Russian navy. Triptych in the Anne S.K. Brown Military Collection, Brown University Library, Providence, USA.

The one that got away! The Russian cruiser Aurora, now a world famous museum ship because of the role it played in the October 1917 Revolution, also took part in the battle of Tsushima against Admiral Togo's Japanese fleet on 27-28 May 1905. It managed to escape to neutral Manila (Philippines) where it was interned by the U.S. authorities. Launched in 1900, it is still officially in commission and can be visited at St. Petersburg, Russia. It is one of the best preserved warship from that era and is presented here to show what such ships actually looked like compared to the prints reproduced in this book. Its displacement was 6,731 tons, speed 19 knots and was armed with eight 152mm (6 inch) guns, twenty-four 75mm guns, eight 37mm guns and three torpedo tubes (two underwater).

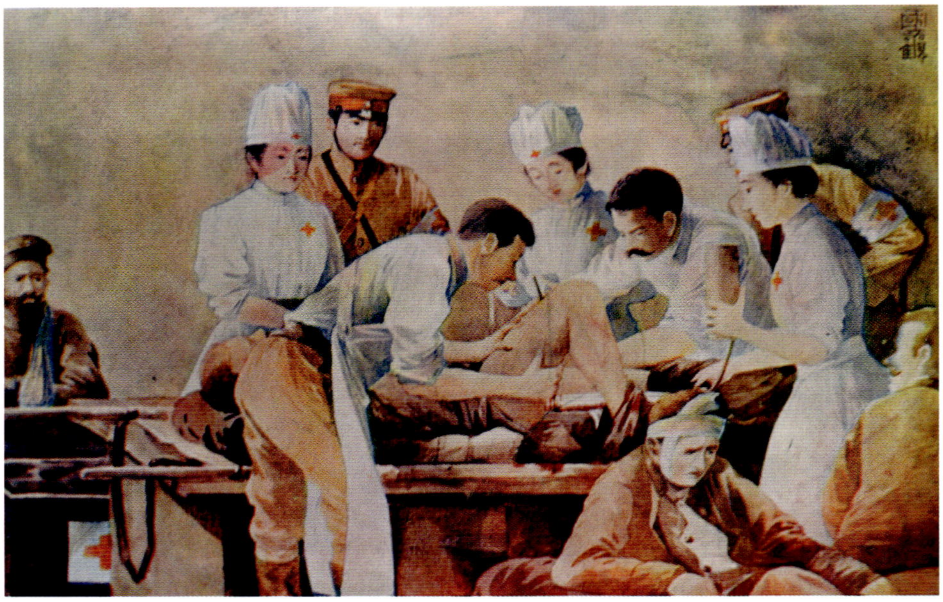

Operation room of a Japanese field hospital during the Russo-Japanese War, 1904-1905. Doctors are shown operating a badly wounded Russian soldier assisted by Japanese Red Cross nurses. They wear the white service uniform, the nurses having the Japanese Red Cross's distinctive high cap. The stretcher bearers are infantrymen detached for this type of service. Print in: Pictorial Reports of the Russo-Japanese War (Tokyo, 1904-1905).

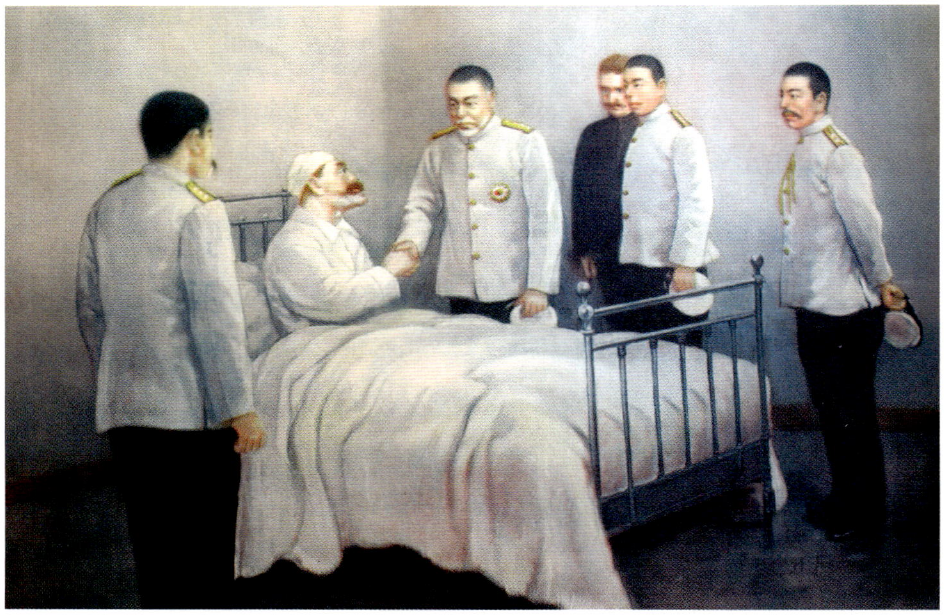

Russian navy Admiral Rojestvenski, who was badly wounded and captured by the Japanese at the battle of Tsushima on 27-28 May 1905, was later visited in hospital by Admiral Togo. Compassionate and philosophical, Togo told Rojestvenski that defeat was part of the fate of a soldier, but "the great point" was "whether we have done our duty." Both men and their sailors certainly had. Togo and his officers are shown wearing the white summer jacket. Print after M. Furoshima. Anne S.K. Brown Military Collection, Brown University Library, Providence, USA.

Russian troop train on its way to the Pacific coast is blown up by a Japanese bomb placed on the railway in eastern Siberia. This triptych is full of dramatic features such as the locomotive going through the ice of a river and men being hurled in the air or jumping out of the railway cars. Anne S.K. Brown Military Collection, Brown University Library, Providence, USA.

A Japanese field hospital during the siege of Port Arthur, 1904. It shows wounded Russian prisoners receiving treatments from personnel of the Japanese army's medical corps. All attendants wear the red cross on white armbands on the sleeves of their uniforms. The inset at the top of the print shows Chinese civilians being abused by Russian soldiers, an obvious propaganda message. Detail from a triptych. Anne S.K. Brown Military Collection, Brown University Library, Providence, USA.

Japanese officers dressed in the old dark blue Attila and the new khaki (at center) field uniform, 1905. L'Illustration, 30 December 1905.

Army officers, 1904-1905. All wear the new blue service jacket or the new khaki uniform. From left to right: infantry lieutenant; cavalry captain and field officer in the new khaki uniform. Copies of Imperial Museum uniform drawings. Anne S.K. Brown Military Collection, Brown University Library, Providence, USA.

and sea, the Japanese were outstanding warriors and they were as well led as in any major European army or navy. Furthermore, their equipment, ships and logistics were equal to anything found in Europe. It was a sobering thought.

The Imperial Army

During the conflict, the army was divided into five field armies that eventually deployed up to about 350,000 men against the Russians in Korea and northern China. The strain on logistics was, on the whole, sustained and the Japanese were noted for hiring tens of thousands of Koreans and Chinese in support functions and for paying for supplies, which gave them local support compared to the Russians who appear not to have been as generous. As noted above, the infantry was excellent and mounted obstinate assaults in good order and with outstanding bravery. During the siege of Port Arthur, the artillery quickly passed from a field role to serving huge siege guns. Engineers also mastered modern siege techniques, notably by their use of large mines.

Cavalry came into its own during this conflict. It fought with success against Russian Cossacks, but perhaps its most valuable role came when daring cavalry groups made remarkable forays deep inside enemy territory. Some penetrated as far as the Trans-Siberian railway and blew up several bridges on this vital rail line. The Russians therefore had to divert substantial numbers of troops to protect this vital rail link, which weakened their forces facing the Japanese in China. This is said to have one of the factors leading to Japan's victory. However, foreign observers were not impressed with the Japanese cavalry because its horses were considered too small and indifferently groomed.

The medical corps was greatly challenged by the huge numbers of wounded and sick soldiers during the war. Contingents of Japanese Red Cross nurses were sent out to China to cope with the situation and they were shown in a few illustrations.

Uniforms

The war started with, basically, the same uniforms as ordered in the 1886 regulations (described and shown in the two previous chapters). The Japanese observers had seen with interest the experiments in various armies with less conspicuous clothing whose color blended into the environment. The British experience, first in India and then in South Africa, was especially noted. Some Japanese conservatism was apparent and the "colonial" helmet was not to be considered, but a step could be made towards what appeared to be an improvement in battle dress. So, just as the war started, a new khaki campaign dress was introduced. Naturally, not all units were served with it right away, and some never would, but khaki started to be seen next to dark blue and white uniforms. American military observers described the new khaki campaign dress introduced in 1904: "The summer jacket and trousers are of khaki drill; the jacket is perfectly plain, and there are no buttons on any of the garments. A strip of white linen is issued to wind around the neck as a collar inside the tunic. The forage cap which goes with this uniform is a marvel of lightness, from which hangs a linen screen to protect the neck ... the trousers are made like riding breeches."

This was a success and a new and improved khaki uniform was soon brought out. The 1905 version of campaign dress was more sophisticated and was termed as "Standard simplified full dress" meant to be used for parades as well as in the field. It now had small pocket flaps, five buttons in front and a collar patch of the service color. The coat sleeves had red piping above the cuffs and the khaki trousers had red piping for all arms of the service. Officers and enlisted men initially had rank stripes around the cuffs, but these were replaced in 1905 by red and yellow shoulder tabs to designate rank. Field service caps were khaki with a red band and red piping for all arms of the service. Khaki wrap around puttees were used for campaign dress with brown shoes. The summer uniform was similar, but made of lighter material and without piping on the coat and trousers.

The dark blue service and full dress was also issued from 1905. Its caps and trousers henceforth had red bands

Japanese imperial guard infantry at the assault of a Russian fort, 1904-1905. All are wearing brown greatcoats, the officer's having a red lining. Anne S.K. Brown Military Collection, Brown University Library, Providence, USA.

and piping. The tunic had five buttons and two breast pockets with buttons and flaps, the collar having the patch in the service color with a yellow unit number and the red and yellow shoulder tabs. White gaiters were worn with the dark blue uniform.

Red Cross nurses were seen in uniform by the British Illustrated London News reporter Melton Prior, who wrote in April 1894 that they, "marched just like soldiers – in step and with swinging arms. Their cap is white calico with a red cross in front, and a rolled-up cloak was swung over the left shoulder. They had rather short, pleated black dresses, and boots and white gloves. They looked very workmanlike, and thoroughly trained for business." Nurses also had a white uniform for duty in the wards and operating rooms.

Weapons

The Arisaka Type 30 (M.1897) infantry rifle was the primary model used during the Russo-Japanese War. Cavalry had the Murata M. 1894, which was the short version of the Murata Type 22 (M.1889) infantry rifle that was also still used by some troops. Six French Hotchkiss machineguns served by 198 troopers were now attached to each cavalry brigade and they were used with great success against Russian Cossack cavalry.

As previously, some officers used the samurai sword blades with more or less regulation Western style hilts.

The army's artillery had "come of age" by the time of the war against Russia. It had large and proficient artillery units that served a wide variety of ordnance for field, siege or garrison purposes. Its potential was realized at the siege of Port Arthur where the Japanese army deployed some 443 guns to pound the place into submission. The Russians had built very strong fortifications there and large guns were required to destroy them. The Japanese batteries thus eventually included eighteen huge 28cm (11-inch) howitzers, seventy-two large 15cm (6-inch) mortars as well as thirty-three naval guns mounted on land to level Russian fortifications. Because of the rapid evolution in world arms technology, guns could now be fired much faster. In all, over 350,000 rounds were fired by the Japanese artillery during the siege, which was the first large scale operation to deploy such modern weapons. Ammunition production in Japan could not keep up with the demand and the government had to import some from other countries.

The Imperial Navy

The imperial Japanese navy was, in a sense, a revelation to the world as a result of the war with Russia. Everyone in the West was astounded that it crushed the imperial Russian navy. The battle of Tsushima was heralded to be as decisive as the Trafalgar of the East and it was an accurate assessment. Japan's warships, once dismissed as poor imitations of western crafts, were suddenly seen as equal to anything afloat and, perhaps more important, its officer corps and men were

Gun crew of the Japanese warship "Fuji" at the battle of Port Arthur, February 1904. The officer is artillery commander Yamanaka. Behind him is a midshipman. The details shown on the sailor's uniforms are remarkable and even include the small gold anchor embroidered at the end of their cap ribbons. Triptych print after Kiyochika Kobayashi. Anne S.K. Brown Military Collection, Brown University Library, Providence, USA.

Army officer's uniforms, 1904-1905. All wear the new blue field service jacket. From left to right: infantry field officer (mounted); lieutenant general; major general of the paymaster's department and lieutenant colonel of artillery. Copies of Imperial Museum uniform drawings. Anne S.K. Brown Military Collection, Brown University Library, Providence, USA.

seen as thoroughly professional and competitive with any western navy. In naval terms, Japan would remain supreme in eastern Asia and the Pacific until the middle of the 20th century.

The navy's uniforms were almost similar to those worn since the 1880s with allowances for changing fashion styles expressed in the 1896 dress regulations. The dark blue undress frock was the consecrated garment worn by officers on service as well as on dress occasions and in battle. At least according to prints and paintings of the period. The most noticeable change was the officer's white summer jacket that now had no edging lace and fastened with buttons instead of hooks and eyes. Admiral Togo and his officers are shown wearing this jacket in a 1905 print. Sailor's were armed with a specific navy rifle during the Russo-Japanese War, the Arisaka Type 35 Navy (M. 1902).

The Arts

While war raged in the Far East, a new opera by Giacomo Pucini was presented in Italy during 1904. It was "Madame Butterfly" whose romantic and ill-fated story was set in Japan based on late 19th century novels by J.L. Long and Pierre Loti. This enormously successful opera was set in Japan, the very nation that was making headlines all over the world in 1904-1905.

Japanese traditional print production was again very active depicting many battle scenes, both on land and sea that occurred during the Russo-Japanese War. The Japanese were depicted with much accuracy and some prints correctly showed the first khaki uniforms introduced in 1904. Next to these traditionally produced prints were increasingly numerous lithographic color prints that showed vivid actions, but in less subtle compositions. Some of the inspiration was western rather than Japanese. The example given here is the Japanese lithographic print of the 1904 battle fought near Hsimucheng, Manchuria that was inspired from Ernest Meissonnier's 1863 painting of Napoleon III at the 1859 battle of Solferino. Naval battles featuring battleships were especially standard and could be compared easily with illustrations seen in western magazines and newspapers. From this, it is obvious that Japanese traditional printing was in competition with the cheaper prints produced by the mass production news media.

The events of the war also brought forth paintings by Japanese artists that had mastered western academic documentary art. Takeshiro Kanokogi's canvass of the entry of Marshal Omaya and his staff in Mudken on 10 March 1905 is an outstanding example of this type of war art. Even more famous in this school of art is Shotaro Tojo's canvas of Admiral Togo with his officers on the bridge of the battleship Mikasa going into the battle of Tsushima on the morning of 27 May 1905. Because of the fame of this battle, this painting has since been reproduced in nearly all the history books that mention this engagement. Such success obviously filled a desire by the Japanese public for documentary illustrations that seemed more realistic than the traditional art prints.

During 1904-1905, the Western press sent many reporters, photographers and illustrators to the Far East in order to satisfy its readers' curiosity. The "new" Asiatic empire that seemed so progressive yet so different than anything they knew drew special attention. Daily newspapers ran many article and periodicals produced many illustrations of the battles, its participants and, in particular, the Japanese in Japan as well as in the field against the Russians in China. For the first time, Japan was being massively shown to the European and American public through the eyes of Western correspondents and illustrators. As can be seen by the examples published in this chapter taken mainly from the Illustrated London News and Le Petit Parisien, it was quite a different view than the traditional Japanese prints.

Emperor Taisho, c. 1912. Born in 1879, Taisho (whose personal name was Yoshihito) became the 123rd emperor of Japan on 30 July 1912. Plagued by various illnesses since childhood, he was hardly ever seen in public. His condition deteriorated and his son Hirohito was named regent in 1921. Emperor Taisho passed away on 25 December 1926. On this colored photo of the period, he wears the full dress dark blue tunic for generals and marshals, which was hardly altered since the 1870s. The gold lace, embroidery is very lightly colored and appears somewhat silvery on this image. The two rows of buttons are made invisible by the emperor's many orders and medals. The red sash edged blue worn over the right shoulder is the grand cordon of the Order of the Chrysanthemum, Japans highest honor. The stars are of the orders of the Paulownia Flowers, of the Sacred Treasure and of the Rising Sun. Private collection.

6

ASIATIC EMPIRE

1906-1930

In early August 1914, hostilities broke out in Europe between all the major powers. On one side, Germany, Austria-Hungary and Turkey, on the other France, Great Britain, Russia, Italy and a number of smaller countries. For Japan, which had signed treaties of mutual assistance with Great Britain in 1902 and 1905, it would obviously take part in the coalition led by France and Britain against Germany. The German protectorate of Tsingtao (also spelt Tsingtau and now called Qingdao) on the Chinese coast was the Japanese's immediate concern. Ceded by China for ninety-nine years since 1897 following the murder of German missionaries, Tsingtao was a 200 square miles enclave with a population of 200,000 Chinese and some 4,000 Germans besides its garrison of about 4,000 men. It was the base for the German navy's Far Eastern squadron. It was therefore vital for Japan to secure it as soon as possible.

Tokyo's ultimatum for Germany to return Tsingtao to China being ignored, Japan declared war on 23 August. On 5 September, a large Japanese fleet landed an army of some 24,000 men that besieged the German enclave, now completely cut off. On 11 September, a Japanese plane dropped a few small bombs on Tsingtao while troops secured the surrounding countryside. On 24 September, a British force of 1,200 troops (including 300 of the Indian army) joined the Japanese. Misfortune struck the Japanese fleet on 17 October when the old cruiser Takachiko was sunk by a lucky torpedo from the German torpedo boat S-90 that broke through the naval blockade. The German coastal guns also damaged the British cruiser HMS Triumph. The Austro-Hungarian cruiser Kaiserin Elizabeth took part in the defense, its guns being later mounted on shore batteries, the ship itself being scuttled. However, the land forces methodically advanced on Tsingtao taking by assault the various outworks. After a gallant defense against overwhelming odd, Tsingtao surrendered on 7 November. The Japanese forces also proceeded with the peaceful occupation of the German Pacific islands in the early part of the war.

Japan was not otherwise actively involved in the war effort until 1917 when it was agreed to dispatch a naval force to the Mediterranean. From April 1917, a force of fourteen destroyers with the cruiser Akashi under the command of Admiral Sato Kozo were based in Malta, then the largest British naval base in the Mediterranean. They played an important part in protecting convoys against enemy submarines. On 11 June 1917, the destroyer

Japanese observation planes fly over the German port of Tsingtau in Chana, which is bombarded by Japanese navy ships during the fall of 1914. Print published by Shobido and Company in Tokyo. Anne S.K. Brown Military Collection, Brown University Library, Providence, USA.

Japanese navy landing parties overcome German defenses near Tsingtau in early September 1914. Print published by Shobido and Company in Tokyo. Anne S.K. Brown Military Collection, Brown University Library, Providence, USA.

Sakaki was torpedoed off the coast of Crete by the Austro-Hungarian U-27 submarine; sixty-eight officers and men were lost but the damaged destroyer was salvaged and repaired.

On the whole, it was a quiet war for Japan until the middle of 1918. The 1917 Russian Revolution had first taken that country out of the world conflict, but then plunged it in a bitter civil war opposing the radical communists "reds" against the more conservative "white" Russians. The allied nations fighting Germany and Austria-Hungary were concerned that the 50,000 men Czech Legion on the collapsed Russian Eastern Front would be trapped behind enemy lines and that huge stockpiles of war supplies in Russian ports would fall to the communist Red Army. The allies decided to occupy certain ports and, in April 1918, British and Japanese naval landing parties took over Vladivostok in Eastern Siberia. From August, allied troops arrived at Vladivostok including a 12,000 men Japanese army that eventually grew to 70,000. Another 16,000 men, half of them Americans with 4,200 Canadians, 2,400 Italians, 1,500 Britons and 800 French troops arrived in Vladivostok. Meanwhile, the Czech Legion was fighting its way east along the Trans-Siberian Railway and made contact with Japanese troops moving west in early September. By November, much of coastal eastern Siberia and territories inland up to the Transbaikal city of Chita had been occupied by Japanese troops.

In Europe, the Great War ended on 11 November 1918, but the Russian Civil War went on between the Red Army and several groups of White Russians. Western powers were exhausted by the Great War and, in early 1920, opted to withdraw from Russia. Their troops left Siberia during the summer of 1920 including the Czech Legion in early September. Fearing that communist influence would spread to northern China, Korea and Japan itself, the Japanese government opted to keep its troops in eastern Siberia. The Red Army, which eventually may have exceeded 600,000 men deployed in that area, secured most of Siberia during 1919 and moved east against the Japanese and about 100,000 remaining White Russian troops. It was obvious that Transbaikal could not be held and an agreement for Japanese troops to evacuate that area was signed in July 1920 leaving the White Russians to their fate. Japanese troops continued to hold on to Vladivostok and the Pacific coast, but this was increasingly criticized in Japan as well as abroad. Facing a deadlock on all sides, the Japanese government announced its withdrawal from Siberia in June 1922; by the end of October, the last Japanese troops had evacuated Vladivostok.

Japanese infantry overcomes a German battery at Tsingtau, 7 November 1914. The unknown Japanese illustrator of this western style action print has omitted the red piping edging the coat cuffs and the cap crowns of the Japanese soldiers. One of the imperial navy's four French-built Maurice Farman seaplanes used successfully during the siege is shown at upper right. Anne S.K. Brown Military Collection, Brown University Library, Providence, USA.

Japanese naval personnel takes possession of the German Marshall Islands in the Soutth Pacific during the fall of 1914. This print published by Shobido and Company in Tokyo somewhat exaggerates the event. There were no European Germans troops in these garrisons, only a small force of native constabulary with German cadres. Anne S.K. Brown Military Collection, Brown University Library, Providence, USA.

Officer and private, c. 1906. They wear the dark blue, actually black, uniform issued following the Russo-Japanese War. The officer has the fur-trimmed overcoat, the private wears the parade uniform. The French artist had forgotten the star and made the crown's piping too wide on the private's cap. Detail of a print after Geoffroy. Private collection.

Army

In 1914, the army had a peace establishment of seventy-six infantry regiments (each having 1,814 officers and men), twenty-seven cavalry regiments (505 officers and men), twenty-five field artillery regiments (each serving thirty-six guns with 662 men), nineteen engineer battalions, nineteen train battalions plus the various staff and service corps

The 1911 regulation uniform. From left to right: cavalry officer (mounted), infantry officer, intendance sergeant and train enlisted man. Copies of Imperial Museum uniform drawings. Anne S.K. Brown Military Collection, Brown University Library, Providence, USA.

The 1906 regulation khaki uniform for officers. From left to right: 3rd Artillery, cavalry, imperial guard cavalry, accounting and general (mounted). Copies of Imperial Museum uniform drawings. Anne S.K. Brown Military Collection, Brown University Library, Providence, USA.

for a total of some 250,000 officers and men. This was raised to about 350,000 during the First World War although it was really between 1918 and 1922 that the army was deployed on active service in Siberia. Following the Siberian episode, the delicate economic situation followed by the disastrous 1923 earthquake no longer warranted such a huge standing army and the Japanese Parliament voted sizeable reductions for a peacetime establishment. From 1922 to 1925, four divisions were disbanded and the army was reduced by 85,000 officers and men to a force of 210,000 officers and men serving in seventeen divisions and corps. It was still quite a sizeable force that was thoroughly modern and second to none in the Far East.

The experiences of the Russo-Japanese War and of the First World War brought a number of innovations into the army. Heavy "garrison" artillery evolved into units of field heavy artillery such as seen on the 1914-1918 Western Front. In 1922, a battery of mounted machineguns was attached to each infantry regiment. There were also two railway regiments, two telegraph regiments, a balloon corps and, from 1925, a tank corps and an anti-aircraft artillery regiment. More motor vehicles were also being increasingly used by the army's support services.

Uniforms

The changes brought in during 1905 were incorporated in the model 1906 uniforms. These included a dark blue and a khaki uniform. The "dark blue" uniform was actually made from large stocks of black material that were available, a practice that was occasionally resorted to previously. Indeed, the blue was so dark that prints often showed it as being black. The 1886 uniforms were simplified in 1906 with regards to branch of service colors. All branches now had red cap bands, piping and shoulder tabs, the branch color being only shown at the collar tab. As time passed, the dark blue, actually black, uniform was seen less and less. The army's preference rapidly went to the new khaki uniform that, when spotless clean and impeccably pressed and adjusted, could be used for all parades as well. The khaki uniform remained largely unchanged from 1905 to 1930. The tunic had the standing collar with the service color patch and the red and yellow shoulder tabs. The most important uniform regulations during this period were promulgated in 1911. They refined and further codified the khaki uniform in use since the Russo-Japanese War. Leather belts, pouches, shoes and boots were henceforth all brown. Khaki henceforth became the army's uniform for all occasions and, except for high-ranking officers at court, the dark blue uniform practically disappeared from view. In 1930, the red piping at the coat cuffs, at the trousers and edging the crown of the cap was abolished and the hue of the khaki became more olive green than formerly. Most of all, a khaki steel helmet was henceforth issued to all troops in the field. It was only in 1938 that the tunic's standing collar was superseded by a small fall down collar, but it was common to see Japanese troops still wearing the pre-1938 model jacket during the Second World War.

Following the end of the war with Russia, the service branch colors remained generally the same into the 1930s. The colors were:

Infantry: red
Artillery: yellow
Cavalry: medium green
Engineers and pioneers: maroon
Train: blue
Medical: green
Pharmacy: green
Veterinary: green (purple from February 1912)
Intendance: sky blue (later light grey)
Accounting: silver-brown
Justice: white
Gendarmerie: red (black from February 1912)
Technical: yellow
Aviation: sky blue (from April 1925)

To distinguish the imperial guard, a gold wreath consisting of two cherry branches with two buds was added to the

The 1906 regulation khaki uniform for officers. From left to right: medical corps, infantry and engineers. Copies of Imperial Museum uniform drawings. Anne S.K. Brown Military Collection, Brown University Library, Providence, USA.

star for its cap badge from 1905 with the new khaki uniform.

Weapons

At the end of the Russo-Japanese War, the new Arisaka Type 38 (M.1905) 6.5mm infantry rifle was introduced and gradually replaced the earlier models. It remained the primary rifle in service until 1939. It had a fine reputation and many were sold to Great Britain and Russia. Ironically, some armed the Red Army during the Russian Civil War that caused Japan's intervention in Siberia. Officer's swords continued to officially be of Western models until 1930 when the samurai type sword made a comeback after nearly sixty years. The regulation officer's sword now again had the traditional "buke-zukure" hilt and grip in the fashion of those used from the 1530s to the 1860s. Enlisted cavalrymen continued to carry Western type sabers.

Army Air Corps

Hot air balloons were used for observation of the enemy during the 1904-1905 Russo-Japanese War. The army purchased its first biplanes in 1910 and the first pilots returned from training in France during 1911. About half a dozen planes were deployed by the Japanese army during the siege of German Tsingtao during the fall of 1914. However, serious development of an air component only came after the First World War when, in 1919, an air command was created within the imperial army. A French military mission was sent to help organize an air arm and the first aviation school was opened in January 1920 while many surplus French and British planes were bought and used in Siberia. In June 1925, the air corps was created. In 1927, the air corps already had about 3,500 men and 500 planes. Thereafter, Japan rapidly developed its own modern aircraft industry and, by the 1930s, had the most powerful air arm in Asia. The uniforms of the air corps were the same as the rest of the imperial army. From 1925 it was granted the branch color of sky blue.

The Imperial Navy

Following its outstanding victories over the Russian navy in 1904-1905, the Japanese navy was confirmed as one of the most powerful fleets in the world and it thus became the naval guardian of the Far East and the Western Pacific. On the eve of the First World War, it consisted of fourteen battleships, fourteen armored cruisers, sixteen light cruisers, fifty-two destroyers,

The 1911 regulation uniform for enlisted men. From left to right: medical corps, infantry and engineer. Copies of Imperial Museum uniform drawings. Anne S.K. Brown Military Collection, Brown University Library, Providence, USA.

LEFT: Japanese artillery bulger at Tsingtau, 1914-1915. The yellow collar tabs indicate he is a gunner. Notes taken at Tsingtao by a German resident following its occupation by Japanese troops. Anne S.K. Brown Military Collection, Brown University Library, Providence, USA. MIDDLE: NCO of the 1st Infantry Regiment with battalion flags, 1914-1915. He wears the 1911 regulation khaki uniform, the red collar tabs and numeral denoting the 1st Infantry Regiment. At the NCOs rifle is fixed the 2nd battalion's color. The pattern of the 1st, 2nd and 3rd battalion flags are sketched above. Notes taken at Tsingtau by a German resident following its occupation by Japanese troops. Anne S.K. Brown Military Collection, Brown University Library, Providence, USA. RIGHT: Infantry private soldier, uniform of 1911. Plate by Benjamin M. Dale, Philadelphia Public Ledger, July 1917. Anne S.K. Brown Military Collection, Brown University Library, Providence, USA.

sixteen torpedo boats and thirteen submarines. The armament on the capital ships included 305 mm (12-inch) guns, one armored cruiser having even 365 mm (14.3-inch) cannons. Japan declared war to Germany on the 23 August 1914 and the imperial fleet sealed off Tsingtao and occupied the German Marianas (excluding American Guam), Marshall and Caroline Island groups in the Western Pacific. Admiral Graf Spee's German Far Eastern squadron dispersed because it knew it could not hope for success against the powerful Japanese navy. Japanese imperial navy destroyers were based at Malta in 1917-1918. After the war, the navy took part in operations against the Bolsheviks in eastern Siberia. During the early-1920s, the imperial navy had fifteen battleships, seven battle cruisers, about fifty cruisers and various types of heavy coast defense ships and gunboats, 130 destroyers and torpedo boats, about fifty submarines and four aircraft carriers.

Naval Aviation

The first naval aviators came back from training in France during 1912 and a small training field was set up at Oppama near Yokosuka. During the siege of Tsingtao in 1914, four imperial navy seaplanes carried out the world's first successful sea-launched bombing runs from a seaplane carrier ship. This branch grew steadily, especially from 1920 and a distinct naval aviation department was created in April 1927. At that time, it had 108 flying boats and land-based planes and two Zeppelin airships. The real novelty was the four new aircraft carriers that had a number of planes on board. Seaplanes were also fitted on board several battleships and cruisers.

Marines

With Japan assuming an imperial power role as the "policeman" of the Far East since the First World War, the need for a marine corps was increasingly perceived by the government. Naval landing parties temporarily

Japanese troops at Tsingtau, 1914-1915. At left, an infantry officer; at center, a sailor of a landing party and at right, an infantry private. He hold a small national flag that Japanese troops carried in combat, notably assaults. All are in winter dress wearing a khaki hooded overcoat. The red band on the infantrymen's cap's front is made invisible by a removable khaki cover. Notes taken at Tsingtao by a German resident following its occupation by Japanese troops. Anne S.K. Brown Military Collection, Brown University Library, Providence, USA.

Imperial guard cavalry at a parade, c. 1920. Library of Congress, Washington.

The Japanese army air force deployed aircrafts over eastern Siberia between 1918 and 1922. In this propaganda print, older model French-made Farman reconnaissance and light bomber planes fly over a lush, prosperous-looking landscape. Anonymous print published by Shobido and Company, Tokyo. Library of Congress, Washington.

Japanese cavalry taking over the bridge at Khabarovsk on the Amur River, 1918. Completed in 1916, this bridge was an important link of the Trans-Siberian Railway. Previous to its construction, railroad cars had to be ferried across the river by boats. The Red Army troops are dressed in imaginary uniforms in this propaganda print. The Japanese cavalry is correctly shown and even the green collar tabs are visible. Anonymous print published by Shobido and Company, Tokyo. Library of Congress, Washington.

The Japanese army penetrated deeply into eastern Siberia and reached Khabarovsk on the Amur River taking control of the fleet there. This propaganda print shows the Russian Bolshevik troops surrendering. The uniforms they wear are based on the old imperial Russian army styles; the artists working for Shobido and Company in Tokyo obviously had no information on what the Red Army soldiers looked like. The Japanese uniforms are correctly shown. Library of Congress, Washington.

Landing Japanese troops at Vladivostok, Siberia, in August 1918. The soldiers are shown being greeted by crowds of Russians waving Japanese flags. But as events unfolded, it became apparent that many Siberians were not all that anxious to be saved from the Soviet government from Japan and other western nations. As can be seen in this propaganda print published by Shobido and Company in Tokyo during 1921, there is little evidence of the traditional influences of Japanese art seen in this print, which was part of a series. Library of Congress, Washington.

organized from fleet personnel depleted the ship's crews and lowered their efficiency. Therefore, the navy started to experiment with more permanent "marine" type units. In 1928, "Special Naval Landing Forces" numbered regiments were raised that formed, for all intents and purposes, a corps of marines. They were drawn from naval personnel and were under the command of naval officers. They were highly trained elite troops and were first deployed in China during 1932. Their dress uniform consisted of the dark blue naval dress with white canvas gaiters. Field uniform, arms and equipment were similar to those worn by the army. The marines had an outstanding service record until the end of the Second World War, but the study of these troops falls outside the scope of this book.

The Arts

Although Japan was on the allied side during the First World War and also participated in its sequel intervention in eastern Siberia, the armed forces were not heavily involved in these hostilities. Between the bloody 1904-1905 war with Russia and the 1930s operations in China, there was a dearth of war actions to portray. The military illustrations that did appear were notably westernized in their approach. Shotaro Tojo's painting of the naval review showing the emperor and Admiral Togo was a rendering typical of the European academic school.

The lithograph prints of the 1914 capture of Tsingtao and of the 1918-1922 Siberian intervention were mass media products such as were found in newspapers and magazines everywhere in the world; the subjects and the uniforms shown were Japanese, but everything else and especially the composition, was typical of illustration styles in Europe and America. This continued with early-1930s prints of the campaigns in China.

Gone were the beautiful Ukiyo-e war prints with their original settings and superb colors. The Japanese art market no longer sustained the expensive and hand crafted production of traditional Ukiyo-e prints. The current aesthetic inclination favored more western art expressions although there were still many traditional art forms that continued to flourish, notably in textiles and pottery as well as in paintings. The mass media

LEFT: Navy officer, c. 1914-1916. Plate by Benjamin M. Dale, Philadelphia Public Ledger, July 1917. Anne S.K. Brown Military Collection, Brown University Library, Providence, USA. MIDDLE: Infantry private, 1930 service dress. RIGHT: Infantry officer, 1930 service dress. The samurai style sword was now officially allowed for officers. From the 1944 U.S. handbook on Japanese forces. Canadian War Museum, Ottawa.

was, however, largely converted to Western technology and artistic influence for its illustrations. The impact of photographic reproductions, which gradually increased in quality, was also felt in Japan just as it was elsewhere in the world. As early as 1914, colored photos of the siege of Tsingtau were produced.

In the 19th century Western nations, Japanese art had gained a lasting influence. Its aesthetic values were often expressed in paintings and posters of the pre-First World War "La Belle Époque" years. Many advertising posters and paintings tried to capture a Japanese artistic atmosphere, a good example of this trend being American artist Marietta Andrews' evocative "Japanese Tea Room" of about 1905, as well as the works of Alphonse Mucha and other "Art Nouveau" movement artist. The "New Art" movement was partly inspired by the curved lines, patterned surfaces, contrasting voids and flatness of Japanese prints. This influence now extended to architecture, first in "Art Nouveau" buildings, and eventually in great force as expressed in the outstanding works of the great American architect Frank Lloyd Wright.

In a sense, Japanese art came to be known in the West thanks to its exquisite prints, and a substantial part of these beautiful prints depicted warriors, fortifications and battles. Just as the prints showing scenes of everyday life or of natural sites, the military prints confronted European and American viewers with a profoundly different way of showing war, its actors and its technology.

One may wonder why such a fine art as Ukiyo-e prints vanished. Whether the Japanese's profound commitment to creating beauty by mastering the fine arts was swept away by the Meiji reforms remains an open and debated question. The fine arts have always been the privilege of the elite in any society and so it was in Japan, although it could be argued that the less expensive Ukiyo-e prints were available to a larger number of Japanese homes. It should also be pointed out that, even as it mastered everything from shipbuilding to motor vehicle manufacturing, a proportion of Japan's population remained, and remains to this day, strongly attached to its traditions and to the pursuit of beauty through the arts. M. Léra, an early 20th century French observer, noted that the Japanese who avidly adopted all forms of European products in public life reverted to traditional values when in the

Emperor Meiji (center) and Admiral Togo (right) preside a review of the Japanese navy, 1906. The emperor and the officers wear the service dress jacket, even on the solemn occasion of an imperial review, a sign that this jacket was becoming the recognition hallmark of Japan's navy officers. Print after Shotaro Tojo. Anne S.K. Brown Military Collection, Brown University Library, Providence, USA.

Navy sailor, c. 1917-1918. This fine pastel by French artist Eugène Burnand most likely portrays one of the crewmembers from the Japanese imperial navy destroyers sent to Malta in the Mediterranean during 1917. The artist thus may have encountered Japanese sailors in Marseille or Toulon. The uniform is much as in the British and American navies, but the ship's name on the cap ribbon is of course in Japanese and the jumper's collar is edged with a single white stripe. Plate from Les Alliés dans la guerre des nations (Paris, 1922).

Navy sailor, c. 1914-1916. Plate by Benjamin M. Dale, Philadelphia Public Ledger, July 1917. Anne S.K. Brown Military Collection, Brown University Library, Providence, USA.

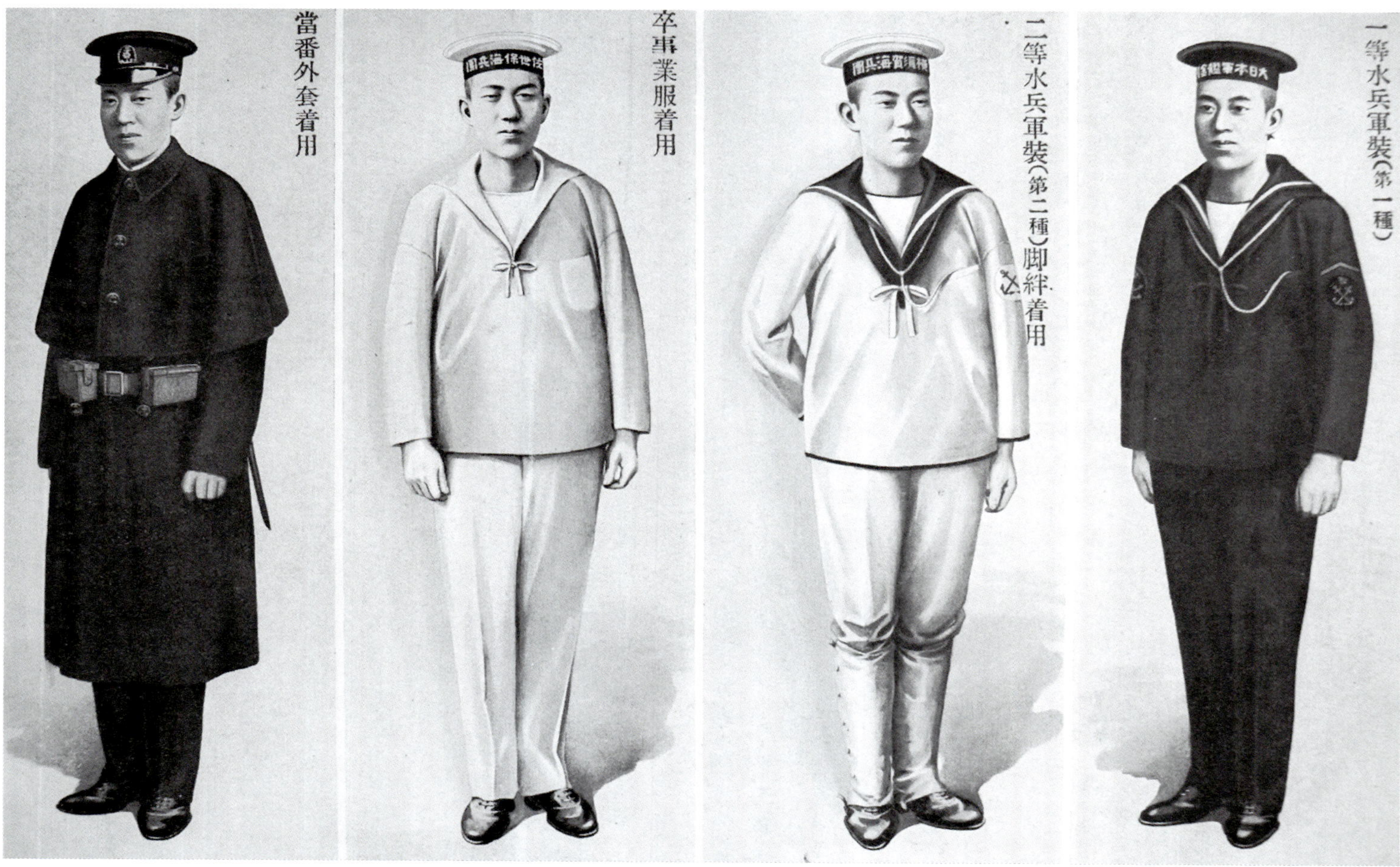

Navy ratings and petty officer, 1914 regulations. Petty officer in dark blue overcoat, equipped for sentry duty. Sailors in tropical ordinary fatigue dress, and service dress. Anne S.K. Brown Military Collection, Brown University Library, Providence, USA.

Navy officers, c. 1914-1915. Captain G. Ishii, Rear Admiral Ijichi, Flag (or Staff) Lieutenant Shimomure (standing), and Captain T. Sato. All wear the dark blue dress frock coat with caps. Decorations have been put on for a dress occasion. Library of Congress, Washington.

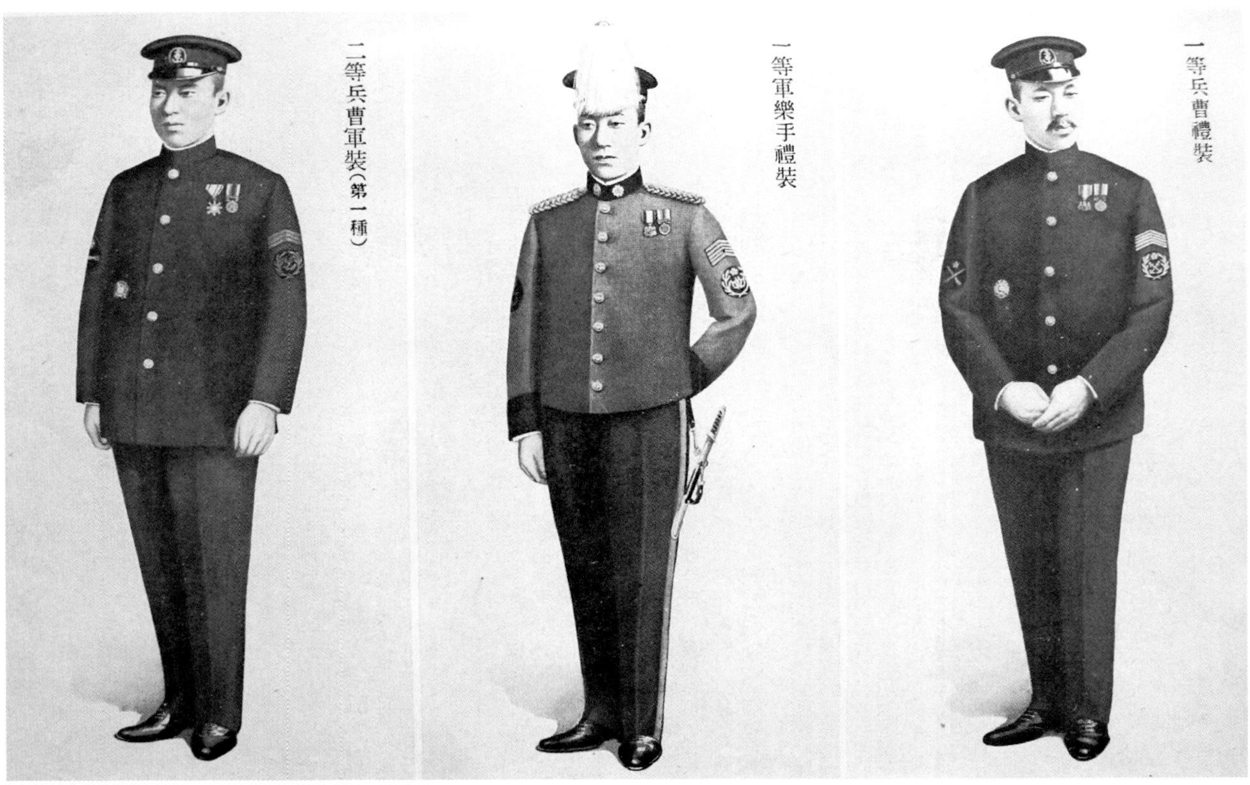

Navy NCOs, 1914 regulations. NCOs at left and right, the bandmaster wears the distinctive red jacket and cap white plume at the center. Anne S.K. Brown Military Collection, Brown University Library, Providence, USA.

Navy officers, 1914 regulations. Dress frock with cap and bicorn for full dress. Anne S.K. Brown Military Collection, Brown University Library, Providence, USA.

intimacy of their homes. There, officers, officials and businessmen exchanged their European uniforms and suits for comfortable kimonos in houses that remained barren of almost any Western furniture. They would consume a meal of rice and raw fish in an environment beautified by "Ikabana" flower arrangements. The spread of Ikabana, the unequalled artistic science of flower arrangements, in all nations during the later 20th century is one example of many of the enduring power of Japanese aesthetics all over the globe.

Japanese personal martial arts such as Judo and Karate have also flourished all over the world. Even more widespread especially amongst the world's young people were the warrior-like "Mangas" – the so-called Japanese comic books – although the dramatic adventures they relate are always tragic, mystical and not necessarily set at a particular era. The earliest Mangas date from the 12th century and some were later occasionally illustrated with wood block prints. They often feature a righteous lone knight or samurai-like hero that battles all sorts of more or less evil creatures. In this, Mangas very much echo the knightly warrior values, not only of feudal Japan, but also those of Medieval Europe: the struggle against evil and the protection of the weak. An essential quality of any successful Manga is its illustrations, which are always most distinctive from American comics and European "bandes dessinées" by their very bold and imaginative style. In a sense, although vastly different, the Manga style appropriates much of the stances and styles found in warriors illustrated in the vanished Ukiyo-e prints.

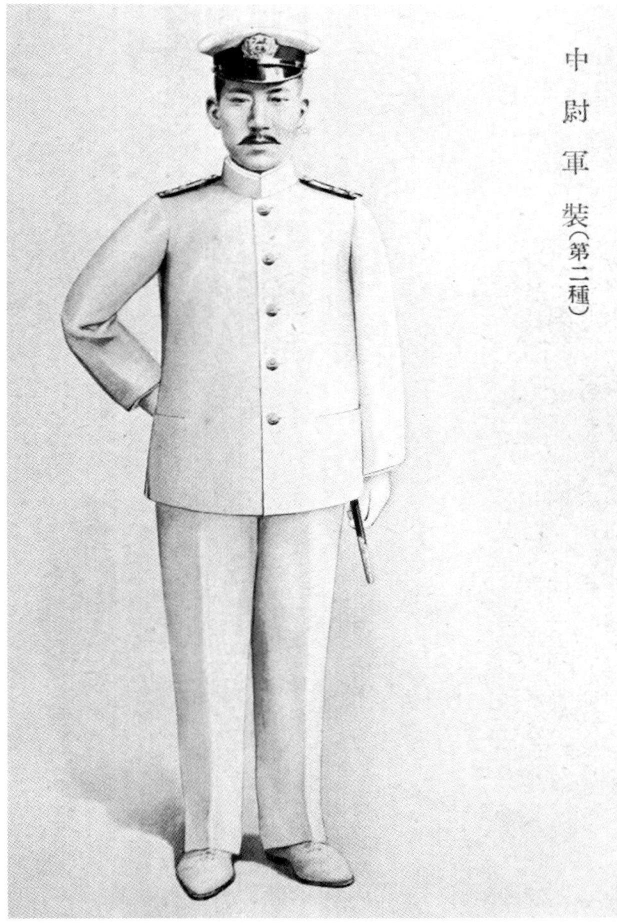

Navy officers, 1914 regulations. Tropical and service dress. The gold aiguillette indicates a staff officer. Anne S.K. Brown Military Collection, Brown University Library, Providence, USA.

Navy officer, 1914 regulations. Bicorn and tailcoat for full ceremonial occasions. Anne S.K. Brown Military Collection, Brown University Library, Providence, USA.

Japanese plane at the 1914 siege of Tsingtau. This French built Farman F7 was photographed at its base along the Tschang-tsun River. Long tubular bomb carriers can be seen on each side of the pilot's windshield. From a photo in The Siege of Tsingtau (Boston, 1915).

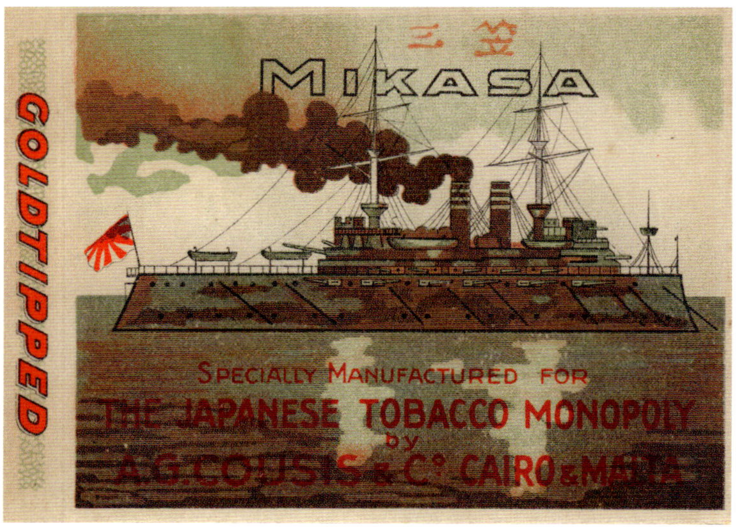

Cigarette pack card showing the Japanese warship Mikasa, of Tsushima fame, c. 1917-1918. This small example of Japanese war art was distributed in Malta on packets each containing ten cigarettes. They were intended for Japan's sailors serving on the imperial navy's squadron based on that island fortress. The illustration has Japanese language characters and is a good example of that nation's mass media and commercial art at the beginning of the 20th century. Private collection.

The Seventh Art also did not escape a strong Japanese influence, which spread around the globe during the second half of the 20th century thanks to the cinema masterpieces made by Akiro Kurosawa and his followers, which led to international recognition of the Japanese film industry. Kurosawa's most famous films were warrior epics, for instance his lauded "Rashomon" (1950), "The Seven Samurai" (1954) and his grandiose "Ran" (1985), all of which allied outstanding scripts set in feudal Japan to some of the finest art ever crafted for the silver screen. Again, while these productions were not strictly war or military art, they were very powerful artistic expressions that centered on warriors and the martial arts.

Perhaps the final irony is that, through the modern mass media, Ukiyo-e prints now enjoy a renaissance and an unheard of dissemination all over the globe thanks to printing presses that now can reproduce high quality images in countless books. Such as this book does to present the progress and many aspects of the pictorial record and dress of Japan's wars and its warriors.

Thus, Japanese War Art is very much with us as never before.

This poster painting of a "Japanese Tea Room" in about 1905-1910 shows the influence that Japanese art and taste was increasingly having in America and Europe. Even as traditional arts and ways were being somewhat overwhelmed in the Land of the Rising Sun, the extraordinary strength of Japan's art and design values was gaining converts all over the western world as shown by this evocative painting by American artist Marietta Minnigerode Andrews (1869-1931). Washington County Museum of Fine Arts, Hagerstown, MD, USA.

Appendices

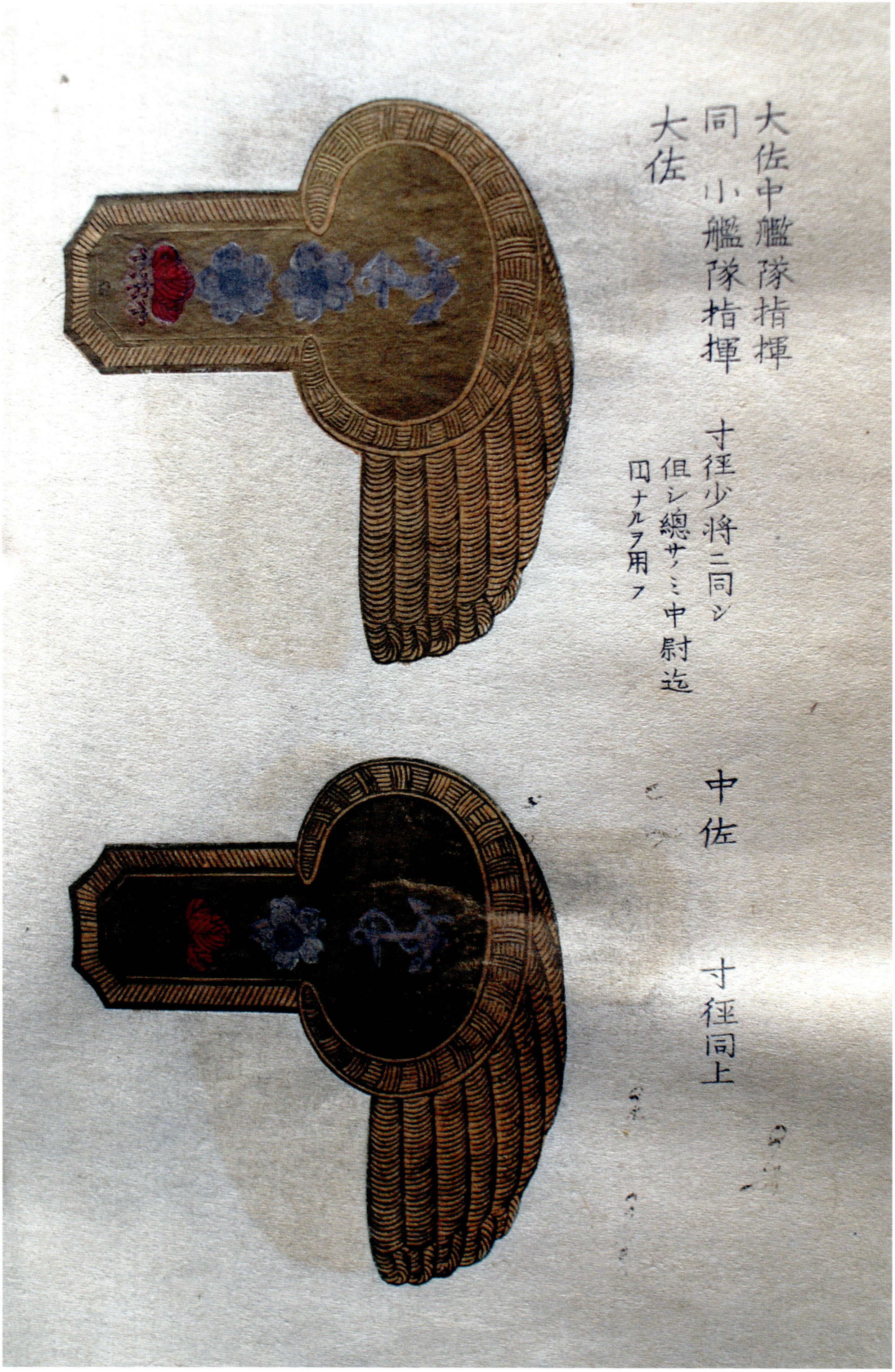

Navy 1873-1874 regulations officer's epaulets. From top to bottom: Captain: anchor, two flower stars, chrysanthemum badge. Lieutenant: anchor, one flower star, chrysanthemum badge. Anne S.K. Brown Military Collection, Brown University Library, Providence, USA.

I

Army Rank Badges

1873-1874 Army Regulations

Officers
All officers of the fighting services had gold lace. **Administrative** and **medical branch officers** had mixed gold and silver lace.

Tunic sleeve laces

General: seven laces with three curls

Lieutenant general: six laces with three curls

Major general: five laces with three curls

Colonel: six laces

Lieutenant colonel: five laces

Major: four laces

Captain: three laces

Lieutenant: two laces

Second lieutenant: one lace

Tunic collar laces

General officers: collar covered with lace

Field officers: top of collar edged with wide lace.

Company officers: top of collar edged with *medium width lace.*

Warrant officers: top of collar edged with narrow lace

Kepi tops

General: six stars

Lieutenant general: five stars

Major general: four stars

Field officer: three stars

Company officer: two stars

Kepi lace bands

General: three narrow and one wide

Lieutenant general: two narrow and one wide

Major general: one narrow and one wide

Colonel: one narrow and two wide

Lieutenant colonel: six narrow

Major: five narrow

Captain: four narrow

Lieutenant: three narrow

Second lieutenant: two narrow

Field service cap central line on branch color band

General officer: three lines

Field officer: two lines

Company officer: one line

Greatcoat cuff stars

General: five stars

Lieutenant general: three stars

Major general: two stars

Field officer: none

Service dress Attila sleeve laces (9mm wide, black on the standard model and white on the summer model)

General: seven laces with three curls

Lieutenant general: six laces with three curls

Major general: five laces with three curls

Colonel: six laces

Lieutenant colonel: five laces

Major: four laces

Captain: three laces

Lieutenant: two laces

Second lieutenant: one lace

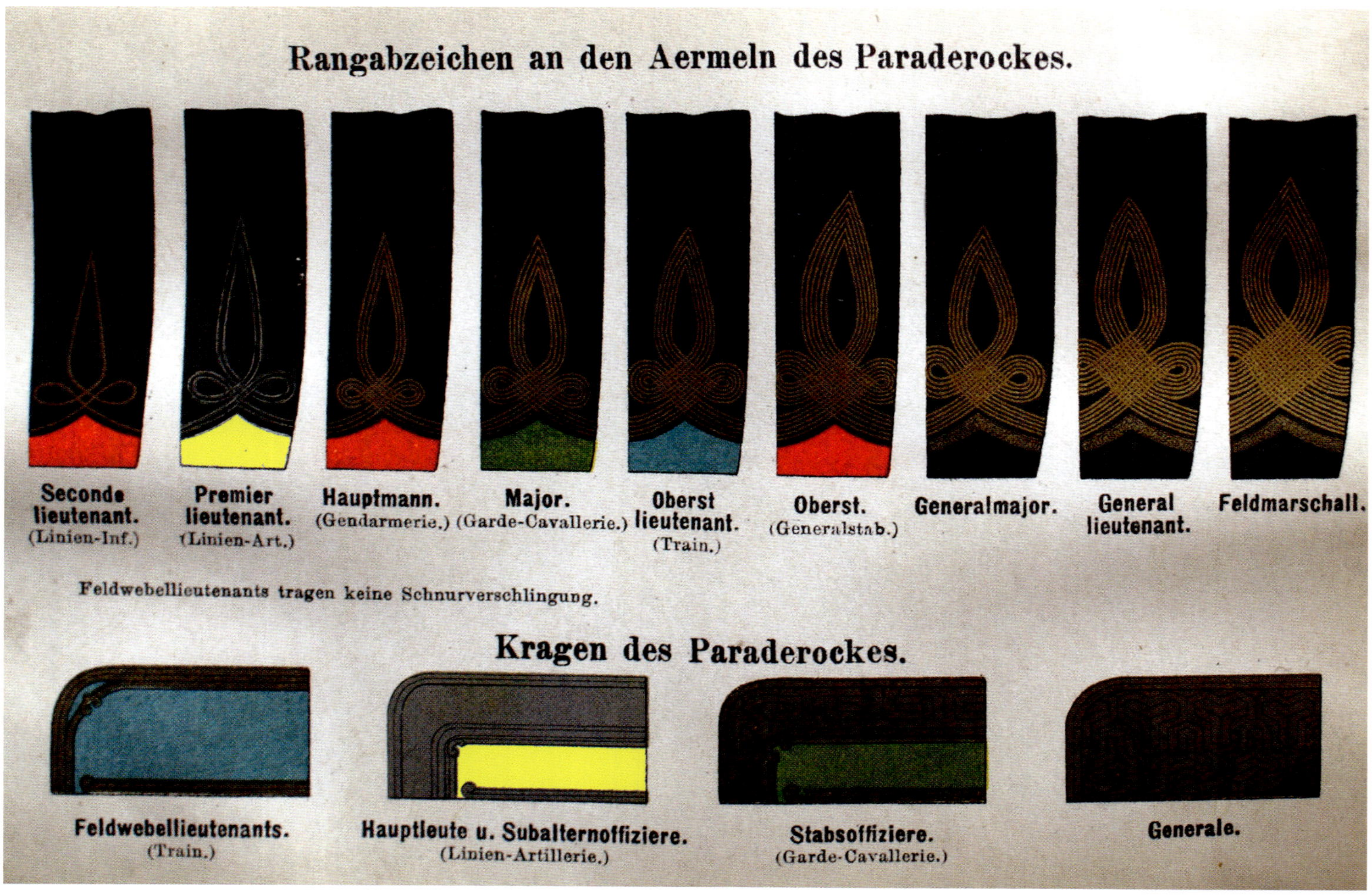

Army officer's sleeve and collar badges of the dress tunic, 1886 regulations. Top: sleeve badges. Bottom: collar badges. The cuffs and collar of the line artillery ("linien-Artillerie") have been digitally colored yellow. The artillery's lace should be gold rather than silver as shown. Print after Moritz Rhul.

1886 Army Regulations

Officers

Tunic sleeve laces

General: seven laces with a wide lace

Lieutenant general: six laces with a wide lace

Major general: five laces with a wide lace

Colonel: six laces

Lieutenant colonel: five laces

Major: four laces

Captain: three laces

Lieutenant: two laces

Second lieutenant: one lace

Tunic collar laces

General officers: collar covered with lace

Field officers: top of collar edged with wide lace

Company officers: top of collar edged with medium width lace

Warrant officers: top of collar edged with narrow lace

Shoulder knots

Gold cord with silver stars. *Administration branches officers* had gold and silver mixed cords and silver stars.

General: three stars on tripe knotted cord

Lieutenant general: two stars on tripe knotted cord

Major general: one star on tripe knotted cord

Colonel: three stars on double knotted cord

Lieutenant colonel: two stars on double knotted cord

Major: one star on double knotted cord

Captain: three stars on single knotted cord

Lieutenant: two stars on single knotted cord

Second lieutenant: one star on single knotted cord

Warrant officers: no star¬ on single knotted cord

Kepi tops

One large star for *all officers*

Kepi lace bands

General: three narrow and one wide

Lieutenant general: two narrow and one wide

Major general: one narrow and one wide

Colonel: six narrow

Lieutenant colonel: five narrow

Major: four narrow

Captain: three narrow

Lieutenant: two narrow

Second lieutenant: one narrow

Warrant officers: none

Field service cap central line on branch color band

General officer: three lines

Field officer: two lines

Company officer: one line

Greatcoat cuff stars

General: three stars

Lieutenant general: two stars

Major general: one star

Field officer: none

Service dress Attila sleeve laces (9mm wide, black on the standard model and white on the summer model)

General: seven laces with three curls

Lieutenant general: six laces with three curls

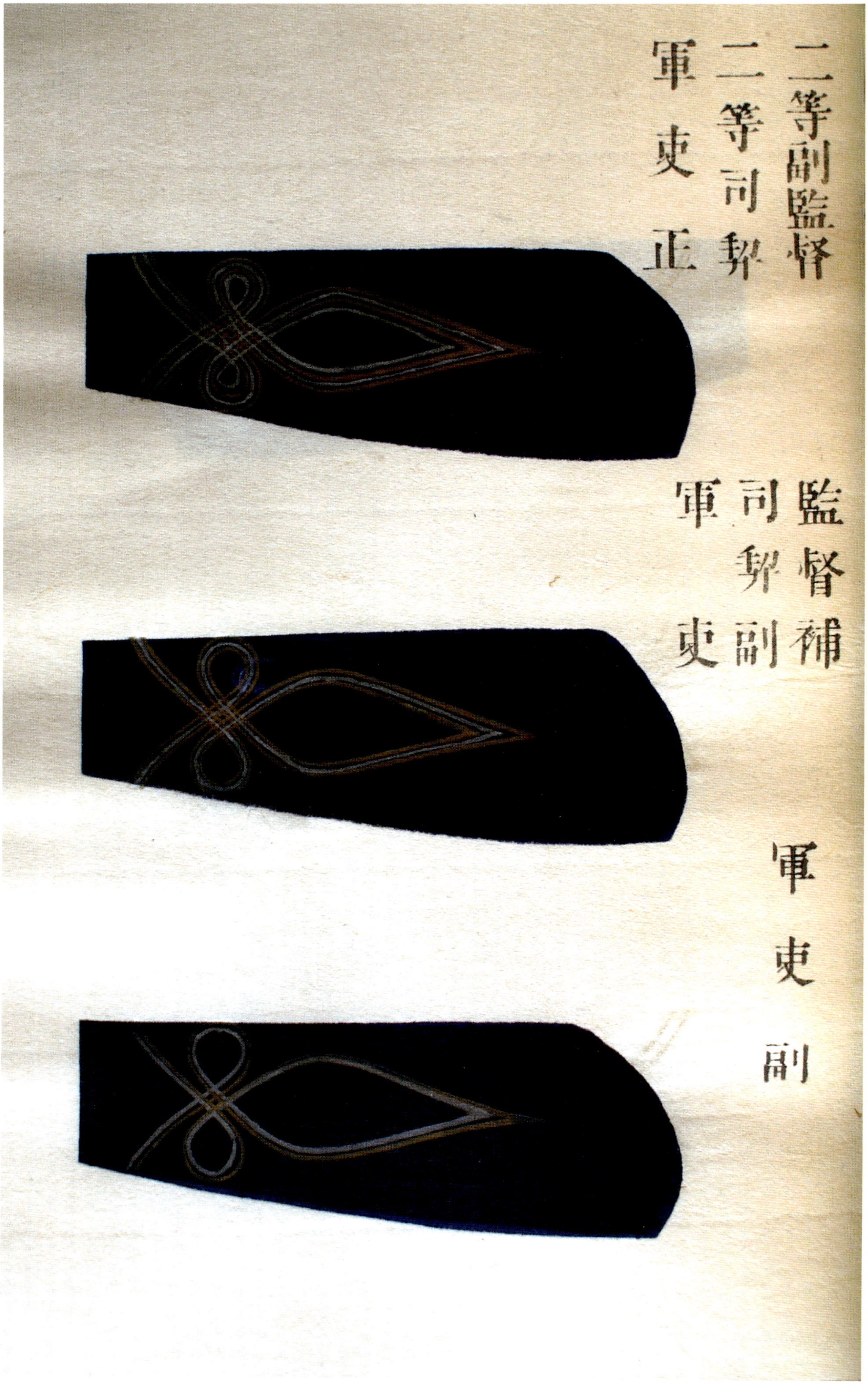

Army battalion officer's tunic sleeve rank badges, 1874 regulations. Top to bottom: major, captain, first lieutenant. Lieutenant colonels had five laces, colonels had six. The laces were always gold except for certain staff functions such as the medical corps that mixed gold and silver as shown here. Anne S.K. Brown Military Collection, Brown University Library, Providence, USA.

Army officer's dress tunic collar lace, 1874 regulations. Subaltern officer's. Captains and field officers had wider gold lace. Generals had their tunic collar fully covered with gold lace. Anne S.K. Brown Military Collection, Brown University Library, Providence, USA.

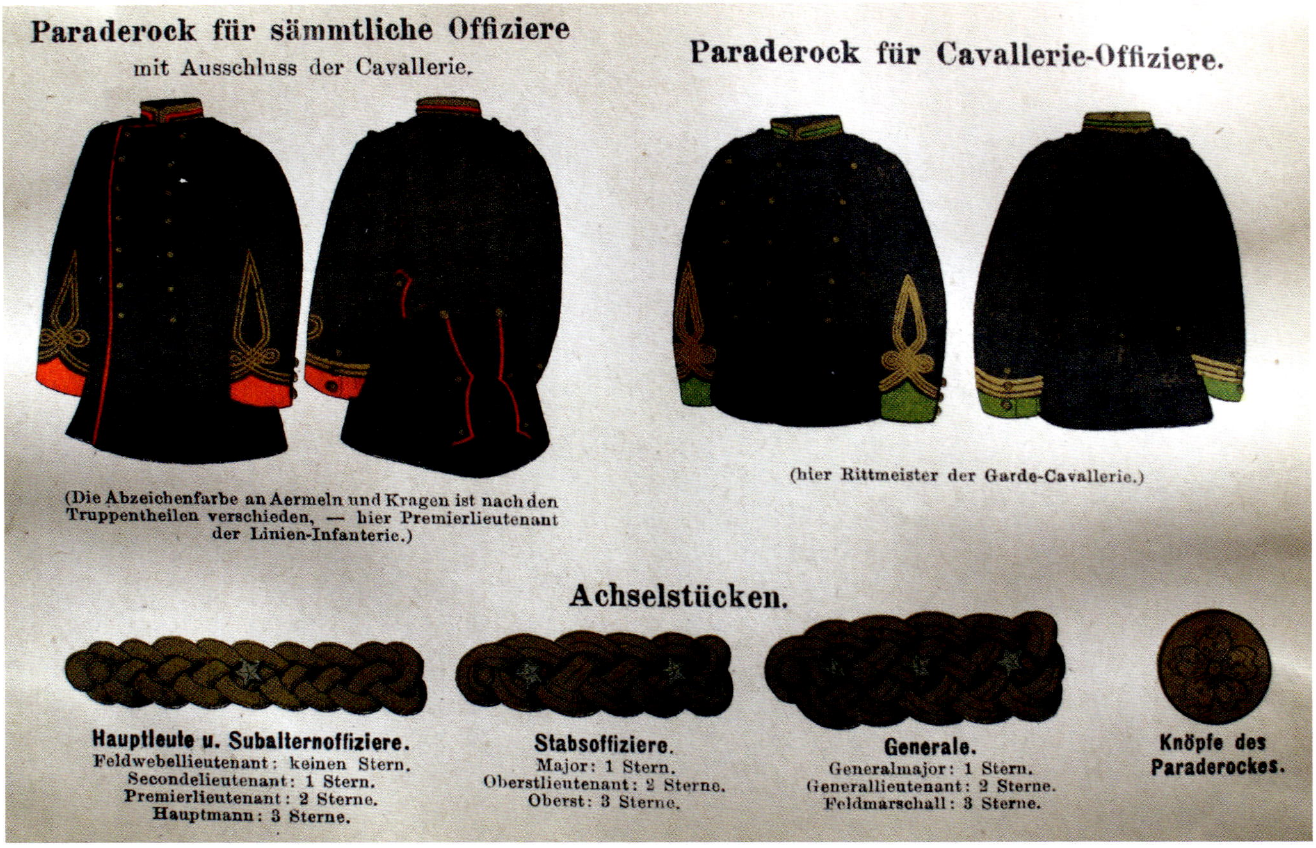

Army officer's tunic, Atilla and shoulder knots, 1886 regulations. Top: line infantry dress tunic and guard cavalry Atilla. Bottom: shoulder knots button of the dress tunic. Print after Moritz Rhul.

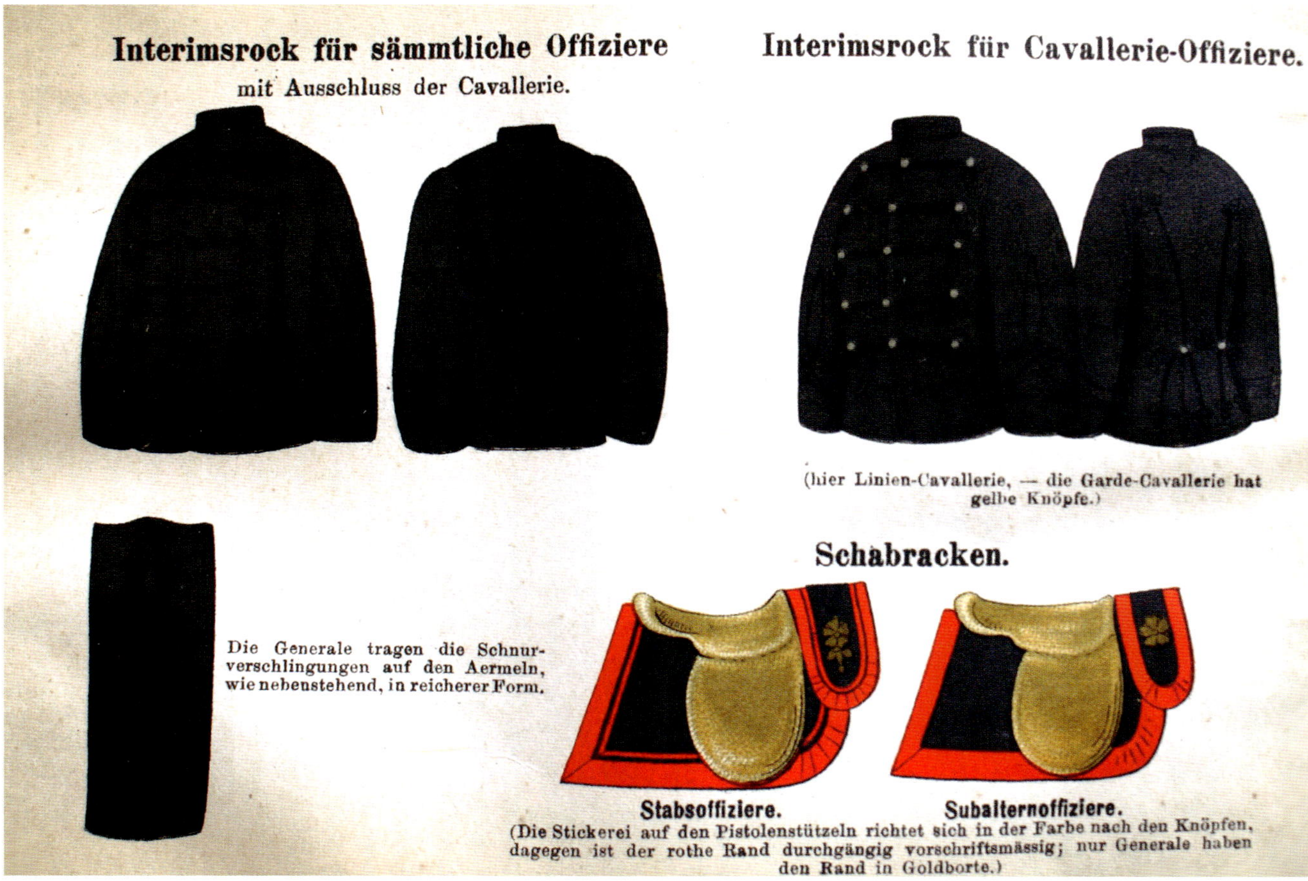

Army officer's Attila and saddlery, 1886 regulations. Top: Attila jackets for senior and junior officers. The line cavalry had gold buttons, not just the guard cavalry as stated in the German caption. Bottom: saddlery for field and subaltern officers. Print after Moritz Rhul.

Army officer's dress kepis and service caps, 1886 regulations. Two top rows: dress kepis, which assumed the shape of a small shako only used in dress occasions from 1886. The line artillery and line cavalry kepis should have gold rather than silver lace, a coloring error. Bottom: service peaked caps. Print after Moritz Rhul.

Major general: five laces with three curls

Colonel: six laces

Lieutenant colonel: five laces

Major: four laces

Captain: three laces

Lieutenant: two laces

Second lieutenant: one lace

Warrant officer: a chevron (no sleeve lace)

1886 Regulation

NCOs and corporal's cuff stripes

Sergeant major: one gold stripe, three branch colors stripes above.

Sergeant first class: one gold stripe, two branch colors stripes above.

Sergeant second class: one gold stripe, one branch color stripe above.

Superior private: three branch color stripes.

Private first class: two branch color stripes.

Private second class: one branch color stripe.

Student or cadet: one pointed branch color stripe.

1900 Army Summer Dress and Frock and 1904 Army Khaki Service Dress

Jacket cuffs

General: three laces with three stars

Lieutenant general: two laces with three stars

Major general: one lace with three stars

Colonel: three laces with two stars

Lieutenant colonel: two laces with two stars

Major: one lace with two stars

Captain: three laces with one star

Lieutenant: two laces with one star

Second lieutenant: one lace with one star

Warrant officer: plain

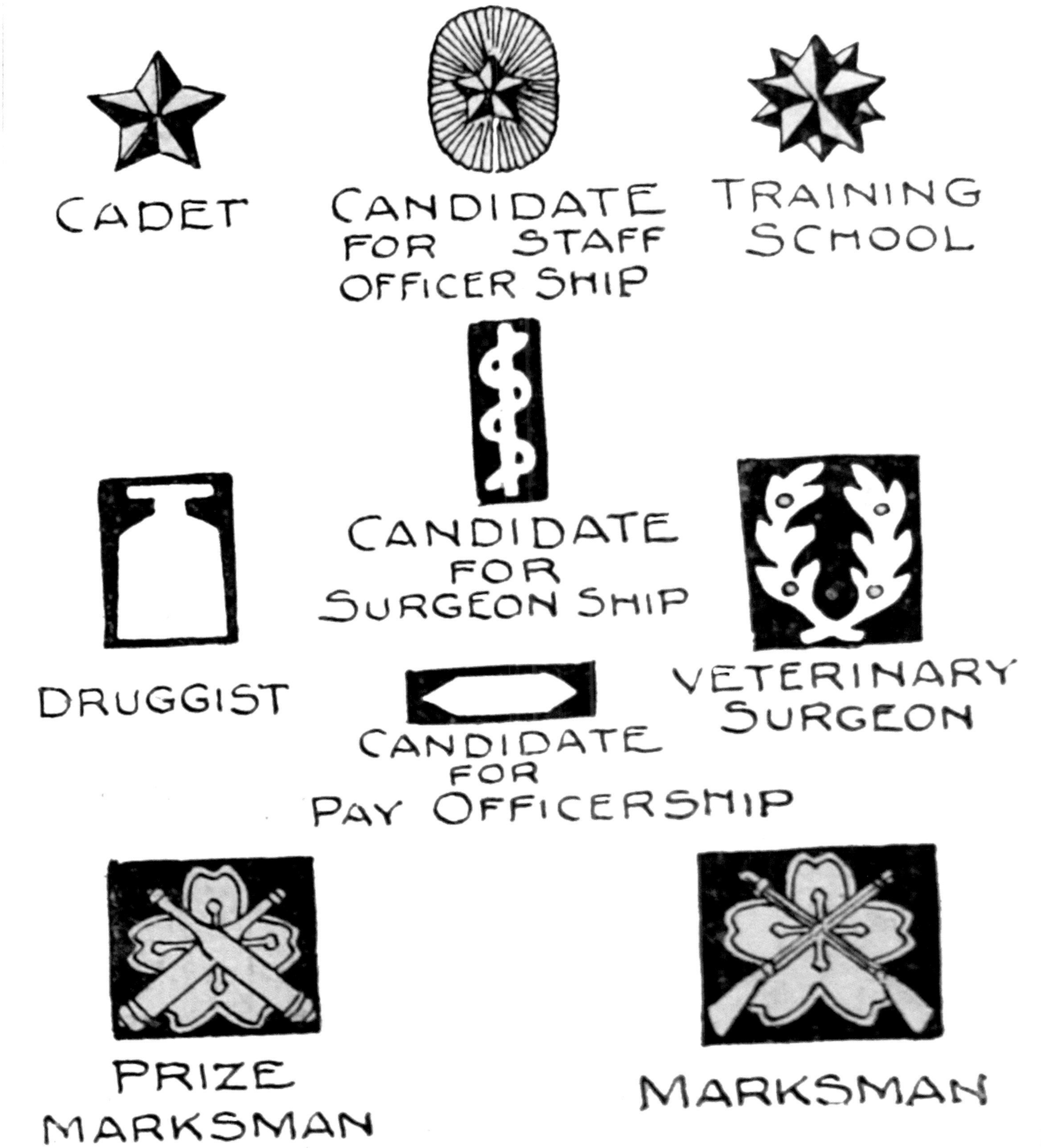

Army collar badges, 1904. As shown in the Illustrated London News of 4 April 1904.

Army sleeve badges, 1904. As shown in the Illustrated London News of 4 April 1904.

1911 Army Dress Regulations

Shoulder rank badges

Officers: red strap with gold lace stripes and gold stars

General: wide central gold lace with three gold stars, narrow gold lace edging each side.

Lieutenant general: wide central gold lace with two gold stars, narrow gold lace edging each side.

Major general: wide central gold lace with one gold star, narrow gold lace edging each side.

Colonel: two gold stripes with three gold stars at center, narrow gold lace edging each side.

Lieutenant colonel: two gold stripes with two gold stars at center, narrow gold lace edging each side.

Major: two gold stripes with one gold star at center, narrow gold lace edging each side.

Captain: one gold stripe with three gold stars at center, narrow gold lace edging each side.

Lieutenant: one gold stripe with two gold stars at center, narrow gold lace edging each side.

Second lieutenant: one gold stripe with one gold star at center, narrow gold lace edging each side.

Warrant officer: one gold stripe with no gold star at center, narrow gold lace edging each side.

NCOs and enlisted men: red strap with yellow lace and stars.

Sergeant major: a yellow central stripe and three stars fixed upon it.

Sergeant: a yellow central stripe and two stars fixed upon it.

Corporal: a yellow central stripe and one star fixed upon it.

Superior private: three yellow stars only.

Private first class: two yellow stars only.

Private second class: one yellow star only.

Note: the rank of *field marshal* existed briefly from July 1872 to 1873 and from 1893. The 1872 field marshal's uniform was never worn. The 1893 uniform was the same as a full general with a red chrysanthemum flower badge added to the three flower stars on the shoulder cord. The emperor wore the full dress uniform of a field marshal.

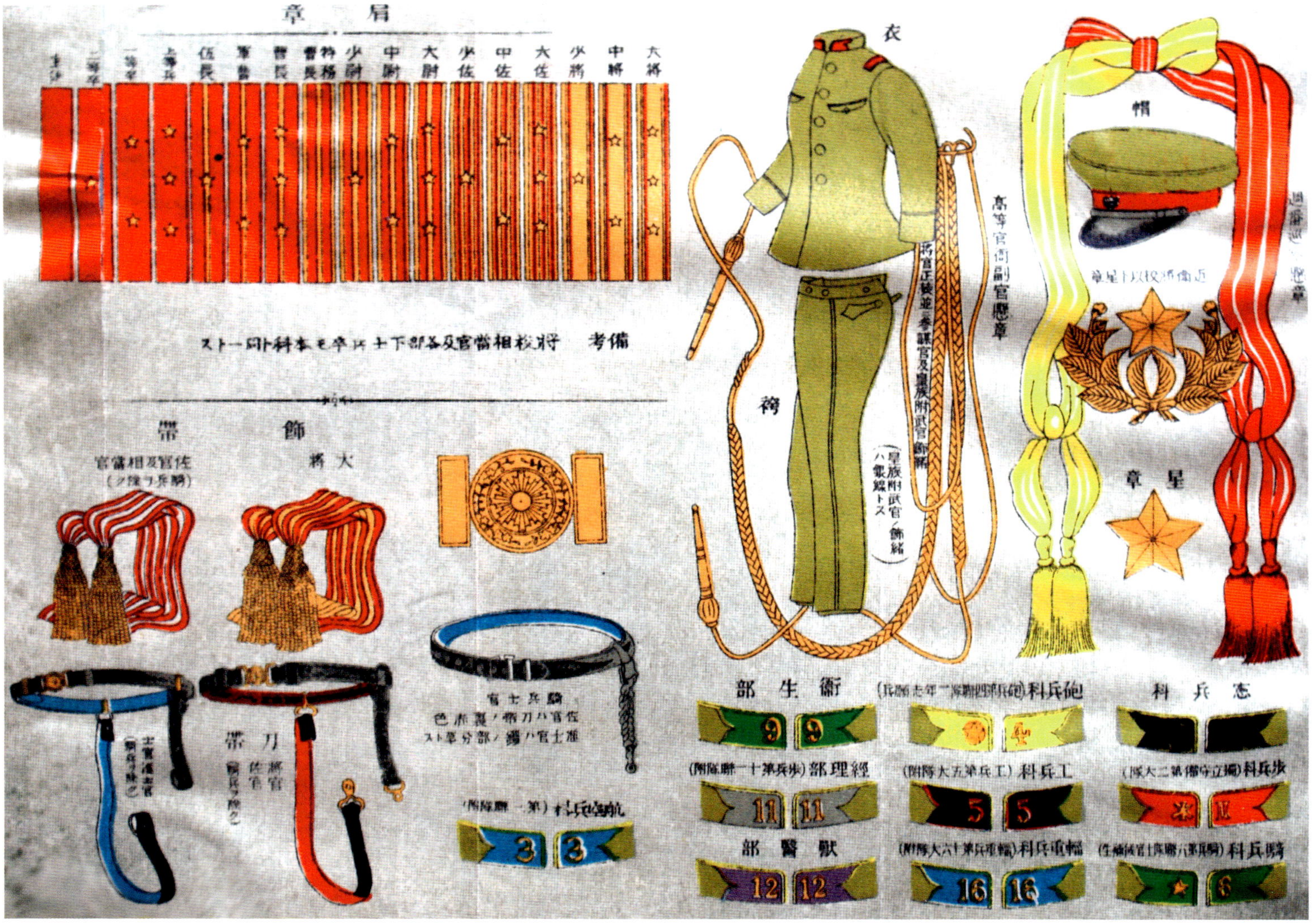

Chart of the 1930 army uniform regulations. This somewhat poorly printed document must have been distributed widely and it provided the features of the army's uniform. At top left, the shoulder tabs for all ranks from cadet to general. At centre, the tunic and trousers surrounded by a staff aiguillette. At top right, the service cap with the imperial guard badge (adopted since 1905) and the other unit's star badge bellow surrounded by sashes for general and staff (red and white) and members of the imperial family (yellow and white). At center left, field officers sashes and standard belt buckle. At bottom left, cavalry officer's sword belt, foot troops field officer's and junior officer's sword belts. Collar tabs, from left to right: 3rd air corps regiment (at bottom center), 9th medical corps detachment, 4th artillery one year volunteer, gendarmerie, 11th intendance regiment, 5th pioneer battalion, 2nd infantry battalion of a detached garrison regiment, 12th veterinary corps detachment, 16th train battalion and 6th cavalry officer candidate. Anne S.K. Brown Military Collection, Brown University Library, Providence, USA.

II

NAVY RANK BADGES

1873-1930 NAVY REGULATIONS

Sea officers

Gold full dress epaulets with silver anchor, chevron lace and flower stars, red chrysanthemum badge.

Admiral: chevron lace, three flower stars, chrysanthemum badge.

Vice admiral: chevron lace, two flower stars, chrysanthemum badge.

Rear admiral: chevron lace, one flower star, chrysanthemum badge.

Captain: anchor, two flower stars, chrysanthemum badge.

Commander: anchor, one flower star, chrysanthemum badge.

Lieutenant commander: anchor, no flower star, chrysanthemum badge.

Lieutenant: anchor, one flower star.

Sub-lieutenant: anchor, one flower star (no fringes).

Acting sub-lieutenant: anchor only (no fringes).

Naval administration officers

Gold epaulets with silver lace edging the strap. Gold flower stars and red chrysanthemum badge. No anchor or chevron.

Vice admiral: three flower stars, chrysanthemum badge.

Rear admiral: one large and one small flower star, chrysanthemum badge.

Captain: three flower stars, chrysanthemum badge.

Commander: two flower stars, chrysanthemum badge.

Lieutenant commander: one flower star, chrysanthemum badge.

Lieutenant: two flower stars only.

Sub-lieutenant: two flower stars only (no fringes).

Acting sub-lieutenant: flower star only (no fringes).

Cuff stripes, from 1871

Sea officers have gold lace with top lace having the executive curl.

Admiral: three wide laces, one lace with curl. From 1883, two wide laces and three laces, the top one with curl.

Vice admiral: two wide laces and one narrow lace between, one lace with curl. From 1883, two wide laces and two laces, the top one with curl.

Rear admiral: two wide laces, one lace with curl.

Captain: four laces.

Commander: four laces. From 1883, three laces and a narrow bottom lace. From 1914, three laces only.

Lieutenant commander: three laces. From 1914, two laces and a narrow bottom lace.

Lieutenant: two laces.

Sub-lieutenant: one lace and one narrow bottom lace.

Ensign or acting sub-lieutenant: one lace.

Midshipman: three buttons. From 1887, one narrow lace with curl.

Warrant officer: one narrow lace with curl, three buttons on the cuff.

Warrant officer (engineers): one narrow lace with curl, narrow violet lace below, three buttons on the cuff.

Non-combatant branches had colored stripes between the laces: engineers violet, medical deep red, engineer constructors brown, ordnance constructors maroon, administration and pay white, hydrographic light blue, pilots blue, chief carpenters (warrant officers) green, bandmasters (warrant officers) grey. They had no executive curls.

Reserve naval officers had narrow gold cuff laces with no curl: six for commander, five for lieutenant commander, four for lieutenant, three for sub-lieutenant, two for ensign and one for midshipman.

Shoulder straps, from 1900

Sea officers

Dark blue with gold lace set length wise and silver badges.

Admiral: wide lace, three flower stars.

Vice admiral: wide lace, two flower stars.

Rear admiral: wide lace, one flower star.

Captain: two laces, three flower stars.

Commander: two laces, two flower stars.

Lieutenant commander: two laces, one flower star.

Lieutenant: one lace, three flower stars.

Sub-lieutenant: Lieutenant: one lace, two flower stars.

Ensign or acting sub-lieutenant: one lace, one flower star.

Midshipman: one narrow lace. From 1904, one lace.

Warrant officer (from 1904): one narrow lace.

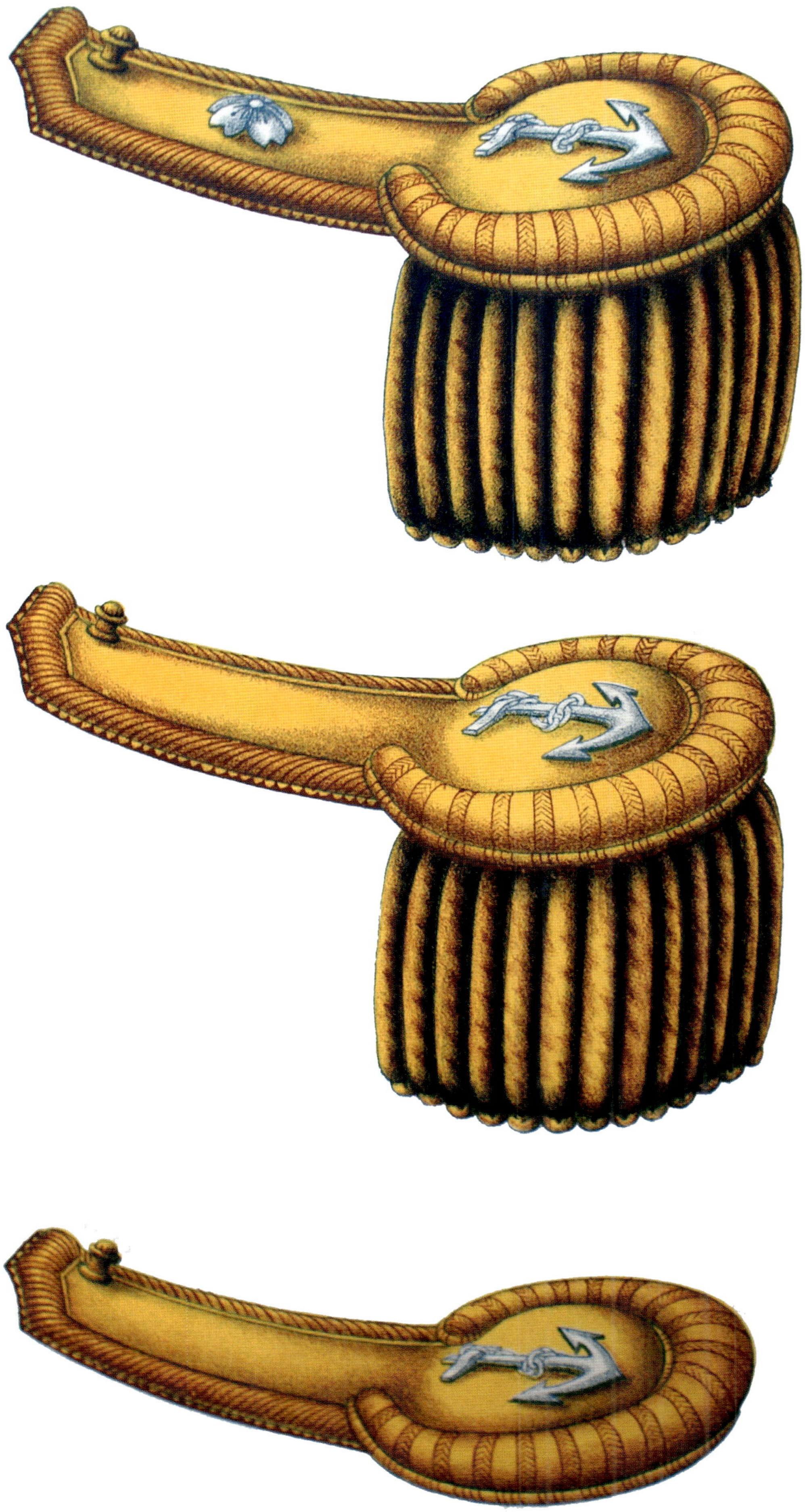

Navy 1883 regulations officer's epaulets.
From top to bottom:
Lieutenant: anchor, one flower star.
Sub-lieutenant: anchor.
Acting sub-lieutenant: anchor only (no fringes).
Anne S.K. Brown Military Collection, Brown University Library, Providence, USA.

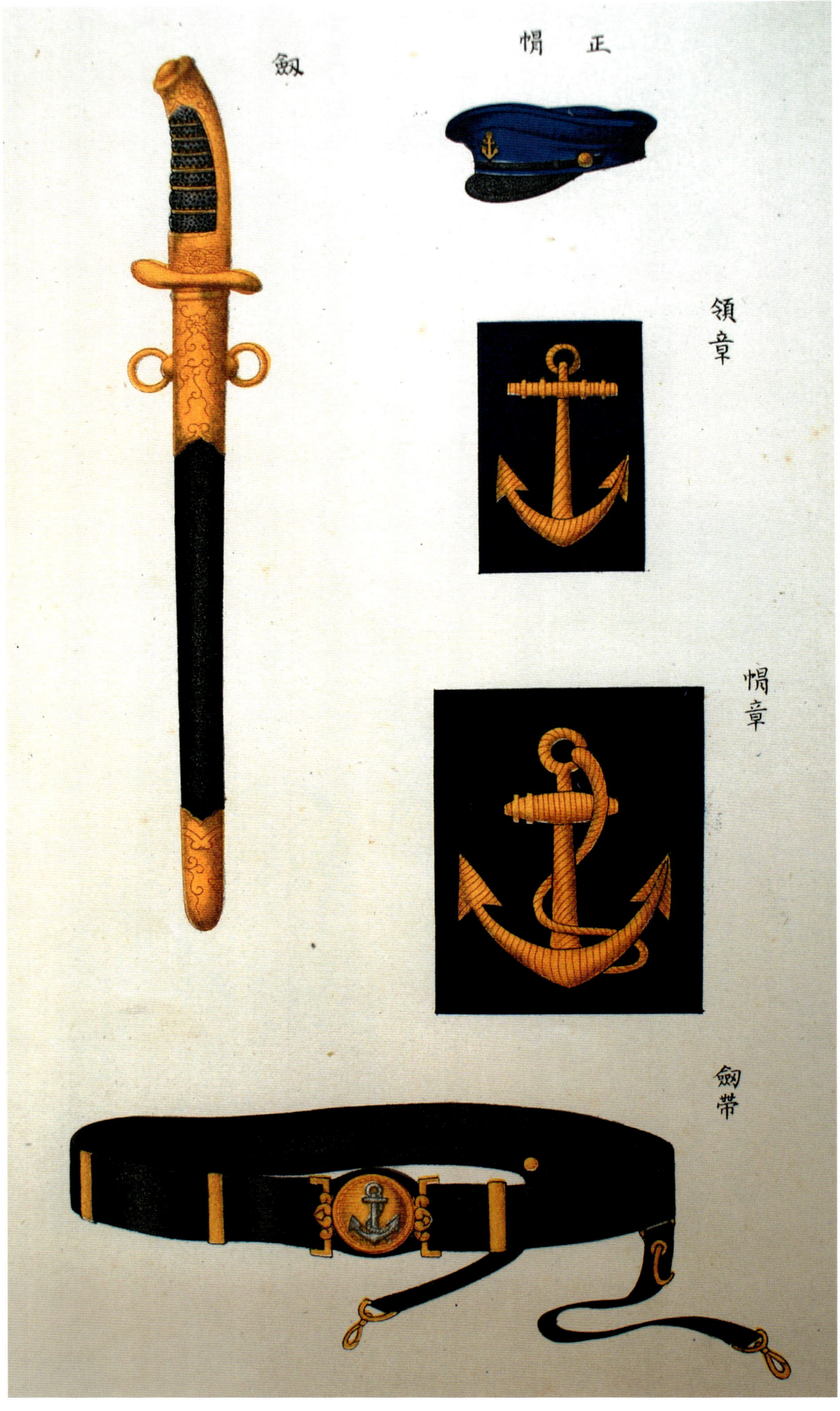

Navy petty officer's cap, badges and dagger, 1883 regulations. Anne S.K. Brown Military Collection, Brown University Library, Providence, USA.

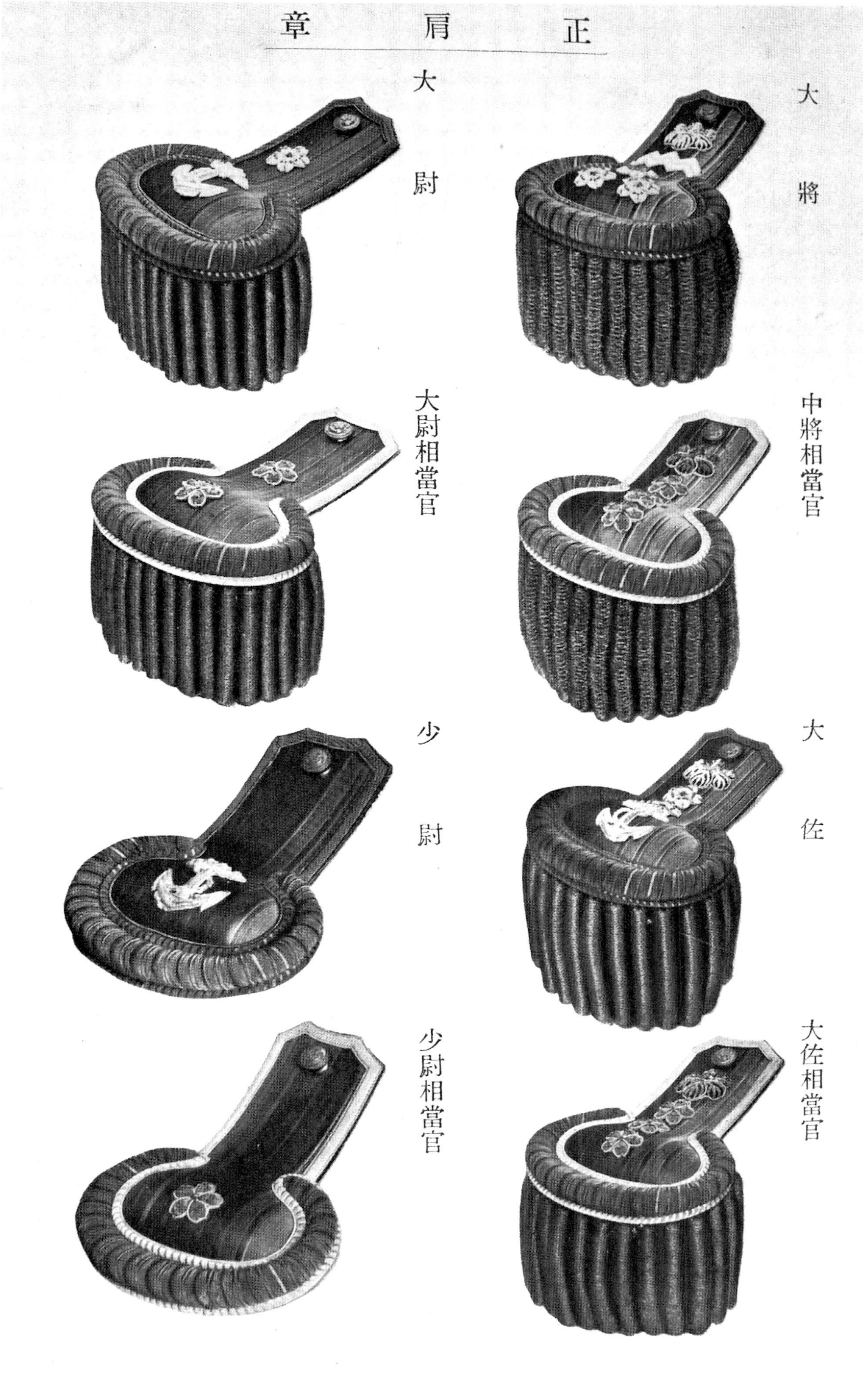

Navy officer's dress epaulets, 1914 regulations. Clockwise: admiral; vice admiral (administration); captain; captain (administration); acting sub-lieutenant (administration); acting sub-lieutenant; lieutenant (administration); lieutenant. Book of naval dress regulations, Tokyo, 1916 and 1930.

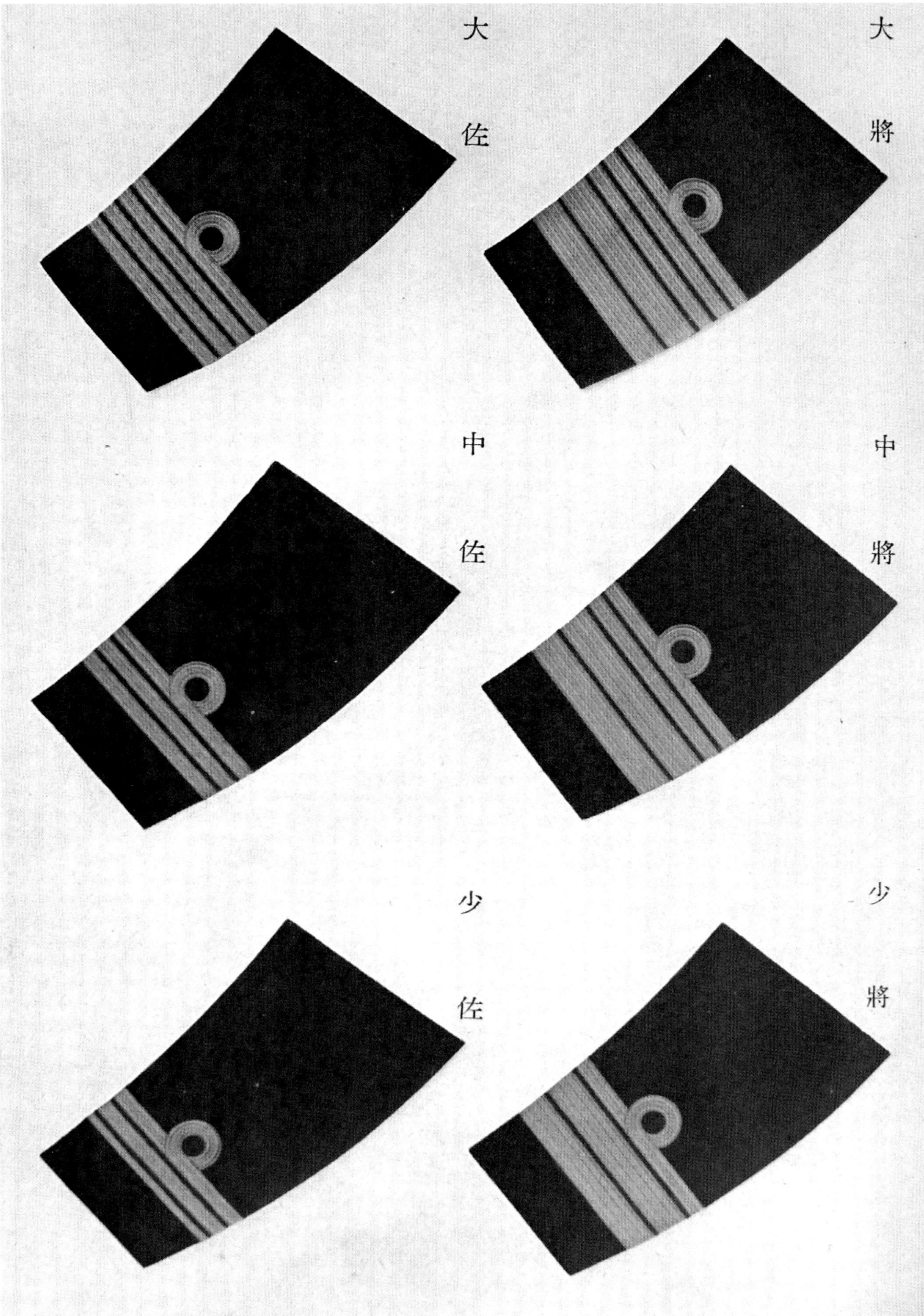

Navy rank cuff stripes. Clockwise: admiral from 1883; vice admiral from 1871; rear admiral from 1871; commander from 1914; lieutenant commander from 1914; captain from 1871. Book of naval dress regulations, Tokyo, 1916 and 1930.

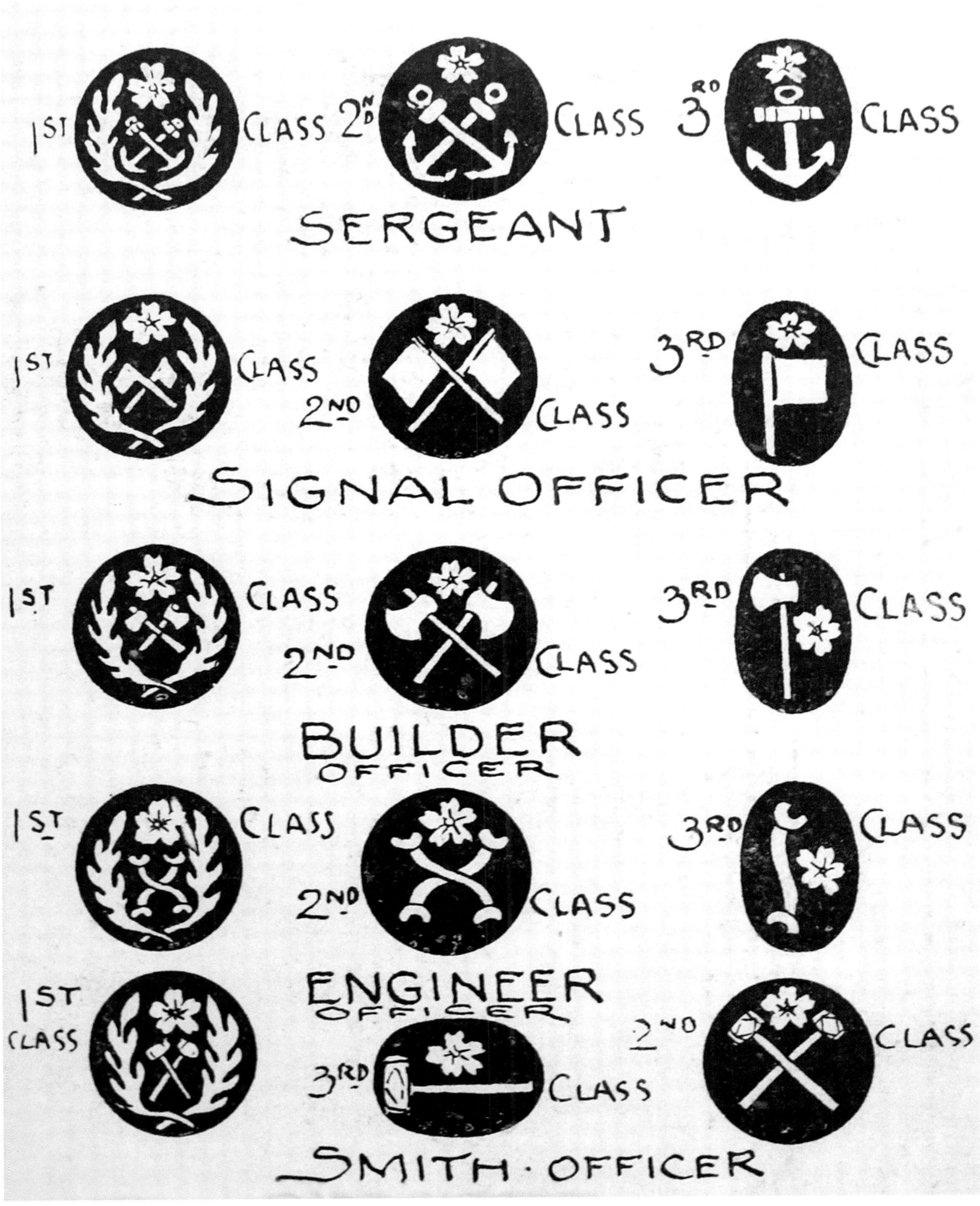

Navy trade and rank badges, 1890s-1900s (1). Illustrated London News, 9 April 1904.

Navy trade and rank badges, 1890s-1900s (2). Illustrated London News, 9 April 1904.

III

Flags and Colors

The emperor's badge was a gold chrysanthemum (or cherry blossom) with sixteen petals that was seen on banners and, from 1870, on flags, some of them quite ornate. In 1889, the emperor adopted as his flag the gold chrysanthemum with sixteen petals on a red field.

The red sun disk in a white field flag known as the "Hinomaru" flag has origins going back to the Middle Ages and, as early as 1854, was used by Japanese ships as the nation's insignia. In 1870, it was confirmed as the national flag and the ensign for merchant ships.

In May 1870, the military "War Flag" consisting of the red sun disk with sixteen red rays was henceforth assigned to the army and the navy. For the army, the sun was in the center of the flag and for the naval ensign, it was slightly to the left.

Regimental colors for regular units consisted of the war flag edged with violet fringes with, at the lower left edge, a small white rectangular panel bearing the regimental designation. The standards of the cavalry regiments were similar to the regular infantry colors, but were smaller in size. Reserve infantry regiments had the same type of colors, but edged with red fringes

Small square white battalion flags with horizontal zigzag lines were carried. In the regular regiments, the 1st battalion had a red zigzag, the 2nd had a red and a black zigzag and the 3rd had a red, a black and a red zigzag. In the reserve regiments, the 1st battalion had a black zigzag, the 2nd had a black and a red zigzag and the 3rd had a black, a red and a black zigzag. In the territorial regiments, the 1st battalion had a blue zig-zag, the 2nd had two blue zigzags. There were no 3rd battalions in the territorial regiments.

IV

Muskets and Rifles

Another helpful tool to date Japanese military prints is to identify the type of rifle depicted. Many details are obscured or rendered inaccurately by artists bemused by this highly complex object, the difficulty being increased by the rapid changes that occurred in firearms design from the 1850s. The prints reproduced merely show the main types used by Japan's troops and are not an exhaustive survey.

Briefly, the Japanese forces went form the 1850s muzzle loading rifled muskets using percussion caps to the later-1860s breech loading rifled muskets and, from the early-1880s, bolt action rifles. Until 1880, most weapons were made in Great Britain and the United States. They were manufactured in Japan thereafter.

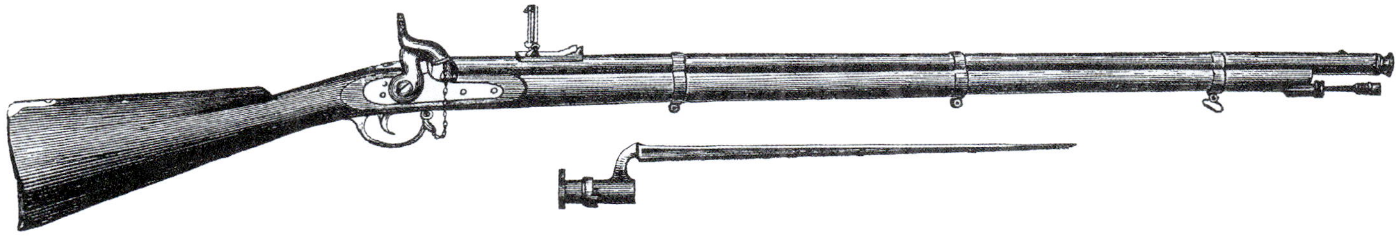

British Pattern 1853 Enfield rifled musket. It was a sturdy and popular weapon that was widely used not only by British forces, but also by Union and Confederate armies, by republican Mexican troops and by imperial Japanese forces. Contemporary print.

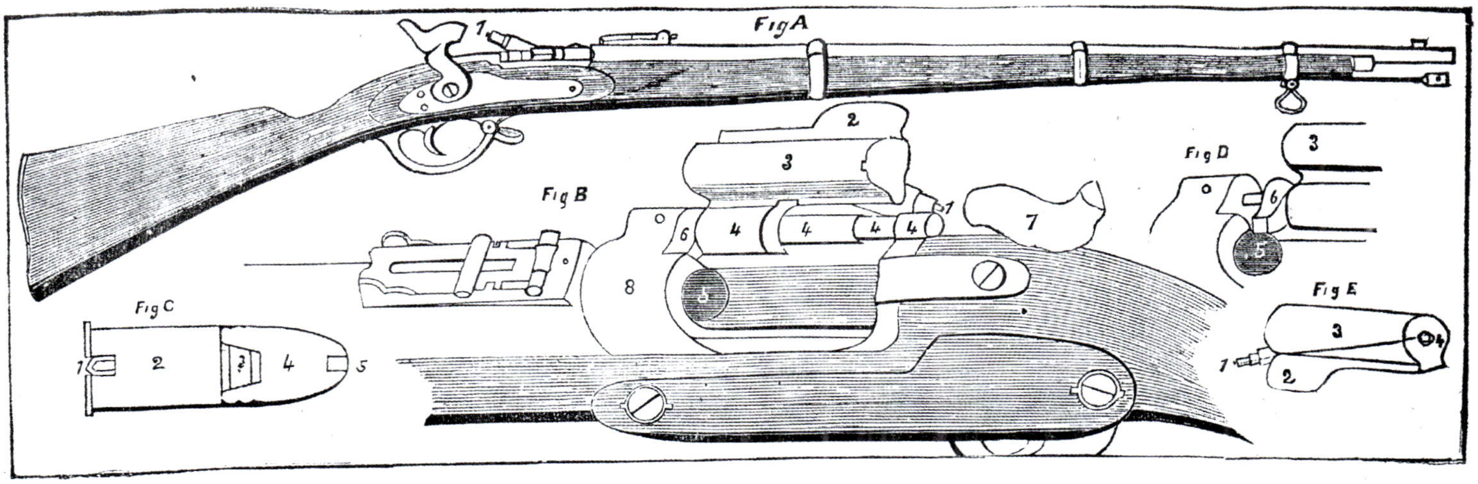

British Snider-Enfield breech-loading rifled musket, 1867. This weapon introduced in the later 1860s was the standard weapon for foot troops in Japan until the advent of the Murata rifle. Print in The Volunteer Review (Ottawa), 27 May 1867.

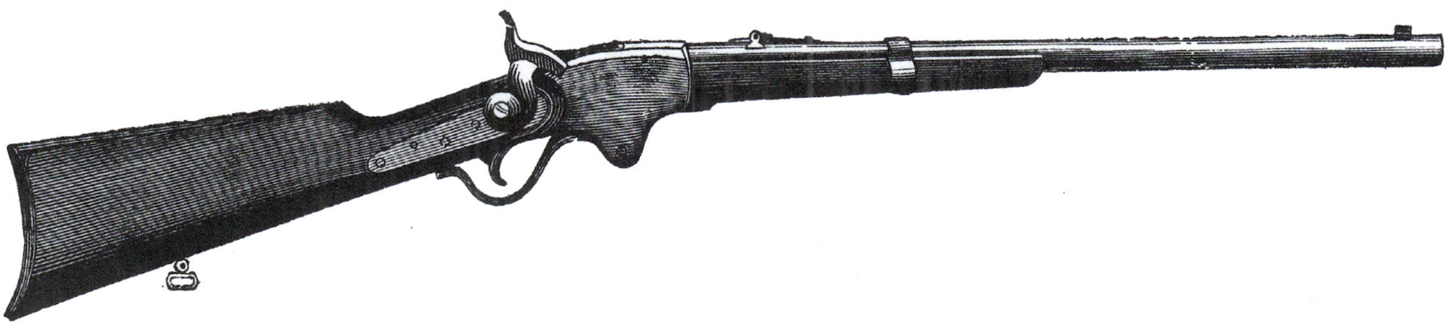

Spencer cavalry carbine, c. 1870. The revolutionary American weapon was breech-loading with a tubular seven-round magazine. Usually used by cavalry in several armies, Spencers were also used in Japan. Contemporary print.

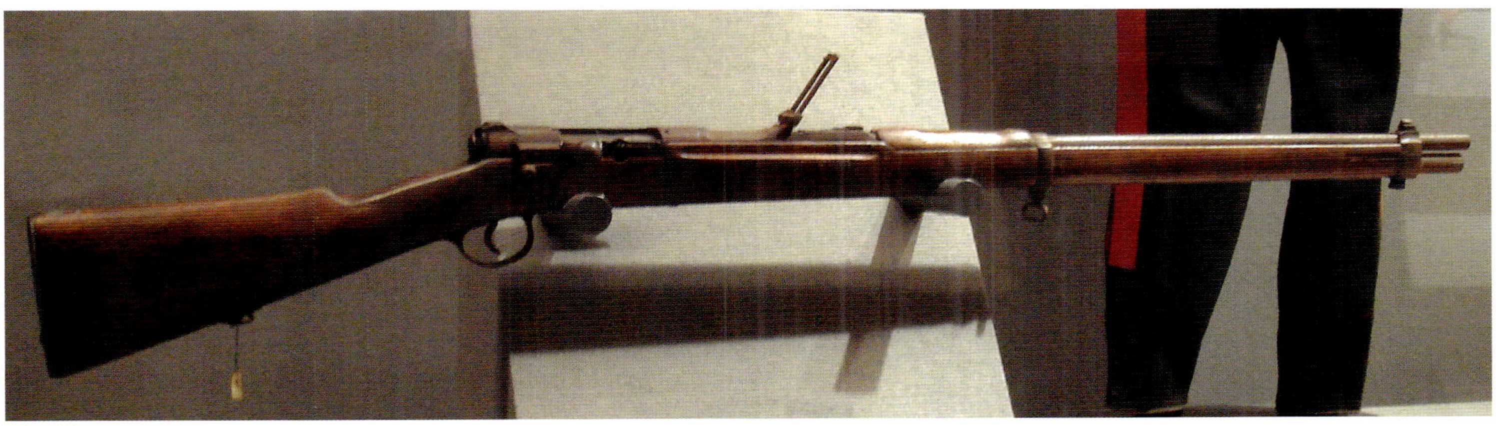

The Murata Type 22bolt action rifle (M. 1889). This was an improved version of the Type 13 (M. 1880) and Type 18 (M. 1885) versions that were single shot weapons of 11 mm caliber. This version had an eight-round tube magazine (its end visible below the barrel) and a smaller 8mm caliber. From an example at Yasukuni Shrine. Wikimedia.

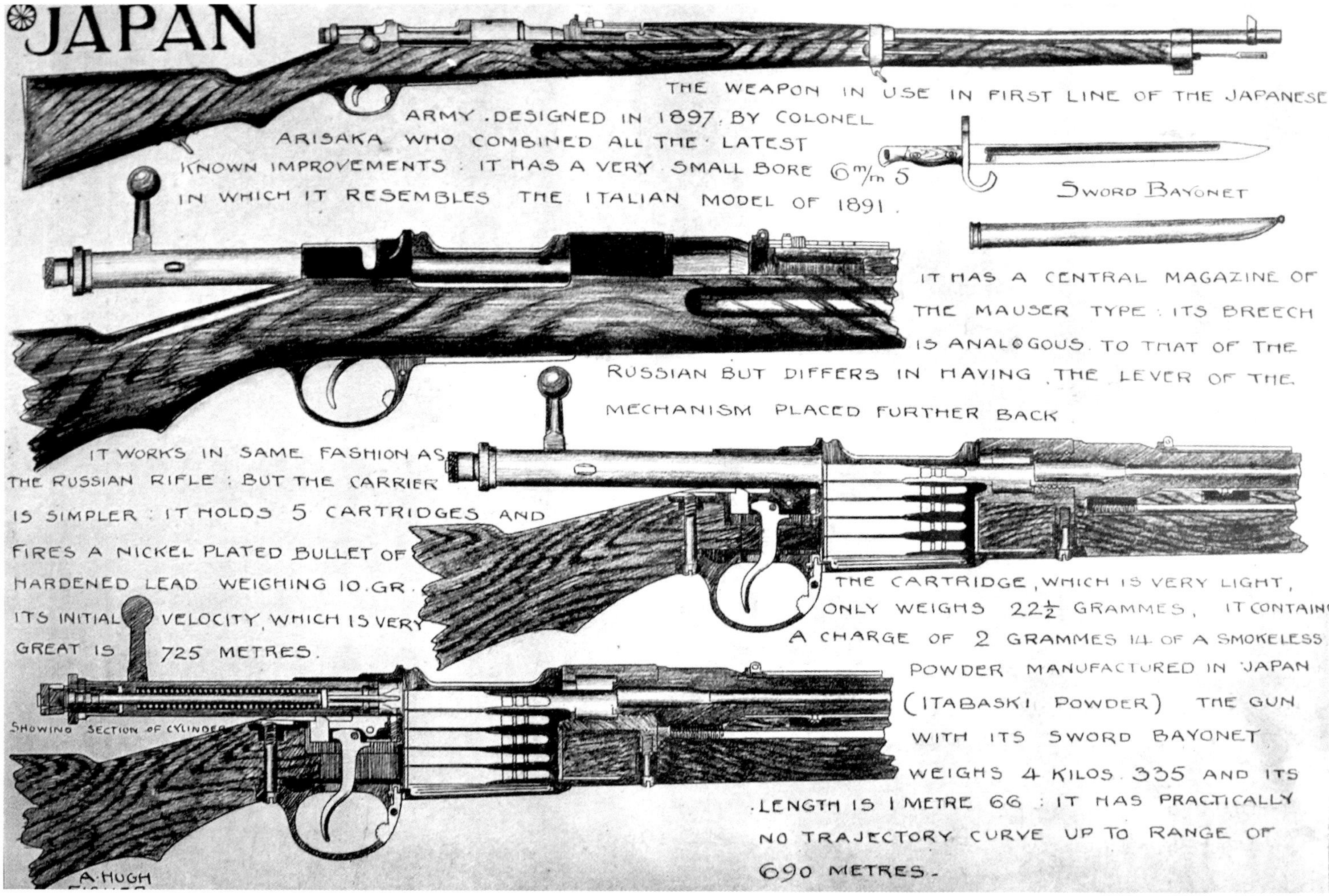

The Arisaka Type 30 rifle (M. 1897). Its caliber was 6.5mm (or .256 inches) and its magazine held five bullets. Print after Hugh A. Fisher. Illustrated London News, 2 April 1904.

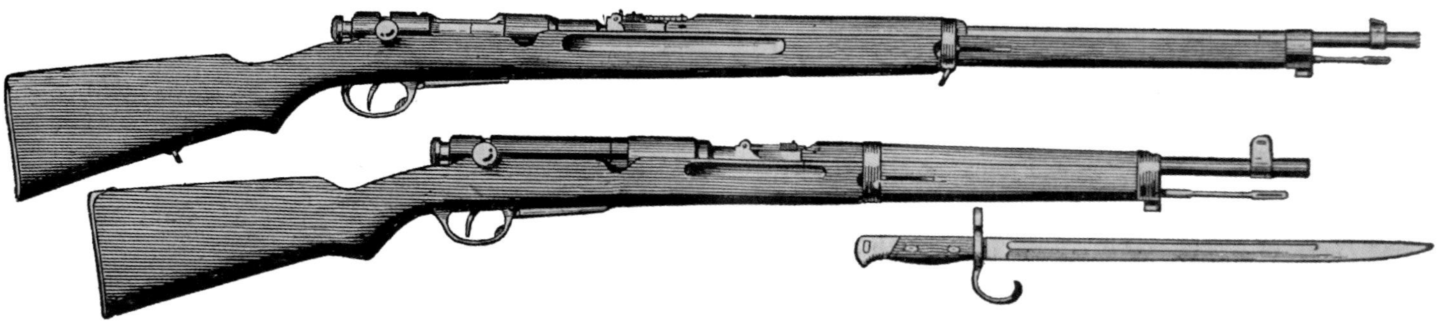

The Arisaka Type 38 (M. 1905) long infantry rifle and shorter cavalry carbine. These were heavily inspired from the German Mauser rifles. The caliber was 6.5mm (or .256 inches) and its magazine held five bullets. Both used the same model of bayonet. Print in a private collection.

Select Bibliography

Adidora, Ronald. "In Nelson's shadow", *Military History*, December 1995, pp. 66-72, 96-98.

Alexandre, Arsène. *Histoire de la peinture militaire en France* (Paris, c. 1888).

Ashmead-Bartlett, Ellis. *Port Arthur: The Siege and Capitulation* (Edinburgh and London: William Blackwood and Sons, 1906)

Balet, J.C. *Military Japan* (Kelly and Walsh: Yokohama, 1910).

Battles of the Nineteenth Century (London: Cassell, c. 1900), multiple authors, Vol. 5.

Blacker, Carmen, Hugh Cortazzi and Ben-Ami Shillony. *The Collected Writings of Modern Western Scholars on Japan* (Curzon: Richmond, UK, 2000, 3 volumes), Vol. 2.

Blakeslee, Fred Gilbert. *Uniforms of the World* (E.P. Dutton: New York, 1929).

Bryant, Anthony J. *The Samurai 200-1500* (Osprey Elite: Oxford, 1991).

Chaïkin, Nathan. *The Sino-Japanese War* (1983). Catalogue of prints in the Basil Hall and another private collection. Good biographies of artists.

Chartrand, René. "La transformation des institutions militaries du Japon 1854-1904", *Tradition* [Paris], No. 245, novembre-décembre 2009, pp. 57-61.

Cini, George. "Malta connection with Japanese Imperial Navy under study", *The Times of Malta*, 23 September 2002.

Clark, Kenneth. *Civilisation* (BBC: London, 1969).

Cleary, Thomas. *La voie du samouraï* (Sagesses: Paris, 1992).

Deniker, J. "La Corée et la guerre Sino-Japonaise", *Le Tour du Monde*, No. 9, 1 septembre 1894, pp. 129-134.

Dixon, William Gray. *The Land of the Morning: An Account of Japan and its People* (Edinburgh, 1882).

Edgerton, Robert B. *Warriors of the Rising Sun* (Norton: New York, 1997).

Fahr-Becker, Gabrielle, ed. *Japanese Prints* (Taschen: Koln, 1994).

Frédéric, Louis. *Japon : l'empire éternel* (Paris, 1985).

Galli, H. *La guerre en Extrême-Orient* (Granier: Paris, c. 1905), 2 volumes.

Harries, Meirion and Susie Harries. *Soldiers of the Sun: The Rise and Fall of the Imperial Japanese Army* (Random House: New York, 1994).

Hinzelin, Émile. *Histoire illustrée de la guerre du droit* (R. Leduc: Québec, c. 1920), 3 vols.

Humbert, Aimé. *Japan and the Japanese* (London, 1874).

Huyghes, René. *L'Art et l'Homme* (Larousse: Paris, 1961), Vol. 3. Outstanding account of world art from prehistoric times to the middle of the 20th century.

Inouye, Jukichi. *A Concise History of the War between Japan and China* (Tokyo, 1895) and Scenes from the Japan-China War (Tokyo, 1895) with plates by Eiki Yamamoto.

Jones, Jefferson. *The Fall of Tsingtau* (Houghton Mifflin: Boston, 1915).

Kitaoka, Snin'ichi. "The Army as a Bureaucracy: Japanese Militarism Revisited", *The Journal of Military History* (Special Issue), 57 (October 1993), pp. 67-86.

Kure, Mitsuo. *Samouraïs* (Éditions Philippe Piquier: Paris, 2003).

Lapeyrère, P. de. *Le Japon militaire* (Plon: Paris, 1882).

Larroumet, Gustave and Philippe Burty. *Meissonier* (Ludovic Baschet: Paris, 1893).

"L'Armée japonaise". *La Revue scientifique* (Paris, 1888), Volume 41, p. 286.

Léra, M. "Au pays du soleil levant", *Le mois littéraire et pittoresque,* juillet 1905, pp. 80-98.

Lundeberg, Philip K. "Japanese prints of the Perry expedition", *Smithsonian*, Spring 1967, pp. 70-74.

Maffe, Jean-Pierre. *L'Histoire des Indes orientales et occidentales* (Paris, 1665), 2 volumes. This work, translated from Latin to French, is a compilation of Portuguese and Spanish discoveries, first published in 1571 and in French in 1603. Maffee (or Maffei) was a Jesuit scholar. Based on primary materials, it received an enthusiastic reception all over Europe. Maffee's work includes much of great value relating to Japan. It is mainly based on Jesuit letters written either about or from Japan between 1549 and 1570. In 1603, the Jesuit Visitor, Valignano, who was writing his history of Japan, wrote from Macao, China: "Of all those who have so far written about Japan, none has done it with greater precision or in better order than Father G.P. Maffee." The French 1665 edition adds some later developments such as the 1603 division of society into five classes and the increasingly hostile attitude towards anything foreign.

Martin, Frederick. *The Statesman's Year-Book* (London, 1872).

McKown, Robin. *The World of Mary Cassatt* (Thomas Y. Crowell: New York, 1974).

Michakov, Valentin, ed. *La Flotte de l'Empire de Russie* (Slavia: St. Petersburg, 1996).

Mossman, Samuel. *Land of the Rising Sun* (London, 1873).

Mouncey, Augustus Henry. *The Satsuma Rebellion* (London, 1879).

Mutel, Jacques. *La Fin du Shôgunat et le Japon de Meiji* (Hatier: Paris, 1970).

Nakanishi, Ritta. *Japanese Military Uniforms 1841-1929: From the fall of the Shogunate to the Russo-Japanese War* (Dainippon Kaiga: Tokyo, 2001). The most helpful work on the subject.

Nakata, Tadao. *Imperial Japanese Army and Navy Uniforms and Equipments* (Tokyo, 1973). A huge compilation of photos with Japanese texts, especially good with Second World war items; the English leaflet inserted is short and inadequate.

Neuer, Roni, Herbert Libertson and Susugu Yoshida. *Ukiyo-e: 250 ans d'estampes japonaises* (Flammarion: Paris, 1981).

Ohnuki-Tierney, Emiko. *Kamikaze, Cherry Blossoms and Nationalism: the Militarization of Aesthetics in Japanese History* (University of Chicago Press, 2002).

Okamoto, Shumpei. *Impressions of the Front: Woodcuts of the Sino-Japanese War 1894-95* (Philadelphia Museum of Art, 1983).

Oriental Cultural Society. *A Glance over Eighty Years of History* (serial publication first issued in Tokyo on 15 November 1933). Japanese text with many seemingly unsigned color plates apparently made in previous years and decades. Examples consulted in the Todd Albums, Anne S.K. Brown Military Collection, Brown University Library, Providence. The prints are a revealing look at events covering the 1860s and early-1870s by obviously well documented illustrators. The art form expressed is in the Western fashion, but has a definite Japanese feeling in the use of nature and interior designs.

Paine, S.C.M. *The Sino-Japanese War of 1894-1895: perceptions, power, and primacy* (Cambridge University Press, 2003).

Peers, C.J. *Medieval Chinese Armies 1260-1520* (Osprey MAA 251: London, 1992).

Pictorial Reports of the Russo-Japanese War (Tokyo, 1904-1905). Monthly publication in Japanese with color plates having English captions.

Revue d'artillerie, Volume 19 (October 1881-March 1882).

Rhul, Moritz. *Die Japanische Armee in ihrer gegenwärtingen Uniformerung* (Author: Liepzig, c. 1896 and 1904).

Ruhrberg, Karl, et al. *Art in the 20th Century* (Taschen: Köln, 2002).

Shimizu, Christine. *L'art japonais* (Flammarion: Paris, 1984).

Smith, Bradley. *Japan: A History in Art* (Doubleday: New York, 1964).

Swinton, Elizabeth de Sabato. *In Battle's Light: Woodblock Prints of Japan's Early Modern Wars* (Worcester Art Museum, 1991).

Takenobu, Yoshitaro, ed. *The Japan Yearbook* (Tokyo, 1928) Vol. 3, Ch. IX.

Taylor, Bayard. *A Visit to India, China and Japan in the year 1853* (New York, 1885).

Terukazu, Akiyama. *La Peinture japonaise* (Albert Skira: Geneva, 1961).

Turnbull, Stephen. *Samurai Armies* (Osprey MAA 86: Oxford, 1979), *The Book of the Samurai: The Warrior*

Class of Japan (Bison: New York, 1982), *The Samurai Swordsman: Master of War* (Tuttle: Tokyo, 2008).

Upton, Emory. *The Armies of Asia and Europe* (London, 1878).

Vecellio, Cesare. *Habiti antichi et moderni di tutto il mondo* (Venice, 1598), republished as: Vecellio's Renaissance Costume Book (Dover: NewYork, 1977).

War Department, U.S. Army. *Bulletin of Military Notes,* (Washington, 1905).

War Department, U.S. Army. *Handbook on Japanese Military Forces,* 15 September 1944 (Washington, 1944).

Webster, Donald B. *Military Bolt-Action Rifles 1841-1914* (Museum Restauration Service: Bloomfield, Ontario, 1993).

Williams, Dion. *Army and Navy Uniforms and Insignia* (Stokes: New York, 1918).

Wichman, Seigfried. *Japonisme* (Thames and Hudson: London, 1981).

Yumoto, John M. *The Samurai Sword: a Handbook* (Tuttle: Rutland, VT and Tokyo, 1958).

NOTES

1 Jean-Pierre Maffe. *L'Histoire des Indes orientales et occidentales* (Paris, 1665), Vol. 2.

2 Suziki quoted in: *Thomas Cleary. La voie du samouraï* (Sagesses: Paris, 1992).

3 Carmen Blacker, Hugh Cortazzi and Ben-Ami Shillony. *The Collected Writings of Modern Western Scholars on Japan* (Curzon: Richmond, UK, 2000, 3 volumes), Vol. 2.

4 Bayard Taylor, *A Visit to India, China and Japan in the year 1853* (New York, 1885), pp. 416, 419.

5 Aimé Humbert, *Japan and the Japanese* (London, 1874), p. 188.

6 Quoted in: Bradley Smith. *Japan: A History in Art* (Doubleday: New York, 1964), pp. 286-287.

7 Quoted in M. Léra, "Au pays du soleil levant", *Le mois littéraire et pittoresque,* juillet 1905, p. 98.

8 Emory Upton. *The Armies of Asia and Europe* (London, 1878), p. 12.

9 Samuel Mossman. *Land of the Rising Sun* (London, 1873), p. 411.

10 Augustus Henry Mouncey. *The Satsuma Rebellion* (London, 1879), p. 193; William Gray Dixon. *The Land of the Morning: An Account of Japan and its People* (Edinburgh, 1882), p. 161.

11 *Revue d'artillerie,* Volume 19 (October 1881-March 1882), p. 172.

12 *United Service Magazine* (London), 1878, p. 89.

13 William Gray Dixon. *The Land of the Morning: An Account of Japan and its People* (Edinburgh, 1882), p. 401.

14 Quoted in: Robin McKown. *The World of Mary Cassatt* (Thomas Y. Crowell: New York, 1974), p. 125.

15 J. Deniker, "La Corée et la guerre Sino-Japonaise", *Le Tour du Monde,* No. 9, 1 septembre 1894, pp. 129-134.

16 On this event and its reaction in Japan, China and elsewhere, see : S.C.M. Paine. *The Sino-Japanese War of 1894-1895 : perceptions, power, and primacy* (Cambridge University Press, 2003), pp. 210-1271.

17 "The Japanese in Formosa," *Harpers Weekly,* 21 December 1895.

18 M. Léra, "Au pays du soleil levant", *Le mois littéraire et pittoresque,* juillet 1905, p. 94-95.

19 U.S. War Department, *Bulletin of Military Notes,* 1905, p. 145.

20 The Russians later claimed that they mistook the Japanese warship for one of their own and fired a salute. The Japanese of course rejected this explanation.

21 The Japanese had "89,000 men in killed, wounded, and sick ... if we include the battle of Nashan, 94,000. Of the former total 64,000 were officially reported killed and wounded, the remaining 25,000 sick, or dead from sickness." Ellis Ashmead-Bartlett, *Port Arthur: The Siege and Capitulation* (Edinburgh and London: William Blackwood and Sons, 1906), p. 474.

22 U.S. War Department, *Bulletin of Military Notes,* 1905, p. 144.

23 Allocution given by Louis Chartrand on the philosophy of Japan's Mangas on 19 March 2010 at the Philopolis Conference hosted in Montréal by McGill University and the Université du Québec à Montréal.